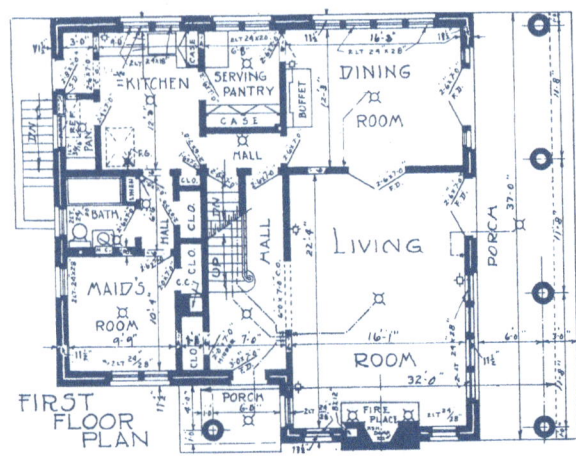

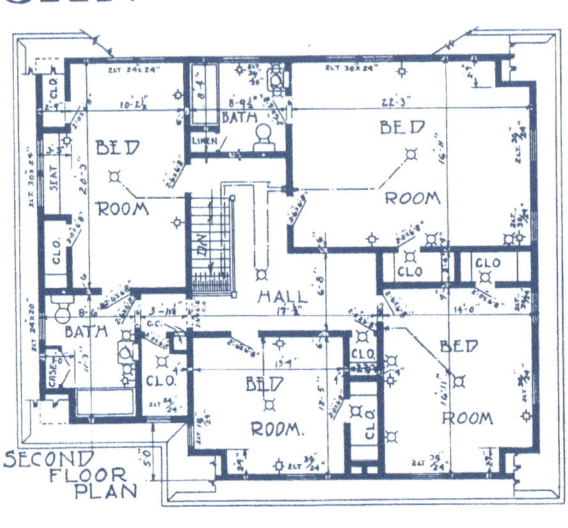

The *ALLEGAN*

FIRST FLOOR PLAN

KITCHEN
SERVING PANTRY
DINING ROOM
CASE
BUFFET
CASE
HALL
MAID'S ROOM
BATH
CLO.
LIVING ROOM
PORCH
ROOM
PORCH
FIRE PLACE

SECOND FLOOR PLAN

BED ROOM
BATH
LINEN
CLO.
SEAT
BED ROOM
CLO.
BATH
HALL
CLO.
BED ROOM
BED ROOM
CLO.

THE MOST POPULAR HOMES
of the TWENTIES

WILLIAM A. RADFORD

With a New Introduction by
DANIEL D. REIFF

DOVER PUBLICATIONS, INC.
MINEOLA, NEW YORK

Bibliographical Note

The Most Popular Homes of the Twenties is an unabridged, slightly altered reprint of the work originally published as *The Most Popular Homes in America* by American Builder, Chicago, in 1925. A new Introduction by Daniel D. Reiff has been provided for the Dover edition; it is followed by eight additional illustrations selected for this reprint.

Library of Congress Cataloging-in-Publication Data

Radford, William A., 1865–
    [Most popular homes in America]
    The most popular homes of the twenties / William A. Radford ; with a new introduction by Daniel D. Reiff. — Dover ed.
       p. cm.
    Originally published: The most popular homes in America. Chicago : American Builder, 1925. With new introd.
    ISBN-13: 978-0-486-47028-3
    ISBN-10: 0-486-47028-8
    1. Architecture, Domestic—United States—Designs and plans. 2. Architecture—United States—History—20th century—Designs and plans. I. Title.

NA7208.R33 2009
728'.370973—dc22

2009000859

Printed in Canada
47028804   2025
www.doverpublications.com

Introduction to the Dover Edition

Daniel D. Reiff, Ph.D.

Illustrated books—used as aids by "those about to build"—have been popular methods of achieving well-designed homes for Americans since the eighteenth century, but their hey-day was in the period of rapid population growth from the mid-nineteenth century onward. Early pattern books provided house designs and some details, which a clever carpenter could copy or creatively interpret. But by 1856, with *Village and Farm Cottages* by Cleaveland, Backus and Backus, one could also purchase measured working drawings for the illustrated houses—the beginning of the mail-order plans business. This service, which continued to grow in popularity in the later nineteenth and early twentieth centuries, was a national movement, and mail-order plan companies could be found in New York, Chicago, Knoxville, Washington, D.C., San Francisco, and elsewhere [1]. Mail-order plans would allow the local contractor to erect the house accurately, enable the owner to see just what the finished product would look like, and permit more accurate pricing of the job.

Another popular way of erecting middle-class—and even upper-middle-class—houses in the early twentieth century was to order plans from companies; in addition to the plans, these companies also supplied low-cost building materials (except for masonry portions of the house), cut and fitted to the exact specifications of the house selected. This pre-cut system had been started by the Aladdin Company of Bay City, Michigan, around 1908; Sears, Roebuck and Company soon imitated them. By the 1920s there were quite a number of firms that would supply the blueprints and all necessary construction documents along with the material, precut by machinery at the factory, which would save the local carpenter (still using hand tools in the 1920s) a great deal of labor [2].

And then there were books of house plans that, essentially, were advertisements for architects! The *Chicago Tribune Book of Homes* (1927) [3] published 99 appealing house designs; while one could order plans for three of them (the prize winners in the newspaper's competition), for the rest, one would have to contact the architect directly—easily done, as their full address was provided with each design.

But what are we to make of the present volume, originally published in 1925 as *The Most Popular Homes in America*? You could not order plans and working drawings of any of the 33 houses; no pre-cut material was available; and architects' names were nowhere to be seen. Actually, one did not need to order working drawings for the designs in the catalog, since most of them had excellent, clear plans, elevation drawings, cross sections, and even included detail drawings. Using these drawings, and the exterior perspective photograph (with the color view providing further information about materials and finishes) and, occasionally, an interior view as completed, a builder could easily erect any of these appealing houses from the information provided.

Thus, it would appear that the aim of the catalog's publication essentially was to inspire and stimulate people to build houses! And it would benefit all aspects of the building industry: Besides the house designs, *The Most Popular Homes of the Twenties* provides a whole range of other things to consider, what today we might consider to be "upgrades" to the basic house. The illustrated essays include "Building on a Small Site," "The Porch as a Living Room," "Built-in Bookshelves," "Modern Plumbing," "Built-in Conveniences," and a host of other useful topics, such as entrance doorways, wallpaper, dining nooks, garages, woodwork, landscaping, electricity, gardens, and so on. The original catalog thus advertised a whole range of amenities, benefiting the entire building industry.

Although ostensibly published by the American Builder Publishing Company of Chicago, the volume is copyrighted by "Wm. A. Radford, Chicago." The Radford Architectural Company was a large and successful firm that issued a huge number of mail-order plan catalogs between 1898 and 1928 and had its own stable of architects, "licensed in the state of Illinois." And they probably obtained many of their designs from other building-trade organizations and materials companies that, in fact, amassed quite a number of designs for this sort of house through national competitions [4]. It seems that these firms shared around their designs, in order to stimulate the house-building business.

The appealing houses in this volume by and large fall into five categories, each having stylistic and cultural associations with popular historic models. The most popular houses were variations on the American/Georgian Colonial; English types; Dutch Colonial; Spanish Southwest; and Italianate designs. Most were for middle-class families (one-car garage), usually consisting of six or seven rooms, though with a full basement (for the furnace, laundry room, root cellar, etc.); one design, "The Akron" (page 77) is even called a "most attractive home for the average American family." However, some designs (houses of eight rooms) could be considered upper-middle-class homes. For example, "The Attica" (page 52), a good English-style home, had eight rooms and three full baths, plus a billiards room in the basement; a "maid's room" was included on the first floor [5]. There were some less-expensive houses as well. "The Alton" (page 88), "a Pennsylvania Dutch Design" [6], is described as a "low-cost six-room home," although it has, in addition to the six rooms, a breakfast nook and small "reception hall"—but only one bathroom. Economy was not ignored in other designs, either. "The Argyle" (page 40), "a five-room Colonial bungalow" with one bath, had an alternate plan that eliminated one room and reduced the size of others, but made up for it by providing two "space-saving beds" (Murphy beds)

that could be let down into the living room! This saved 410 square feet of house construction.

The Most Popular Homes of the Twenties is a "deluxe" compendium of wonderfully attractive homes, made the more seductive by the color plate for each dwelling, and the many intelligent and informative essays. The catalog surely did inspire people to build these houses—and with this Dover Publications reprinting, I suspect the designs' progeny can now be tracked down. But the designs were popular with others as well—the house catalog compilers! Quite a number of these dwellings were copied, almost line for line, in other catalogs [7]. For example, the massive *Home Builders Catalog* of 1927 (which also had all manner of "helpful essays," and, in addition, ads for every conceivable product associated with building and furnishing houses) copied many of these very plates, proving their popularity [8].

The *Home Builders Catalog* reproduces many of these houses almost line for line. "The Ainsworth" (page 68) is reborn as "The Colton," with the same plan, though a few feet smaller; "The Alliance" (page 130) becomes "The Colonial," though with a slightly different plan; "The Acme" (page 136) is reborn as "The Camilla," in mirror image, but with essentially the same plan (only two inches different in width); "The Algona" (page 137) is the somewhat smaller "Cascade," with a variant plan; "The Allenhurst" (page 146) reappears as "The Chenee"—complete with the identical porch grillwork!—but in mirror image, and with a different plan. There were also many houses in the *Home Builders Catalog* that were similar to these and other designs, if not actual copies (as those just cited largely were) [9].

But what is intriguing to note is that a mail-order house plan catalog published that *same year*, 1925, by Standard Homes Co. of Washington, D.C. [10] also includes some dwellings that copy these designs (with slight variants in plan or size). For example, "The Argyle" (page 40) becomes "The Thorndyke"; "The Alma" (page 112) reappears as "The Euclid"; and "The Acme" (page 136) is the model for the somewhat larger "Washington."

A possible explanation for this congruency is found in editorial matter on page 633 of the

Home Builders Catalog: The editors state that the catalog was produced by "the same men who for 12 years have conducted the Architectural & Publicity Bureau—the Bureau whose plan service is used by eleven of the leading Retail Lumber Associations of America." Thus, there was at least one major trade group that prepared and shared these house plans—and over the years could (as with those copyrighted by Radford) develop small house plans that were nearly perfect in style, design, and appeal.

NOTES

1. After mail-order plans for houses were advertised in *Village and Farm Cottages*, others soon followed. Cummings and Miller offered them in their pattern book of 1865, and, in the 1870s, George Palliser and E. C. Hussey did so as well. In the 1880s, books of house designs by R. W. Shoppell and George F. Barber all offered plans for sale. By 1898 one of the most prolific companies, the Chicago firm that became the Radford Architectural Company, was offering mail-order plans too. In the early twentieth century there was a vast number of such firms; Standard Homes Company of Washington, D.C. (beginning about 1921) and Home Builders Catalog Co., Chicago (beginning in 1926) were among the most popular and prolific. The plans could be for frame, for face brick (on frame construction), solid brick, or concrete dwellings. (The *Home Builders Catalog* had a national popularity; the 1927 copy I consulted is inscribed with the name of an owner in Lexington, Kentucky.)

2. Although Chicago, because of its excellent lake and rail connections, was a center for this sort of business, other national firms were also prominent in the 1920s, such as the Ray H. Bennett Lumber Company in North Tonawanda, New York, and the Gordon-Van Tine Company of Davenport, Iowa. Of course, this system was developed for *frame* houses, and the stonework or concrete (for foundations), or brick for chimneys, was explicitly excluded.

3. Reprinted in 2008 by Dover Publications as *Elegant Small Homes of the Twenties: 99 Designs from a Competition* [ISBN 0-486-46910-7].

4. Many building materials organizations sponsored competitions for house designs to encourage homeowners and contractors to use their particular product. For example, the Association of American Portland Cement (Philadelphia) held one for cement houses in 1907; the Building Brick Association of America (Boston), in a 1910 house plan catalog, states that the plans were a "selection from more than 800 drawings submitted in a competition," and their plan catalog of 1912 drew its designs from 666 entries in a competition. Almost every building-trade organization of the day held competitions for house designs of various sizes, as mentioned in their house plan catalogs; some examples are the National Fire Proofing Company, Philadelphia, 1912; Hydraulic-Press Brick Company, St. Louis, 1914; American Face Brick Association, Chicago, 1920; United States Gypsum Company, Chicago, 1925; California Redwood Association, San Francisco, 1925; and Weyerhaeuser Forest Products, St. Paul, 1926. From their catalogs one could purchase low-priced plans and specifications of the houses illustrated—utilizing their particular product, of course.

5. "The Alberhill," (page 33) similarly would be considered a dwelling for upper-middle-class owners, as this fine Dutch Colonial gambrel-roofed home of eight rooms and two and a half baths had, in addition, a "servants' [sic] room and bath, and generous storage space . . . on the third floor."

Having a live-in maid, during the 1920s—an era of fewer "electrical conveniences" (and a lower standard of living)—was common enough for middle-class families, too. My grandparents, living in Spokane, Washington, between 1910 and 1924 in a bungalow much like "The Alton" (page 88), had a live-in maid (usually a local farm girl who wanted to dwell in the city) for cooking and cleaning; my grandmother took care of her two (ultimately six) children. My grandfather was a regional salesman/wholesaler for Peet Brother Soap Company.

6. Though inspired by Dutch Colonial houses of the Hudson Valley, this type of early twentieth century bungalow should really be called a Stickley Bungalow. Gustav Stickley, the New York State furniture designer and architectural reformer, published a plan of the first of this type of house in his magazine *The Craftsman* in February

1905. The "one story" look, with front porch subsumed under the front roof slope and small dormers lighting the second floor, subsequently became enormously popular throughout the United States. The design was included (pages 76 and 77) in Stickley's book *Craftsman Homes* (second ed.) of 1909—from which one could order "architects' drawings." The volume was reprinted by Dover in 1979 (ISBN 0-486-23791-5).

7. Ostensibly, William Radford's copyright of the catalog meant that no one could copy his house designs and publish them elsewhere as their own. This legal issue had been a concern in the profession for many years; it was discussed in *The American Architect and Building News*, a professional journal, in their issue of April 26, 1884, page 203 (as well as Jan. 9, 1886, page 23; May 5, 1894, page 55; and Feb. 16, 1895, page 69). It was recognized, however, that even small changes in the design would "vitiate" the copyright protection.

8. The Home Builders Catalog Company (Chicago and New York) published its first catalog in 1926; the volume I consulted for this essay was the revised and expanded second edition of 1927. House designs (a photograph of the house, often in color, and two floor plans) for 604 houses were the main feature (plus designs for 57 garages); blueprints for each house could be purchased for $20 a set (about $250 with today's purchasing power). But preceding these designs, and occupying pages 33 to 525, were advertisements (fully indexed) for 404 firms producing every product imaginable for home building. Since the catalog also included a section (pages 581 to 632) on "home related" topics (mortgages, selecting the home site, interior decoration, quality of materials, etc.), it did pick up on some of the sorts of essays that *The Most Popular Homes* discussed.

9. Some of the "variants" of *The Most Popular Homes* designs, which can be found two years later in the *Home Builders Catalog*, are very close to—if not quite clones of—their models. Here is a selection of them: For variants of "The Adrian" (page 5), see "The Chaffee"; for "The Alpena" (page 13), see "The Cochrane"; for "The Atwood" (page 34), see "The Colalt;" for "The Argyle" (page 41), see "The Camborne" and "The Comyn"; for "The Ainsworth" (page 68), see "The Crayton" and "The Comstock"; for "The Altamonte" (page 70), see "The Cardonia," "The Claiborne," "The Charleston," "The Corliss" and "The Carrie"; for "The Alcorn" (page 122), see "The Cabinet," "The Cortara" and "The Colgate"; for "The Allendale" (page 123), see "The Chrome"; for "The Alliance" (page 130) see "The Clifford" and "The Clarenden"; for "The Acme" (page 136), see "The Castner" and "The Cautille"; for variants—though here they are all pretty close to copies—of "The Allenhurst" (page 146), see "The Chatfield," "The Camanche" and "The Crilly."

10. *Better Homes at Lower Cost* was published in 1925 by Standard Homes Company of Washington, D.C. This edition was reprinted by Dover Publications in 1999 as *101 Classic Homes of the Twenties* (ISBN 0-486-40731-4), with the ostensible original publisher given as Harris, McHenry & Baker Co., "the Home Builder's Lumber Co." of Elmira, New York. This was, of course, just a local firm that had its name imprinted on the catalog—not the real publisher.

Daniel D. Reiff, Ph.D., is the author of *Houses from Books: Treatises, Pattern Books, and Catalogs in American Architecture, 1738–1950, A History and Guide* (Pennsylvania State University Press, 2000), which won the 2001 Historic Preservation Book Prize from the Center for Historic Preservation, Mary Washington College.

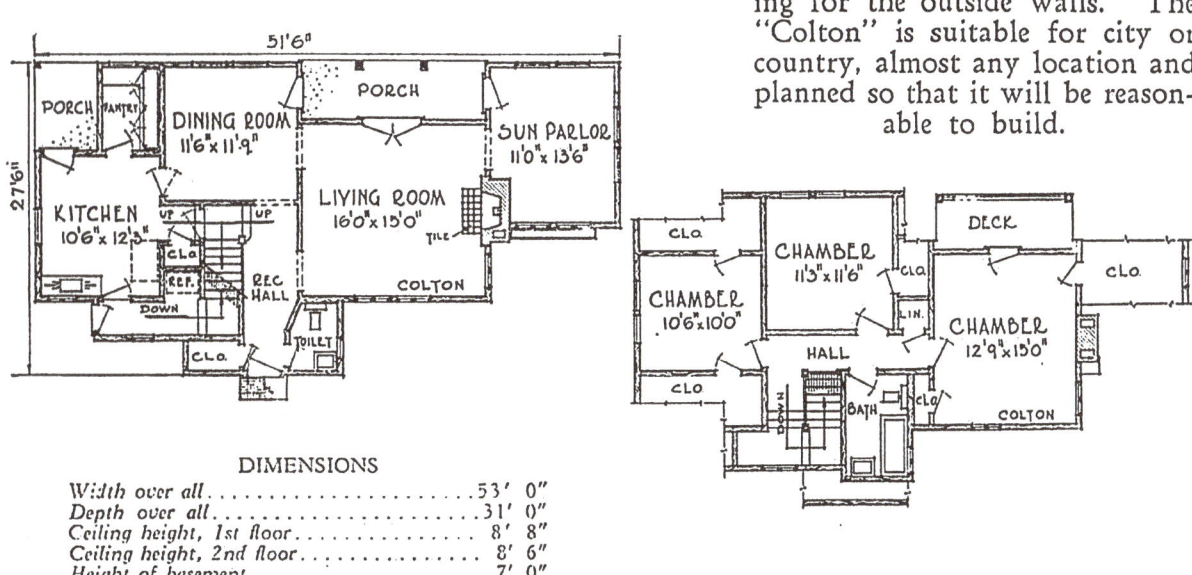

Size 51'6" x 27'6"

6 Rooms, Bath, Toilet and Sun Parlor

The COLTON

IN ITS design this modern American home is suggestive of the ever popular English cottage style—possible because of its steep roof pitch, the half timbered gable and the squatty brick chimney. It is all frame construction with metal lath and stucco covering for the outside walls. The "Colton" is suitable for city or country, almost any location and planned so that it will be reasonable to build.

DIMENSIONS

Width over all . . . . 53' 0"
Depth over all . . . . 31' 0"
Ceiling height, 1st floor . . . . 8' 8"
Ceiling height, 2nd floor . . . . 8' 6"
Height of basement . . . . 7' 0"

Two Complete Sets Blue-Print Working Plans . . . .
One Sixteen Page Classified Guide for Listing Materials . . . . } TWENTY DOLLARS
Two Sets of Specifications and Two Blank Contract Forms . . . .

"The Colton," *Home Builders Catalog* (1927), page 947; based on "The Ainsworth."

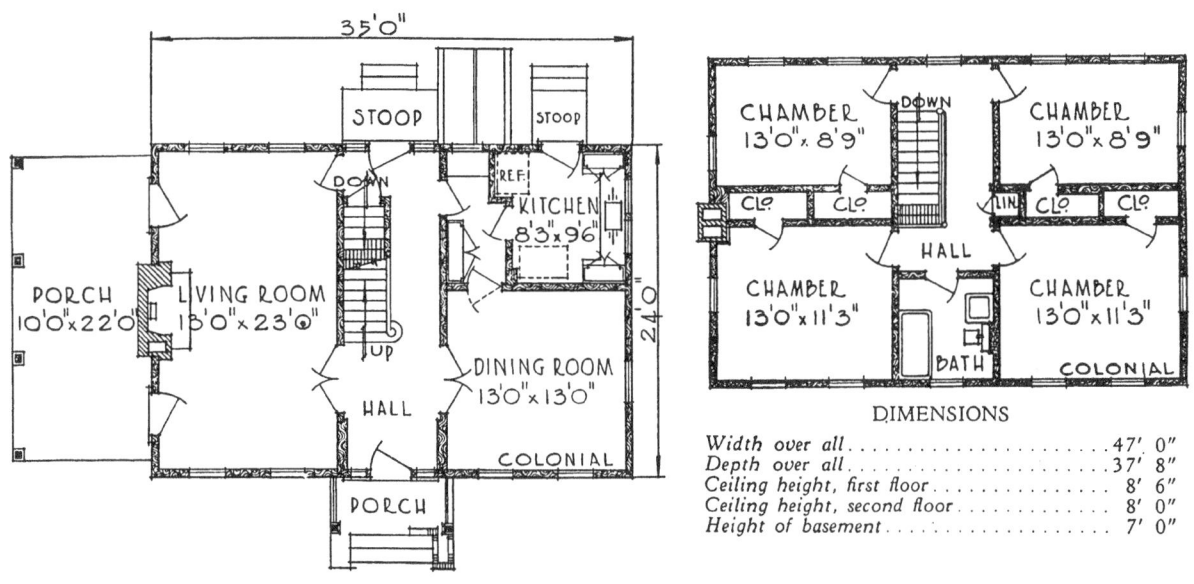

Size 35'0" x 24'0"   7 Rooms and Bath

The COLONIAL

A GREEN shuttered home breathing the peace and luxury of the country-side. A large porch, living room and hall, feature the downstairs. Upstairs the chambers are dispatched in a neat, convenient way. Plenty of windows, but can a home have too many windows?

DIMENSIONS

Width over all . . . . 47' 0"
Depth over all . . . . 37' 8"
Ceiling height, first floor . . . . 8' 6"
Ceiling height, second floor . . . . 8' 0"
Height of basement . . . . 7' 0"

Two Complete Sets Blue-Print Working Plans . . . . ⎫
One Sixteen Page Classified Guide for Listing Materials . . . . ⎬ TWENTY DOLLARS
Two Sets of Specifications and Two Blank Contract Forms . . . . ⎭

"The Colonial," *Home Builders Catalog*, page 702; based on "The Alliance."

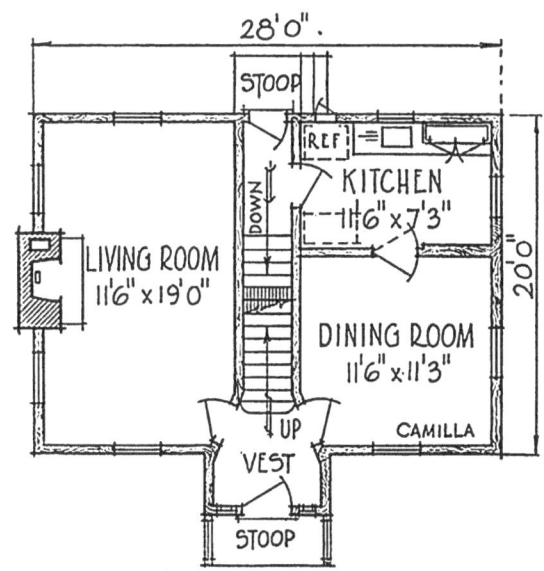

Size 28'0" x 20'0"   5 Rooms, Bath and Sewing Room

The CAMILLA

A SUBSTANTIAL, moderate priced frame house, embodying all modern comforts. By entering the living room from a corner one gets the full effect of the sweep of the room. A sewing room upstairs will please the housewife.

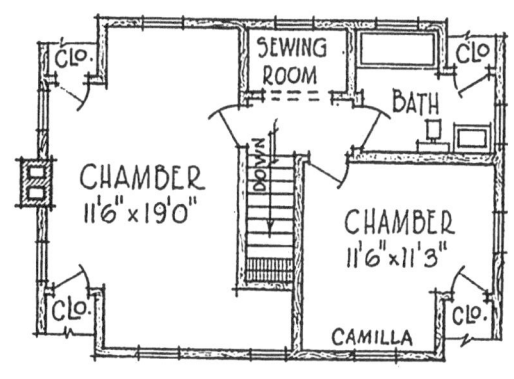

DIMENSIONS

Width over all.........................30' 0"
Depth over all.........................30' 0"
Ceiling height, 1st floor................. 8' 6"
Ceiling height, 2nd floor................. 8' 0"
Height of basement..................... 7' 0"

Two Complete Sets Blue-Print Working Plans....................⎫
One Sixteen Page Classified Guide for Listing Materials...............⎬ TWENTY DOLLARS
Two Sets of Specifications and Two Blank Contract Forms...........⎭

"The Camilla," *Home Builders Catalog*, page 833; based on "The Acme."

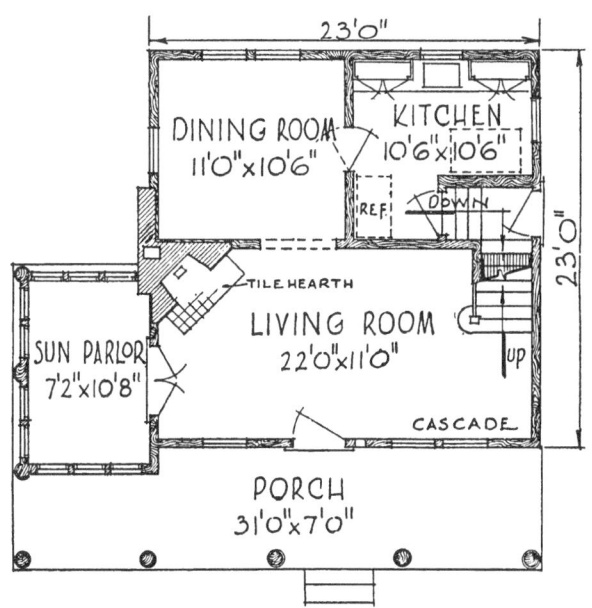

Size 23'0" x 25'0"

5 Rooms, Bath and Sun Parlor

The CASCADE

A FRAME home of the popular type, attractive and inexpensive. The architect has been especially careful in the planning of the interior, each room being of maximum size and within easy access of one another.

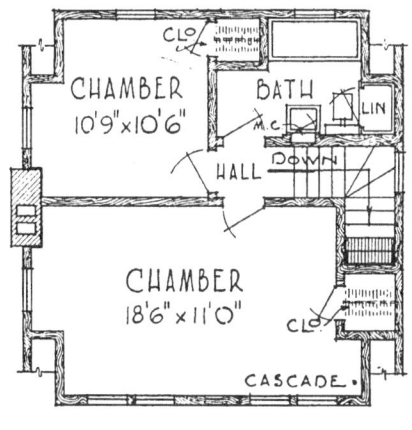

DIMENSIONS

Width over all	31' 6"
Depth over all	31' 0"
Ceiling height, 1st floor	9' 0"
Ceiling height, 2nd floor	8' 0"
Height of basement	7' 0"

Two Complete Sets Blue-Print Working Plans
One Sixteen Page Classified Guide for Listing Materials } TWENTY DOLLARS
Two Sets of Specifications and Two Blank Contract Forms

"The Cascade," *Home Builders Catalog*, page 706; based on "The Algona."

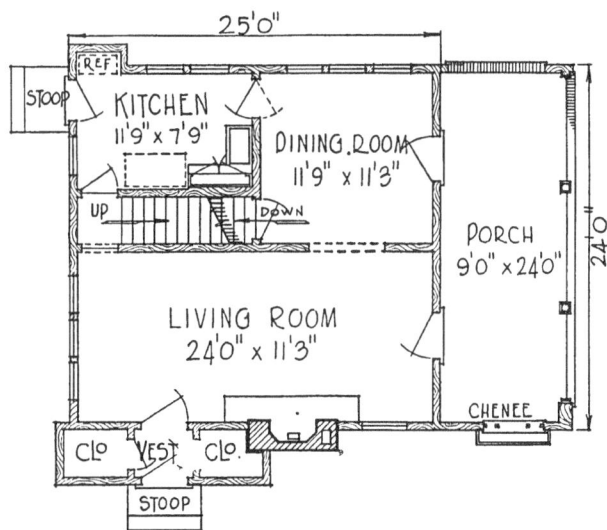

Size 25' 0" x 24' 0"   6 Rooms and Bath

The CHENEE

A HOME for the suburb or country-side. Three large chambers with ample closet room are to be found. A Home of beauty and comfort.

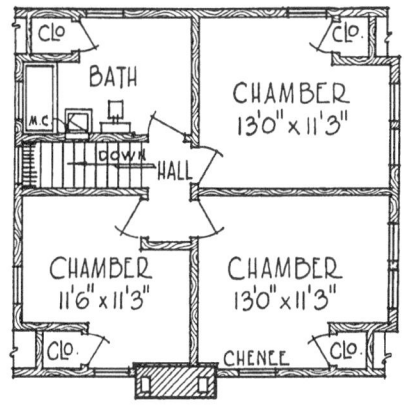

DIMENSIONS

Width over all.....................39' 6"
Depth over all.....................31' 6"
Ceiling height, 1st floor.............8' 0"
Ceiling height, 2nd floor............8' 0"
Height of basement................7' 0"

Two Complete Sets Blue-Print Working Plans.....................⎫
One Sixteen Page Classified Guide for Listing Materials................⎬ TWENTY DOLLARS
Two Sets of Specifications and Two Blank Contract Forms...........⎭

"The Chenee," *Home Builders Catalog,* page 701; based on "The Allenhurst."

The woman who is fair to herself usually stays fair in the eyes of her husband.

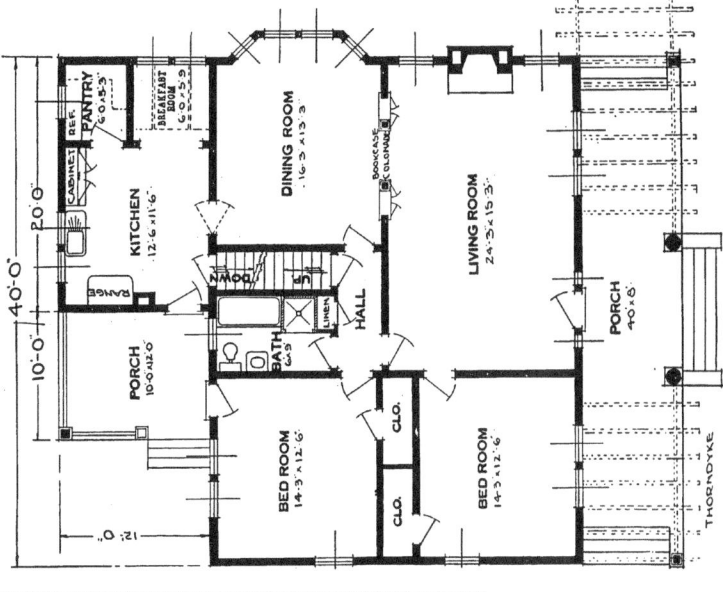

The THORNDYKE (Size 40x42')

Unnecessary work is always unfair work. It is unfair for the housewife to be forced to take hundreds of unnecessary steps in the daily routine of housekeeping because she was not considered in the planning of the home. In arranging the floor plan for The Thorndyke, the architect considered first practical economy for the wife who does her own housework.

"The Thorndyke," *Better Homes at Lower Cost* (1925), page 67: parallel to "The Argyle."

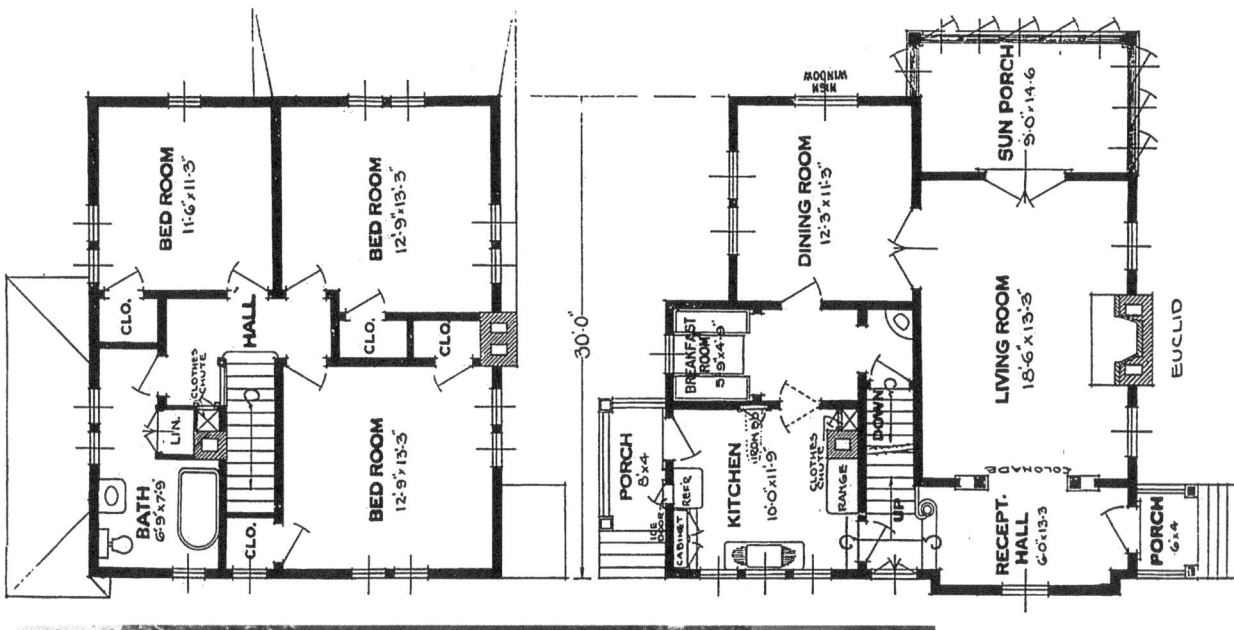

The EUCLID (Size 30x30')

The education that counts in life's competition is the education that elevates and ennobles. The race for supremacy in the sensible pursuit of sane business is not won by the fleet-footed but by the strong. In private homes like The Euclid there is a chance for children to absorb the essentials of a sound, unselfish education.

"The Euclid," *Better Homes at Lower Cost*, page 37; parallel to "The Alma."

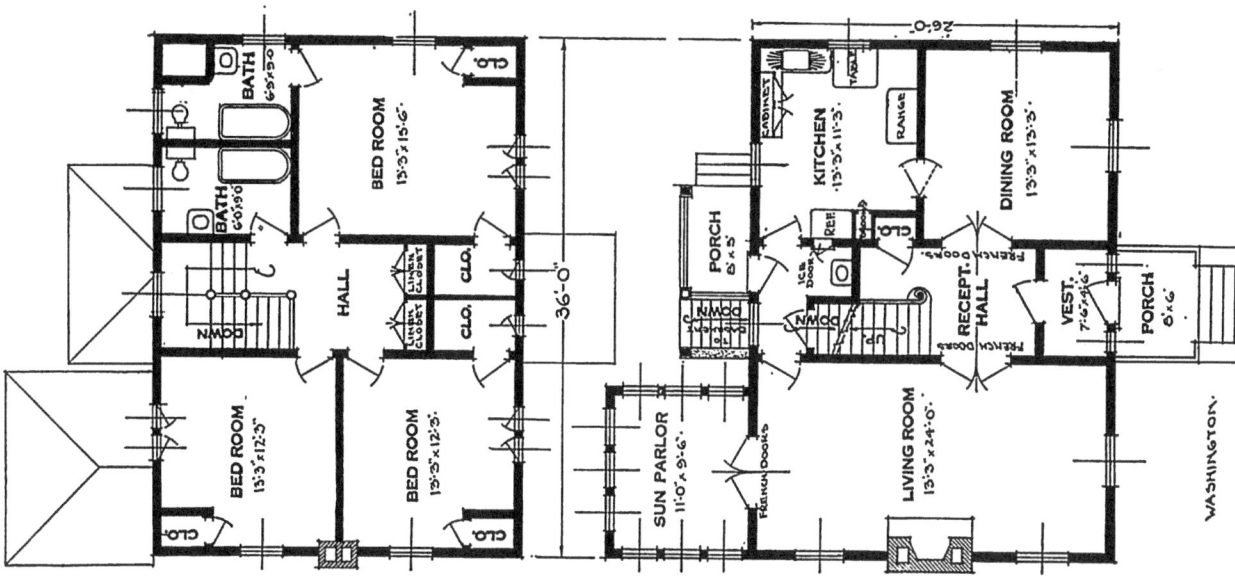

The WASHINGTON (Size 36x26′)

When one looks thoughtfully at the colonial style of architecture as shown in The Washington, his thoughts go back to the days when the love of home and family were the most sacred emotions in the hearts of men. There are yet many with a steadfastness of purpose who inwardly long for the colonial days, and to such The Washington will be an inspiration.

"The Washington," *Better Homes at Lower Cost*, page 19; parallel to "The Acme."

THE MOST POPULAR HOMES
of the TWENTIES

The open door to satisfaction and happiness is the door of the home of your own. This Colonial entrance wreathed with wisteria leads into the "Home, Sweet Home" demonstration house, Washington, D. C.

CONTENTS

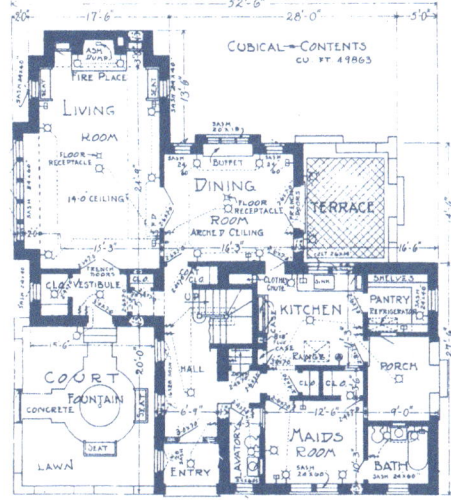

The *ALVARADO*

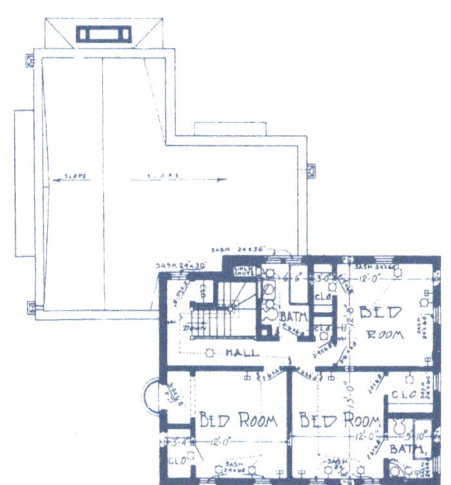

The ADRIAN

OUR Front Cover Home is a Delightful English Cottage. For Complete Building Plans-Working Drawings to Scale See Pages 6, 7, 8 and 9.

Our Front Cover Home

The Adrian

An English Cottage of Shingles and Brick Combined to Form a Distinctive Six-Room House

For Perspective in Full Colors see page 4

A WELL deserved popularity has been accorded to houses of the type represented by Our Front Cover Home. While of no clearly defined style it suggests the English and possesses a distinctive character of its own. The low foundation and walls finished with shingles laid wide to weather give a substantial tone which is ample to carry the rather massive brick chimney and porch and the whole effect is attractively homelike.

On the interior the same thought has been carried out and the design is one of unusual comfort. On one side of the central hall is the dining room while opposite is a large living room with an interesting corner fireplace, built-in bookcase and a doorway opening onto the brick and cement terrace. The rear of the first floor may be reached either through the living room or dining room and here are found a bedroom and bath in addition to the kitchen and a breakfast nook.

The second floor is reached by the stairway leading from the front hall and here are two more bedrooms and a second bathroom. Both these bedrooms are large and one is supplied with a large dressing room. This dressing room has a separate closet while the room off of which it opens is provided with two other closets. The other bedroom has one large closet and a linen closet is a feature of the upstairs hall.

On the front cover this house is illustrated in full colors which brings out the attractive effect of the shingle and brick combination against the background of trees. Floor plans, elevation and detailed sections of building construction are shown on the next four pages and tell in detail the story of Our Front Cover Home.

THE ADRIAN; This Style of House, Finished in Shingles Laid Wide to Weather and With a Massive Brick Chimney Has Earned a Well Deserved Popularity. Floor plans and details of construction will be found on the next four pages.

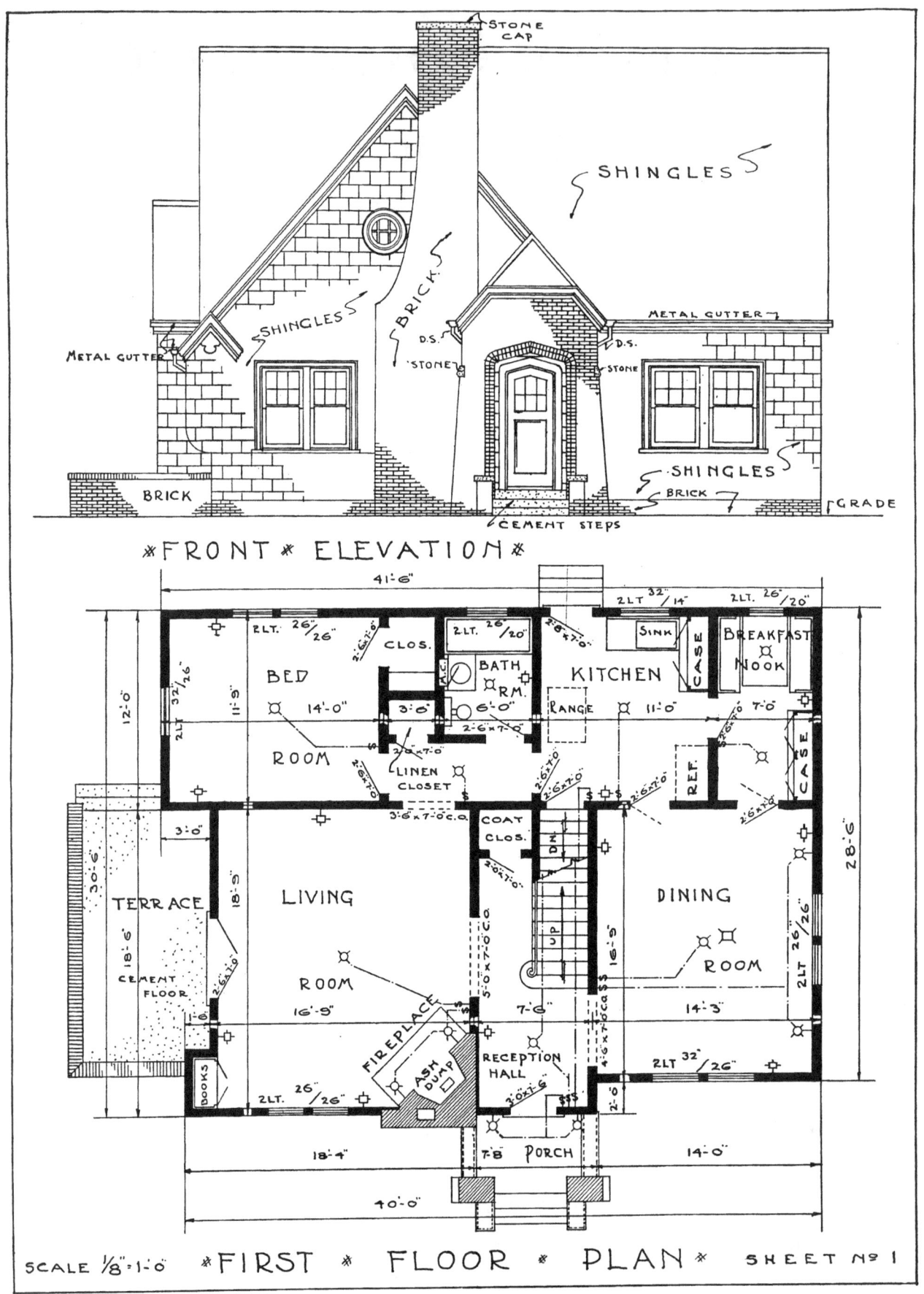

*FRONT * ELEVATION *

SCALE ⅛"=1'-0"   * FIRST * FLOOR * PLAN *   SHEET Nº 1

THE ADRIAN; Elevations and Floor Plans Show What Well Thought Out Planning by an Expert Can Do in
Producing a Convenient and Attractive House Such as That Shown in Colors on Page Four.

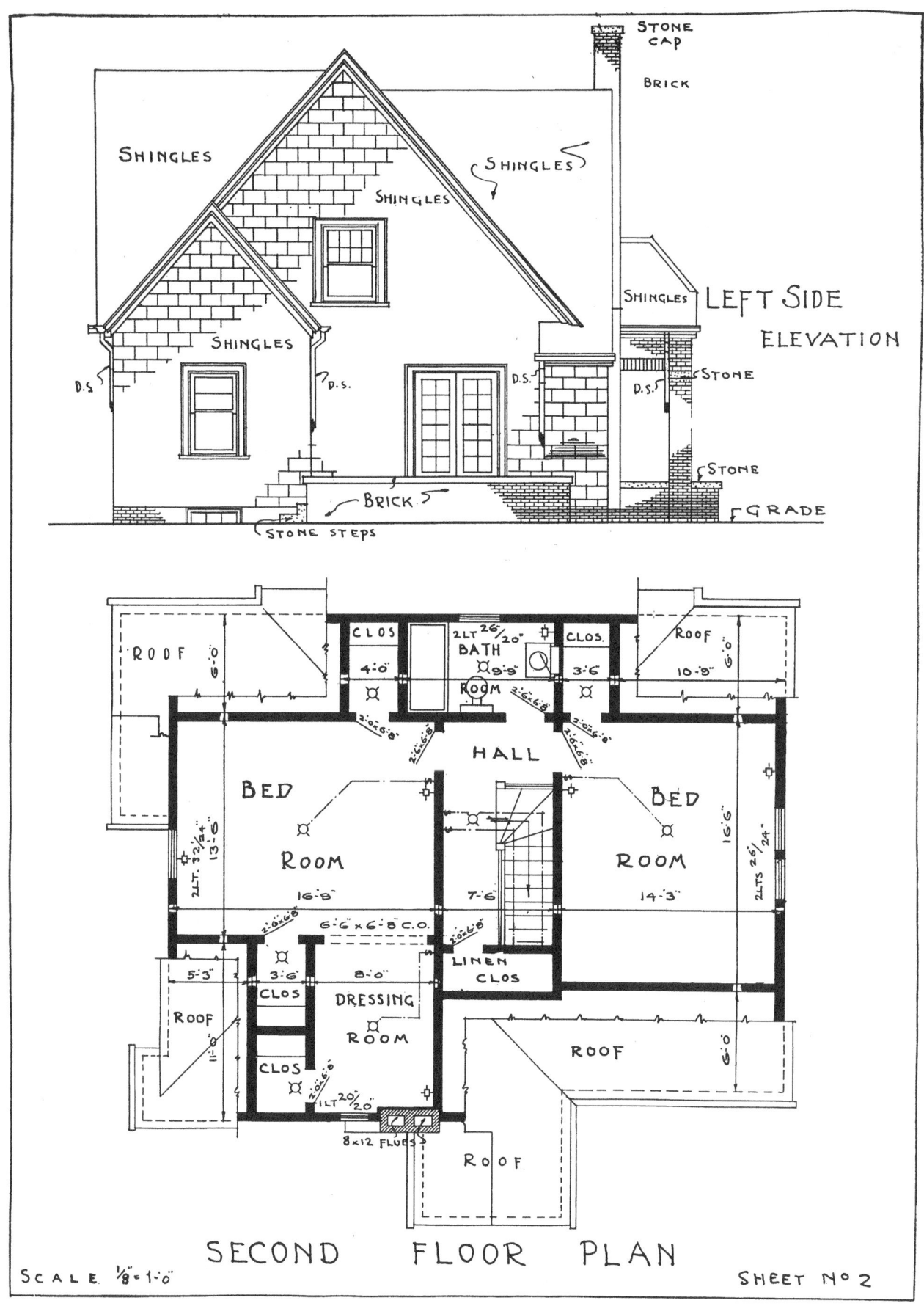

STONE
CAP

BRICK

SHINGLES

SHINGLES

SHINGLES

SHINGLES

LEFT SIDE

ELEVATION

SHINGLES

D.S

D.S.

D.S.

STONE

D.S.

STONE

GRADE

BRICK

STONE STEPS

ROOF
6'-0"

CLOS
4'-0"

2 LT 26/20"
BATH
ROOM
9'-9"

CLOS.
3'-6"

ROOF
10'-9"
6'-0"

2'-0"x6'-8"

2'-6"x6'-8"

2'-0"x6'-8"

2'-0"x6'-8"

BED
ROOM
16'-9"

HALL

7'-6"

BED
ROOM
14'-3"

16'-6"

2LT. 3 2/24
13'-6"

2'-0"x6'-8"

6'-6" x 6'-8" C.O.

2'-0"x6'-0"

LINEN
CLOS

2LTS 26/24

5'-3"

CLOS
3'-6"

8'-0"

DRESSING
ROOM

ROOF
6'-0"

ROOF
6'-0"

CLOS

2'-0"x6'-6"

1LT 20/20

8x12 FLUES

ROOF

SECOND FLOOR PLAN

SCALE 1/8"=1'-0"

SHEET N° 2

THE ADRIAN; There Are Six Rooms in Our Front Cover Home But the Skillful Consideration for Living Comfort Gives it the Adaptability of a Much Larger Building While Preserving a Cozy Homelike Air.

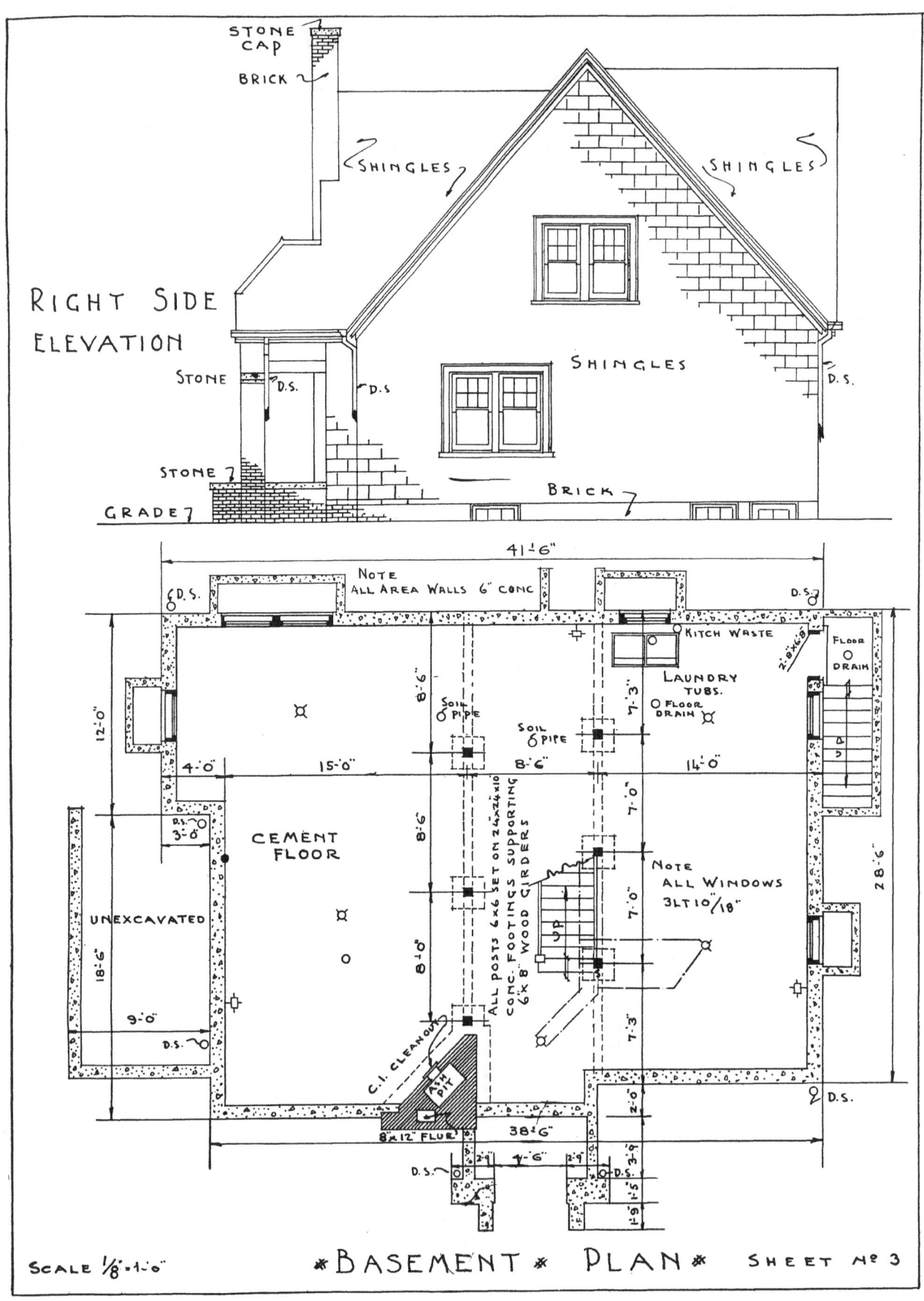

RIGHT SIDE
ELEVATION

BASEMENT PLAN   SHEET № 3

SCALE ⅛"=1'-0"

THE ADRIAN; The Basement Plan and Side Elevation Carry on the Story of the Front Cover Home and Its
Construction Which Is Told on the Preceding Pages.

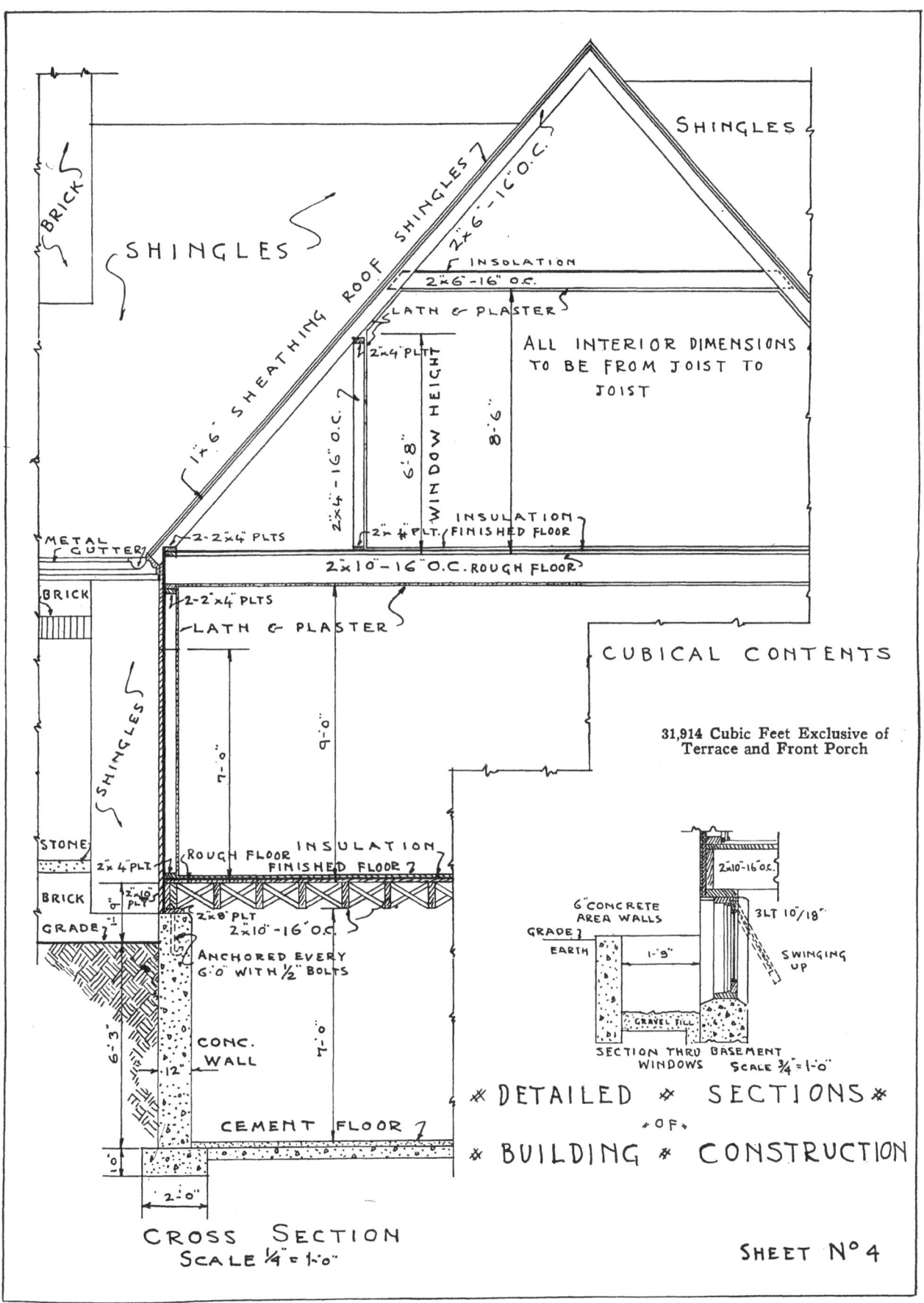

THE ADRIAN; Detailed Sections of Building Construction Are Shown on This Page With Complete Dimensions and
So Round Out the Description of This Front Cover Home.

More Cheerful Home Walls

How Wallpaper Produces Distinctive and Companionable Interiors Far Out of Proportion to the Small Investment Represented

FROM the beginning of time the adornment of the home began with the decoration of its walls. Primeval man brightened his gloomy interiors with crude figures in gay colors. The Egyptian beautified his walls with the stories of his time in weird flat drawings. Our ancestors of the sixteenth and seventeenth centuries decorated their dwellings with rich, gorgeous tapestries and hand-painted papers.

The feeling for beauty and the desire to express it in the adornment of the home finds its happiest and simplest expression today in wallpaper. Decorators' shops are full of bright, cheerful, living papers in warm, rich colors at inexpensive prices; no home need now be dull and unattractive. There are gay chintz patterns for bedrooms in quaint old-fashioned designs, soft two-toned papers best for living rooms and all sorts of queer bizarre effects that are fun to try out in the kitchen.

By some virtue peculiarly its own, wallpaper gives warmth and interest to an interior hard to obtain otherwise. Wallpaper blends with furniture and hangings and gives an intimate friendly air. It reflects personality even, for it makes an otherwise barren room a setting of character and interest. A papered wall becomes an active, truly decorative part of a room, about which everything else centers. It becomes the major theme of a composition, with the hangings and furniture carrying out harmonious details.

Wallpaper is the most flexible medium of decorative expression; with it one can be gay and whimsical or solemn and pretentious, or intimate and informal, or quiet and restful. There are papers for every room and every need, every expression and too, for every purse.

Wallpaper has an economical as well as a decorative value, for aside from the charm and life that wallpaper adds to the home, it is indispensable in protecting plaster walls. When the walls are cracked or blemished it is absolutely essential. It is clean, fresh, sanitary and the means by which any desired effect can be obtained most easily and economically.

In choosing your wallpaper there are three things to consider in order to get the effect you desire: the color, the pattern and the texture. They are very simple things, tremendously effective when correctly, but disastrous when incorrectly used.

Colors in themselves have a very definite effect on the average person. Red stimulates, warms and excites. Blue and green chill and depress. The middle colors of the spectrum, yellow and green yellow, are emotionally indifferent, though yellow by its association with the sunlight seems warm. The so-called neutral colors, the tans and grays, give warmth or coldness according to the dominant note in each. Tan with a yellow or red component is warmer than a tan bordering on gray. Gray may be cold in blue or violet gray and warm in pink or orange grays.

Wallpaper Is the Most Flexible Medium of Decorative Expression. With it one can be gay and whimsical, solemn or pretentious, intimate or informal, quiet and restful. Restful, indeed, is this living room with its plain oatmeal paper and simple decorative border.

These Four-Poster Beds Lend the Required Contrast to the Cretonne or Chintz-Patterned Wallpaper. Small sprays of flowers powdered in a plain ground, fabric effect stripes, or birds—any of these suggest themselves for the bedroom walls.

All this is significant for the home-maker. A room that is too brilliant can be tempered with cold colors. A room that must be as quiet and undisturbing as possible can safely stay in the yellow range or yellow grays. The warm colors, probably because they are exciting and interesting, are more intrusive. They enclose a room and make it smaller. The cold colors tend to recede so that a small room would look larger with light blue or light green paper.

In combining colors, every color has its own complementary. The complementaries of most of the important colors are:

> Red—green—blue
> Orange—blue
> Gold yellow—blue
> Green yellow—violet
> Pure Green—purple.

These complementaries can be used in fascinating ways. If, for instance, you have decided upon a gold yellow room then a touch of blue, if only in a vase or a piece of pottery or a sofa cushion will give character to the setting—each color will emphasize the other.

The most immediately pleasing combinations of colors are usually found, however, not in the exact complementaries but in shades approaching the complementaries.

Wallpaper as an actively contributing factor in the plan of decoration should proclaim the dominant colors of the room and determine all the other color selections. It should always be of a clean tone with some vibrancy, some interest and some reason for existence in itself.

Texture should always be taken into account. Skillfully used it has an expres-

sive value of its own. A rough decided texture increases the appearance of strength in a room. In a living room or library where there are many books this texture is best, for the books are not only heavy but look heavy so that a firm wall is needed to uphold them. Roughness of texture gives a feeling of strength just as the soft depth of a velvet surface gives the feeling of luxury and richness. Damasks and poplins have a mixture of strength with something of the richness of silk. All these textures and many more are available in wallpaper.

Another factor which is most important in the choosing of wallpaper is the nature of the line and

An Always Popular Handling of the Dining Room Walls. White enameled panelling and above that tapestry effect wallpaper in any of the splendid range of patterns now available.

the scale of the pattern. There is as definite a response to line as there is to color and texture. The vertical line is erect. It is dignified, aloof and rather restrained. A room with a strongly emphasized vertical line seems formal and a trifle remote. The horizontal line, on the other hand, is the line of rest and repose. So it is evident that a pattern with an emphasis on the horizontal line would serve to make a room restful, to put it at ease. Too strong and too unrelieved a horizontal, however, might make it seem lifeless and inert.

Broken and curved lines both give the feeling of movement. The broken line in proportion to the shortness of the sections and the angles and also the variety of directions in which it scatters is nervous, agitated and conflicting. A pattern consisting of many broken lines going in various directions would therefore be incorrectly used in a room where a quiet, peaceful effect is desired. A line jointed in long sections moves with more control and ease. Its effect is more calm. The long gradual flat curve moves slowly and with repose. The short, deep, heavy curves move rapidly. For a quiet effect horizontal or long gradual curves are best. If one feels the need of freshness and vitality, short broken lines and deep curves are best. Patterns with sets of lines running in different directions can be used effectively as long as the lines compensate each other, so that the whole pattern can be brought to a balance.

The importance of line cannot be overemphasized. An informal room cannot be definitely vertical and still retain its ease and relaxation. Many rapid curves and sharply broken lines are necessarily de-structive of a restful effect. A room that wants to be gay and cheerful can obtain its effect only by playing upon curves and broken lines. So a room in very bright colors that are themselves intentionally gay should not in line contradict this character by being stiffly vertical or quietly horizontal. The quality of the line, in short, must be consistent with the purpose of the room.

The living room is perhaps the most difficult to choose suitable paper for, because it is so heterogeneous in character. It usually combines the three functions of the drawing-room, sitting-room and library and contains a widely assorted combination of furnishings. There are a few wedding presents, some pieces donated by relatives and all kinds of ends of ornaments and books. Two-toned damask has, therefore, been found successful in many living rooms. This has quiet necessary for the background as well as the touch of dignity that is desirable. Especially attractive are grass cloths or grass cloth finished papers. For a little more vitality and interest there are these same cloths in damask patterns with the pattern lightly outlined in metal—silver or gold. The self-color stripe with the stripe indicated only by a different texture can also be used to advantage. If the room is very informal as is, for instance, the living room of a country cottage or a New England farmhouse, the stripe might be one of those that are lightly dotted in a contrasting color, faintly reminiscent of cotton prints.

For a rich background that will not be too decided there are the tapestry papers. These range all the way from the vague verdure effects, that are hardly more than massed lights and shadows in two or three tones of the color to the rather clearly drawn landscapes, and they come not only in the conventional greens and blues but in soft grays and browns as well. Especially interesting is a recent issued English paper of which the design is adapted from a French Gothic tapestry with medieval gentlemen pursuing quaint beasts through a thick and flowery wood indicated in flatly drawn superimposed shrubs and flowers.

Where there is opportunity for more decided patterns the closely drawn, continuous designs such as those which William Morris made so beautifully are very good. Ideal examples are his Pimpernel and Honeysuckle. And finally for the living room that is quite English and rather more like a morning-room in character there are the chintz papers. But these forbid much ornament in the room.

For bedrooms in country houses there are cretonne or chintz patterns having bright colors on a white or light colored ground. Small sprays of flowers powdered in a plain ground, narrow floral or fabric effect stripes, or in all-over scrollage, sometimes introducing birds among the foliage and flowers are all appropriate designs.

Perhaps, after all, the greatest fun in decorating can be had with the kitchen. That is the one room in the house that should not be taken too seriously. Here one can try out all those papers that are too strange, or too vivid and bizarre to be attempted elsewhere. There are delightful garden effects with fruit trees showing bright, ripe fruit and informal landscapes, landscapes that give a widening effect. The kitchen because it is devoted to dull labor need never be dull. Out-of-doors effects are especially satisfying, further help to relieve the long weary hours that often must be spent in the kitchen.

With the great variety of papers to choose from today every room in the house can be dignified, gay and cheerful. In color and designs are mediums of expression that can be nicely attuned to every varying need and pocketbook. Wallpaper makes cheerful, livable homes more possible than ever before and gives an opportunity for the expression of individual character and taste within the means of everyone.

An Informal Room Cannot Be Too Definitely Vertical and Still Offer Ease and Relaxation. Curves and intentionally gayly patterned wall paper give distinction and comfort.

The Alpena

This English Cottage Style Home, in Brick and Stucco, is the Product of a High Standard of Planning and Construction

HERE is an English cottage style house in which quality is the dominating characteristic. It is one of a group, built in Des Moines, Iowa, which were planned with the thought that those who are in the market for small homes of five or six rooms desire and appreciate the same high type of construction which is most generally associated with the larger and more costly dwellings. How well this ideal was carried out is graphically pictured in the illustrations on this and the two following pages.

A pleasing combination of brick and stucco is used for the exterior while the roof is appropriately covered with shingles laid wide to weather. The lines of the house are harmonious and the one story sunroom at the left is balanced by the pergola over the driveway

at the opposite side. A decorative touch is added by the use of flower boxes at the windows and small trees at either side of the entrance. This entrance is simple but effective and is perfectly fitted to the house to which it gives access.

The interior shows the same careful planning and construction throughout that is found in large and costly houses. On the first floor there are three major rooms, a sunroom and a breakfast room. This floor is divided by a central hall. At the left is the large living room with a neat brick fireplace at one end, flanked by built-in book-cases. French doors open into the sun room which is almost completely enclosed with glass on three sides.

Across the hall is found another cheerful room. The

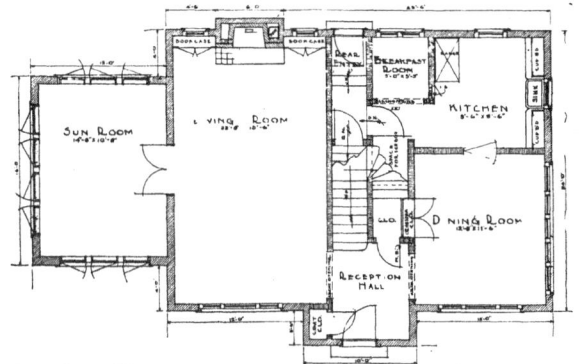

The Floor Plans Allow for the Efficient and Economical Use of Lumber and Other Materials.

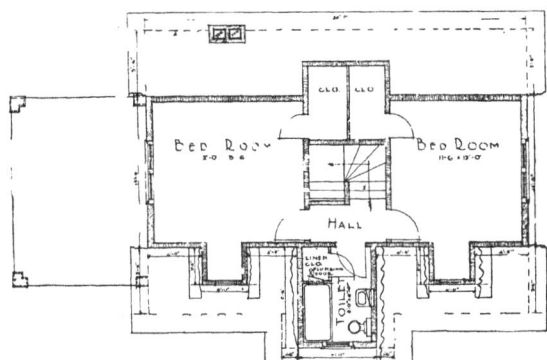

Two Adequately Large Bedrooms with a Bath and Large Closets Are on the Second Floor.

A successful house the attractive, English cottage style of which is backed by skilled and careful planning and high quality of construction, making a home of real permanence.

Including the comforts and conveniences ordinarily found in much larger and more expensive houses has contributed greatly to the success of The Alpena. Here is the sun room which is a part of this five room house, shown on the preceding page. Its sunshiny character is well carried out in the furnishings which have been used.

The Fireplace, with Its Flanking Bookcases, Is an Attractive Feature of This Pleasant Living Room.

ample closets and a bathroom. Both bedrooms have windows on two sides and adequate space for all necessary furniture. A linen closet is included in the bathroom plan.

The dining room of The Alpena is a light and cheerful place for the family to gather at meal times.

dining room is well lighted by windows on two sides. It is directly connected with the kitchen at the rear. This latter room is all that the modern housekeeper could ask in cleanliness and convenience. White tile is freely used and the white enamel sink is surrounded with handy built-in cupboards, both above and below.

Just off this kitchen is a breakfast room of the approved Pullman type and near the door into the hallway are found the rear entrance and basement stairs. At the front of the hall a stairway leads to the second floor. This floor is divided into two large bedrooms with

In the Spotless Kitchen the Glistening White Tile and Dainty Curtains Will Attract the Housewife.

The Amarillo
A Bungalow in the Spanish Style
New Note in Residence Architecture Struck by Adaptations of Spanish
Pioneer Models, With High Chapel-Roof Interiors

For Perspective in Full Colors, see page 21.

"DON'T you think the modern renaissance of the Spanish type of residence worth featuring?" asks not one home builder, but many. We do. The color sketch on page 21 and the photo below, with the following floor plans, is as smart a home as ever graced a building site. It is,—well, rather exotic. It owes its American being to the Spanish pioneers who reproduced in the New World the typical architecture of old Spain. Like Spain, too, we have extremes of temperature which vary from the boasted California climate to the more rigorous New England winter, and the bungalow is of a kind of construction which can be both cool in summer and warm in winter.

The exterior is of a vari-colored stucco, against which the brightly colored awnings stand in bright contrast. The warm red of the roof tiles and the grass-defined flags of the walk and driveway are two other effective color touches. Reference to the detailed plans following shows a *Chapel Roofed Living Room*—

The living room, entered from the terrace entry has the popular style of chapel ceiling, extending upward to the roof. It is a very well proportioned room, and the presence of colored electric light bulbs inside the wood cornice enables different colors to be thrown against the ceiling. In fact, the whole character of the room may be changed by judicious manipulation of these indirect lights, controlled as they are by a switch near the door. The French doors opening on the front terrace look out upon a semi-patio; the enclosed patio typical of real Spanish homes seems not to be preferred in American adaptations.

There is a dining room, with terrace; a kitchen, small, but so compact it is of great convenience; three bedrooms and a bathroom.

THE AMARILLO; The Gaily Colored Baldachin Awnings on this Home Give a Lively Note to the Picture. They are helped by the vari-colored stucco and the warm colored tiles, and the flowers and potted shrubs on the front terrace. Working plans presented on the four pages following.

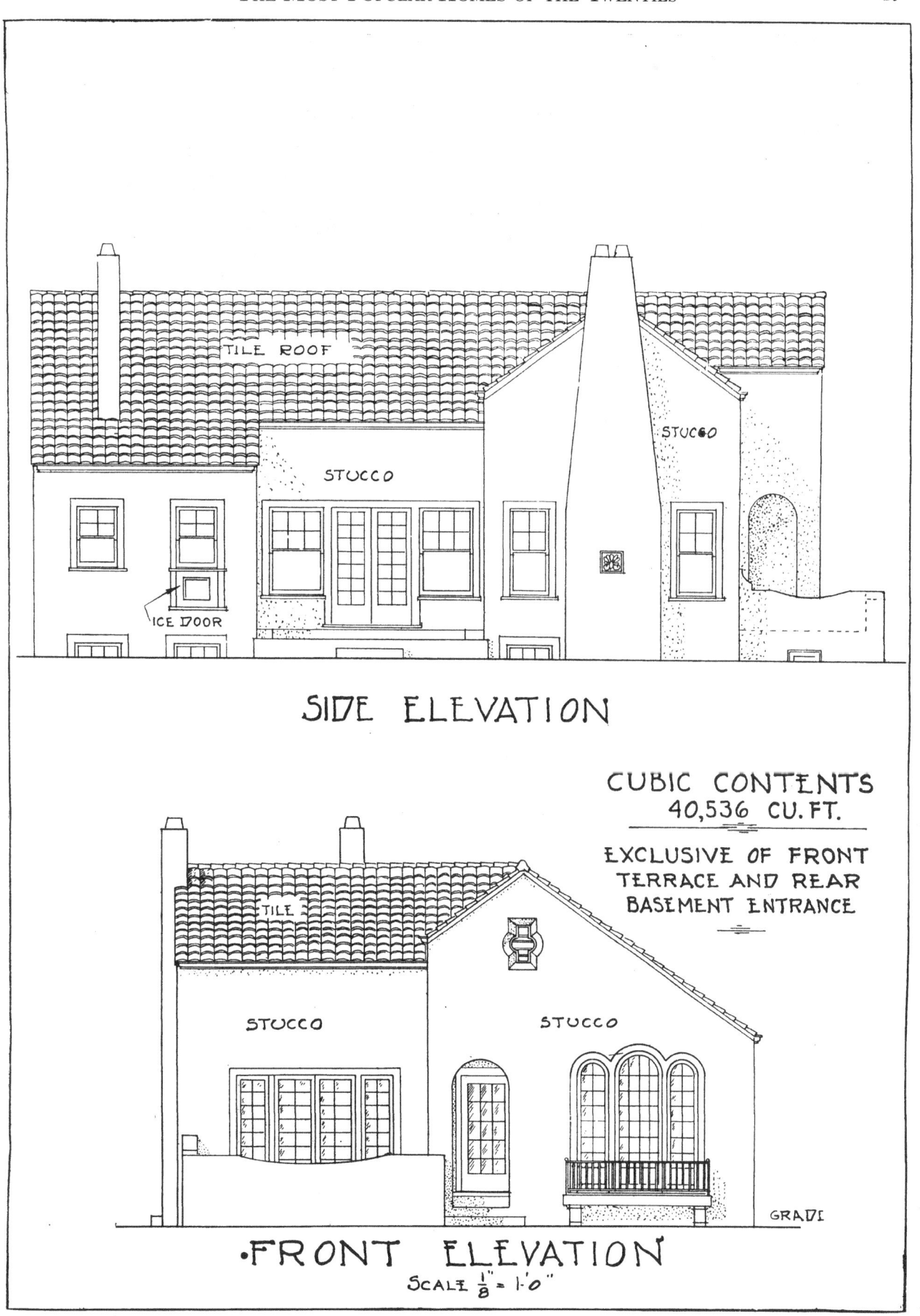

SIDE ELEVATION

CUBIC CONTENTS
40,536 CU. FT.

EXCLUSIVE OF FRONT
TERRACE AND REAR
BASEMENT ENTRANCE

TILE ROOF

STUCCO

STUCCO

ICE DOOR

TILE

STUCCO

STUCCO

GRADE

·FRONT ELEVATION

SCALE $\frac{1}{8}$" = 1'·0"

THE AMARILLO; Front and Side Elevation. Observe that, structurally, the design is very simple, and requires merely tiled roof, arched windows, wrought iron railing and colored stucco to give it its picturesque Spanish character.

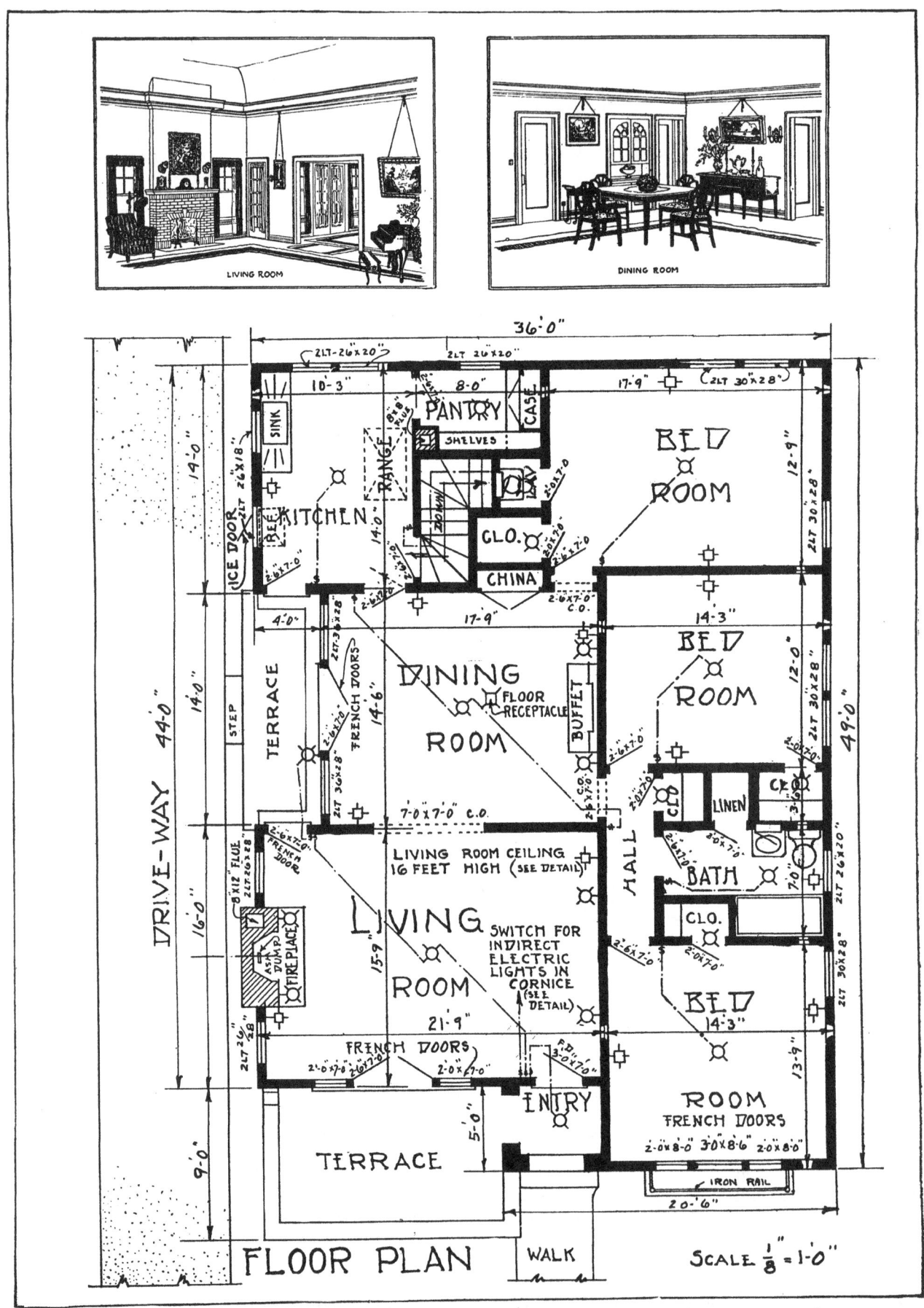

LIVING ROOM

DINING ROOM

FLOOR PLAN   WALK   SCALE ⅛" = 1'-0"

THE AMARILLO; Six Rooms—Living Room, Dining Room, Kitchen and Three Bedrooms, Are Grouped Conveniently Within the Rectangular Plan which is 36 Feet by 53 Feet Over All.

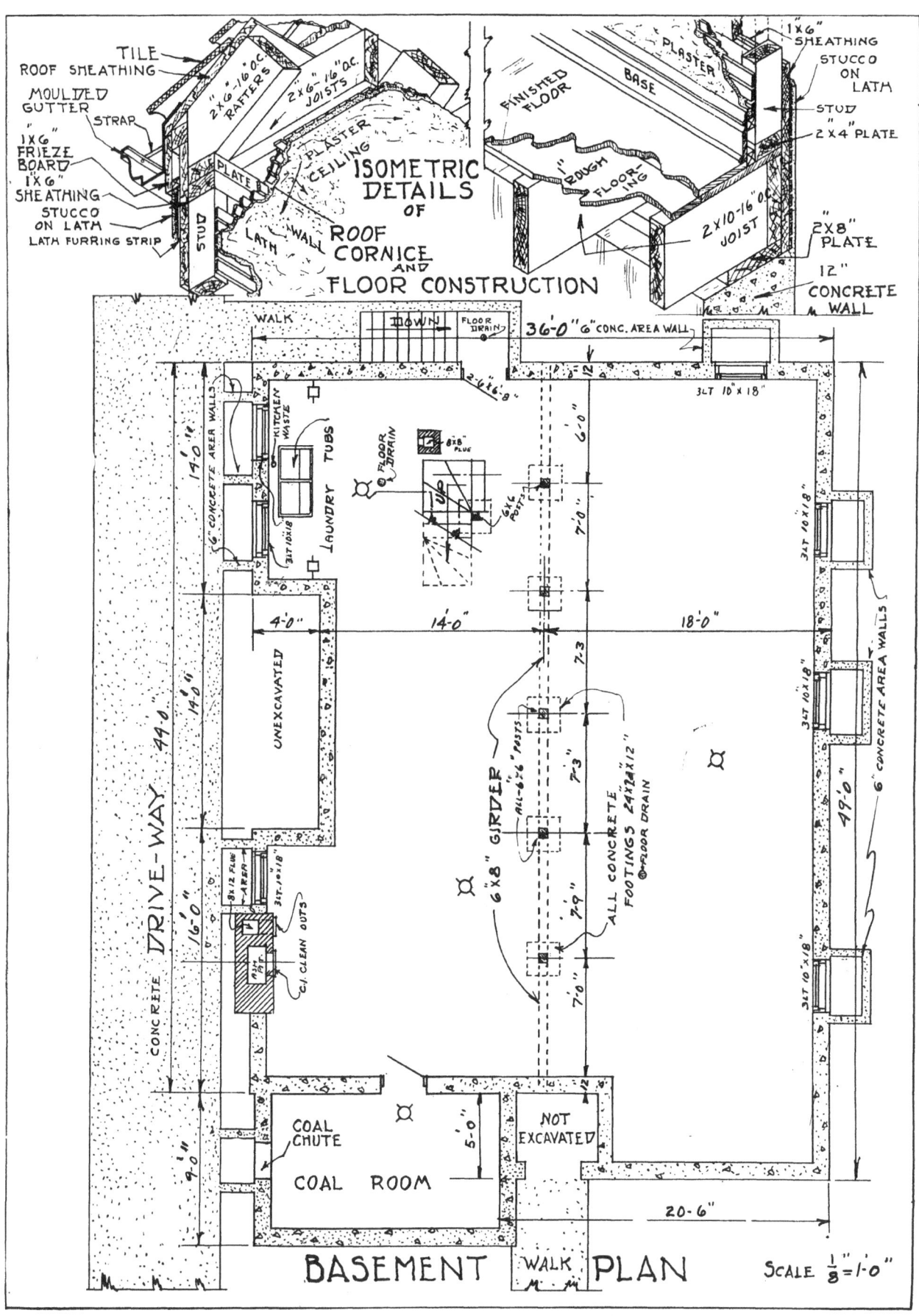

ISOMETRIC DETAILS OF ROOF CORNICE AND FLOOR CONSTRUCTION

BASEMENT PLAN

SCALE ⅛" = 1'-0"

THE AMARILLO; Isometric Details of Roof, Cornice and Floor Construction and Basement Plan. The Coal Room and Heater space are away from the Laundry Tubs and Clothes drying space.

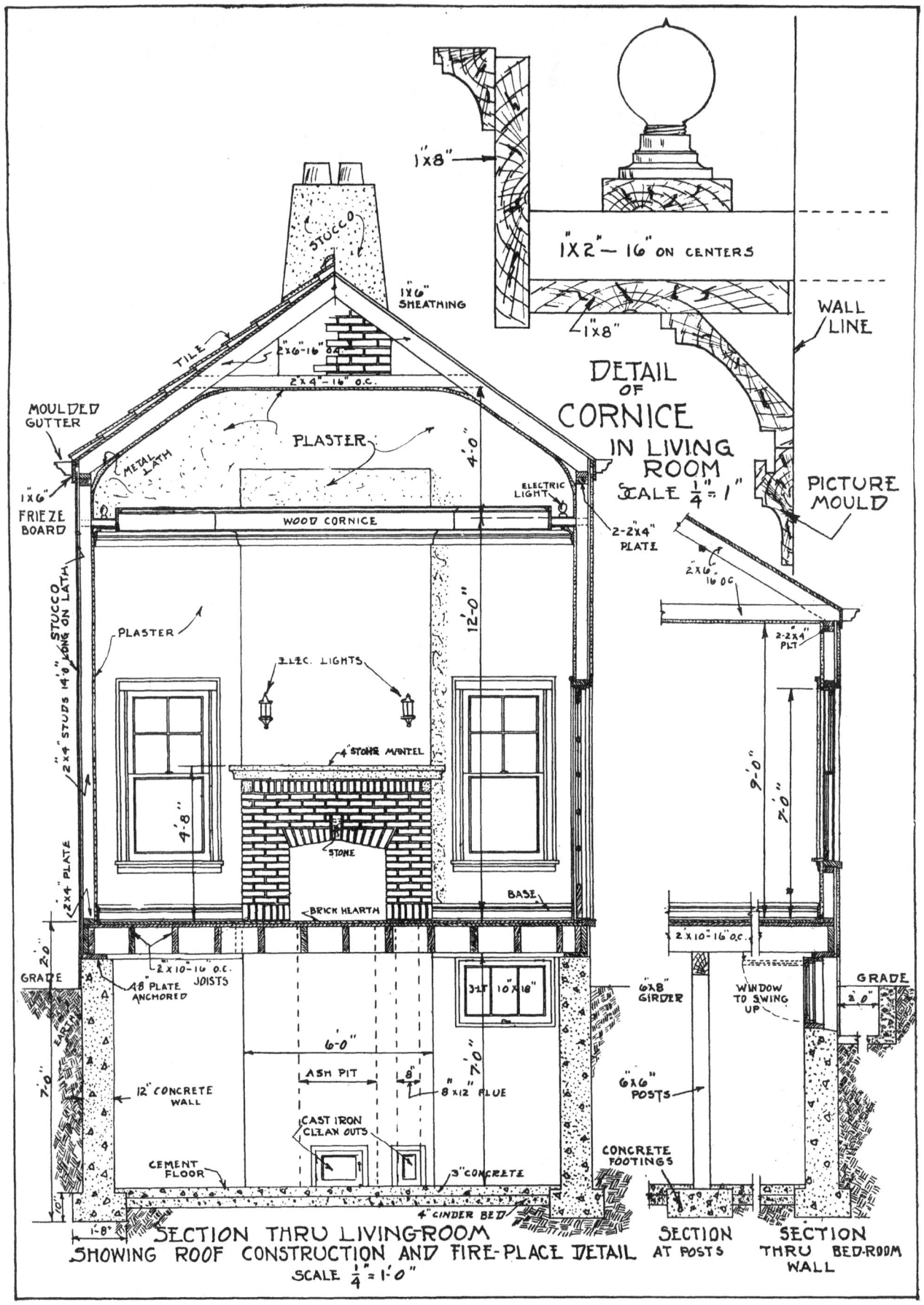

THE AMARILLO; The Cross Section Shows the Living Room with Its Chapel Roof, and the Wood Cornice Moulding
Which Conceals the Colored Light Bulbs. Below, foundation structural details.

The *AMARILLO*

A BUNGALOW In The Spanish Style. For Complete Building Plans-Working Drawings to Scale See Pages 17, 18, 19 and 20.

The ALBION

A PLEASING Western Style Colonial. For Complete Building Plans-Working Drawings to Scale See Pages 24, 25, 26 and 27.

The Albion

A Pleasing Western Style Colonial

Either in Winter Colors or Summer Landscaping, This 6-Room, Sun-Parlor, and 2-Bath Home Wins on the Three Essentials—Economy Convenience and Good Looks

For Perspective in Full Colors, see page 22

EQUALLY pretty in winter or in summer is the verdict on The Albion. We consider it so good, both exteriorly and interiorly, that we have felt justified in devoting to it six pages: Page 22 in full colors, this page, and the four pages of plans following. These are shown in exact scale, enabling you to reconstruct this splendid home to meet the requirements of any intending home builders in your locality.

The pleasing outward appeal of this house is due to the intelligent use of comparatively simple structural details. The interior arrangement is no less admirable, the porch giving into a roomy reception hall, with a handsome Colonial staircase, and closet at the end for outdoor wraps. To the left of the hall opens the living room, 23 feet long by 13 feet 3 inches wide, and with a well proportioned fireplace.

Observe the clear wall spaces which lend themselves to the proper backgrounding of the home furnishings; and how the sun parlor, reached through its double French doors, helps give a most agreeable impression of airiness and comfort.

Crossing the hall again and going through double French doors we are in the dining room. This is 13 feet 3 inches by 14 feet, and will display any dining room furniture to good advantage. Double French doors lead out to the porch, and give a very pleasing prospect, as dining room doors and windows should. At the rear of the dining room we find the breakfast nook, for morning meal or children's lunch or before bedtime snack. The built-in china closet close by saves steps. Now we are in the kitchen, with everything truly arranged to make work a joy; well-placed range, refrigerator and sink with ample shelving; pantry, and rear entry.

Upstairs is a master's bedroom with bath; also two more bedrooms, and hall bathroom.

THE ALBION; This Shows this beautiful Home in Its Summer Dress. Simple but intelligent landscaping helps to make it doubly enjoyable. It is a modified Colonial design, suitable to any locality. Working plans presented on the four pages following.

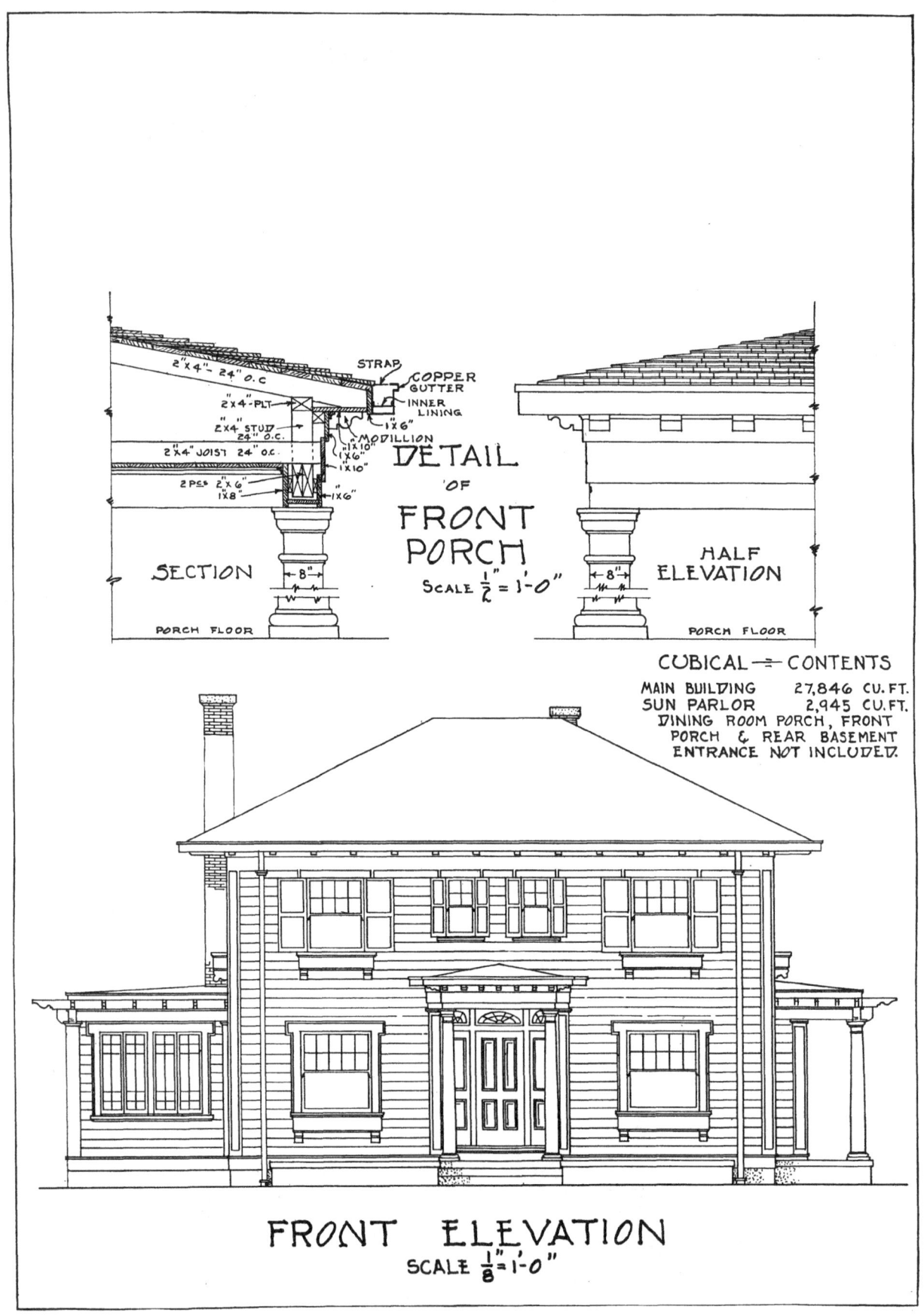

DETAIL OF FRONT PORCH

SCALE ½" = 1'-0"

SECTION

HALF ELEVATION

STRAP
COPPER GUTTER
INNER LINING
1"X6"
MODILLION
2"X4"— 24" O.C
2X4"-PLT
2"X4" STUD 24" O.C.
2"X4" JOIST 24" O.C.
2 PCS 2"X6"
1X8"
1X6"
1X10"
1X10"
1X6"

PORCH FLOOR

CUBICAL — CONTENTS

MAIN BUILDING   27,846 CU. FT.
SUN PARLOR   2,945 CU. FT.
DINING ROOM PORCH, FRONT
PORCH & REAR BASEMENT
ENTRANCE NOT INCLUDED.

FRONT ELEVATION

SCALE ⅛" = 1'-0"

THE ALBION Has a Simple Rectangular Plan. This offers the utmost saving in construction costs and gives most room in the interior. The over all dimensions are 46 feet by 27 feet.

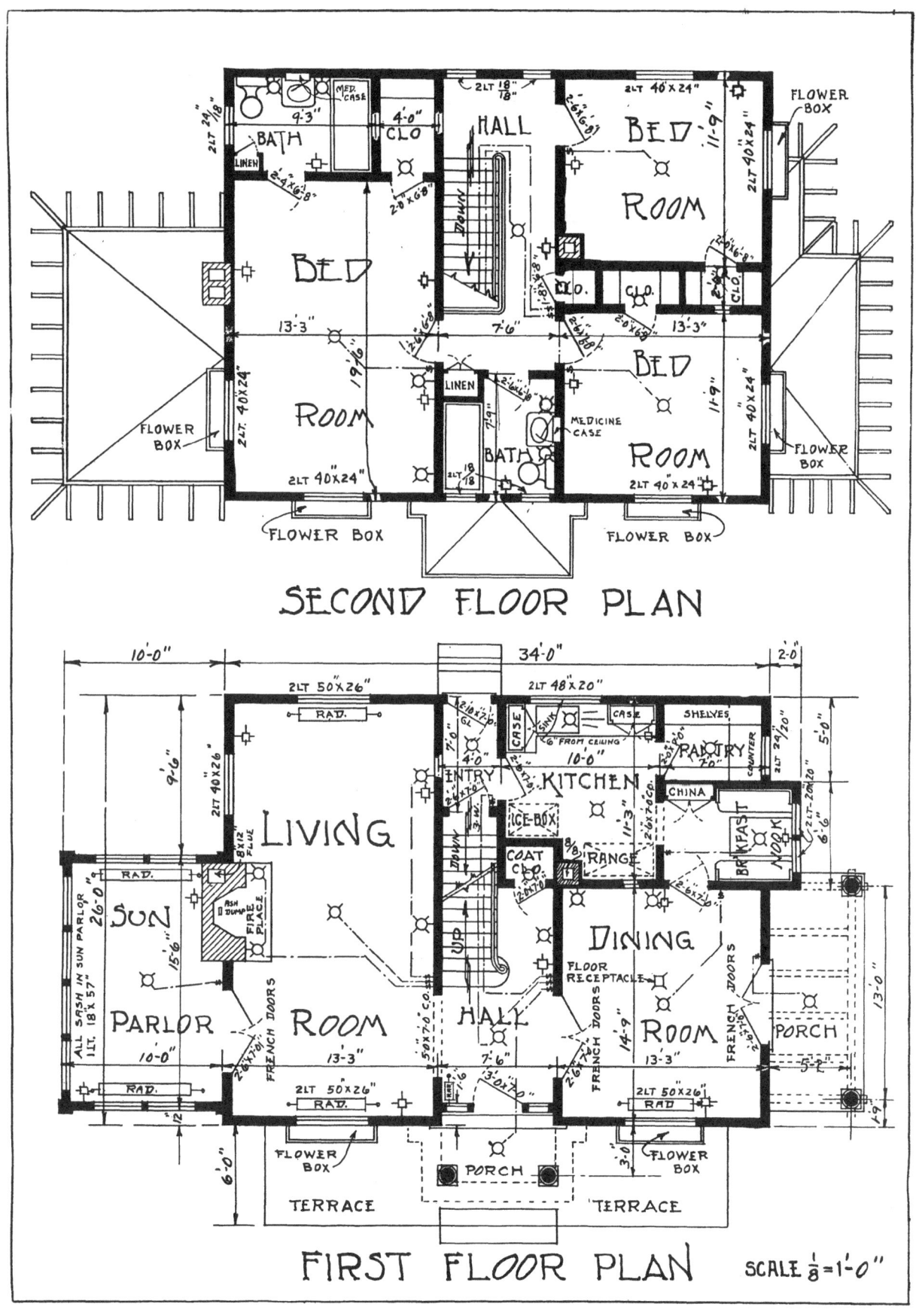

SECOND FLOOR PLAN

FIRST FLOOR PLAN

SCALE ⅛=1'-0"

THE ALBION; On the First Floor We have Reception Hall, Living Room, Sun Parlor, Dining Room, Kitchen, Breakfast Nook, Pantry and a Rear Entry Hall. On the second floor are master's bedroom and bath, and two other bedrooms, with bathroom off hall. Full provision is made for modern use of electricity.

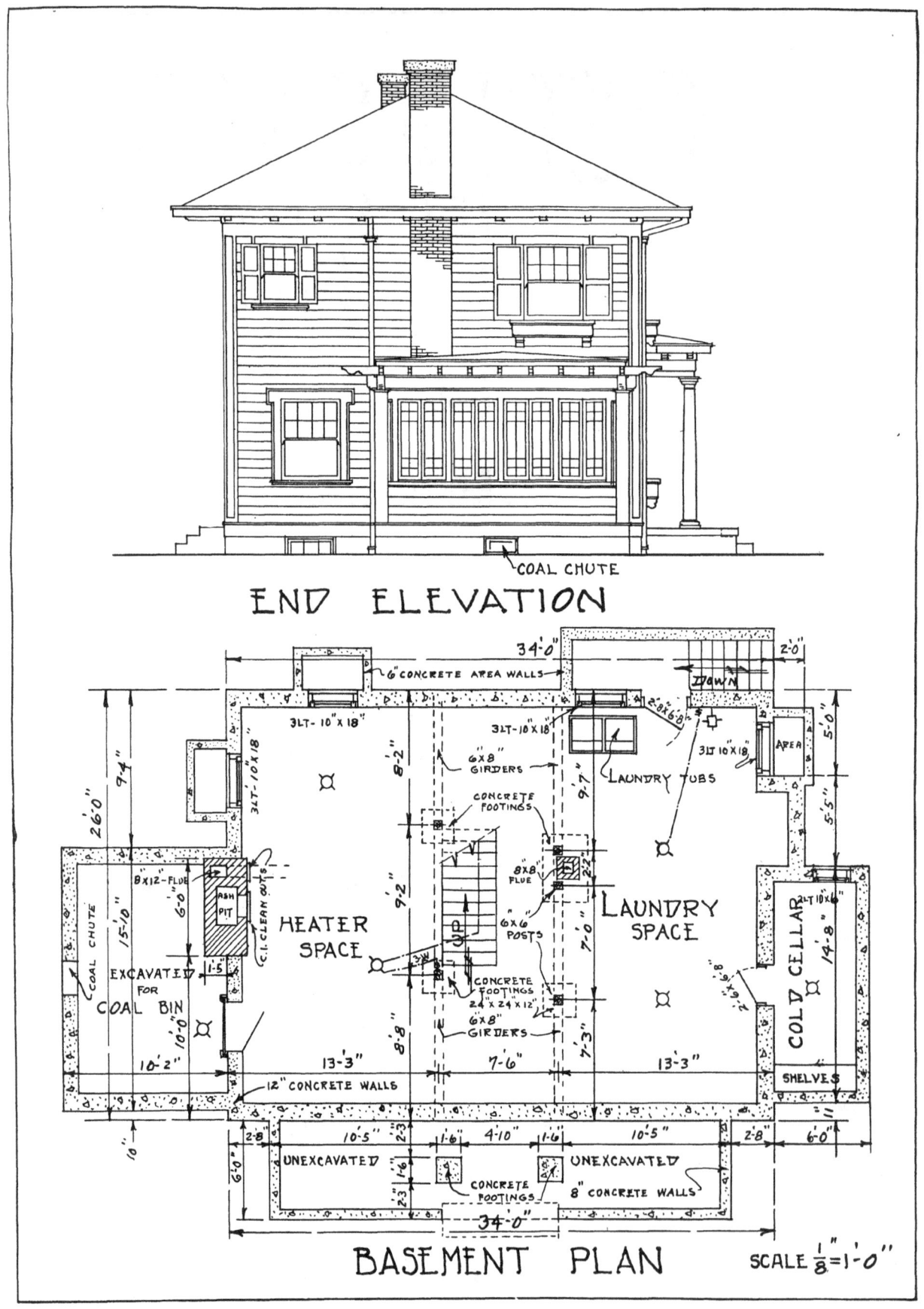

END ELEVATION

COAL CHUTE

BASEMENT PLAN

SCALE ⅛" = 1'-0"

THE ALBION; The End Elevation Is Calculated to Present as Pleasing an Appearance as the Front, and Therefore Makes the House Position Reversible, to Fit a Narrower Lot. The house has commodious, well-arranged basement, with coal bin, heater and laundry space.

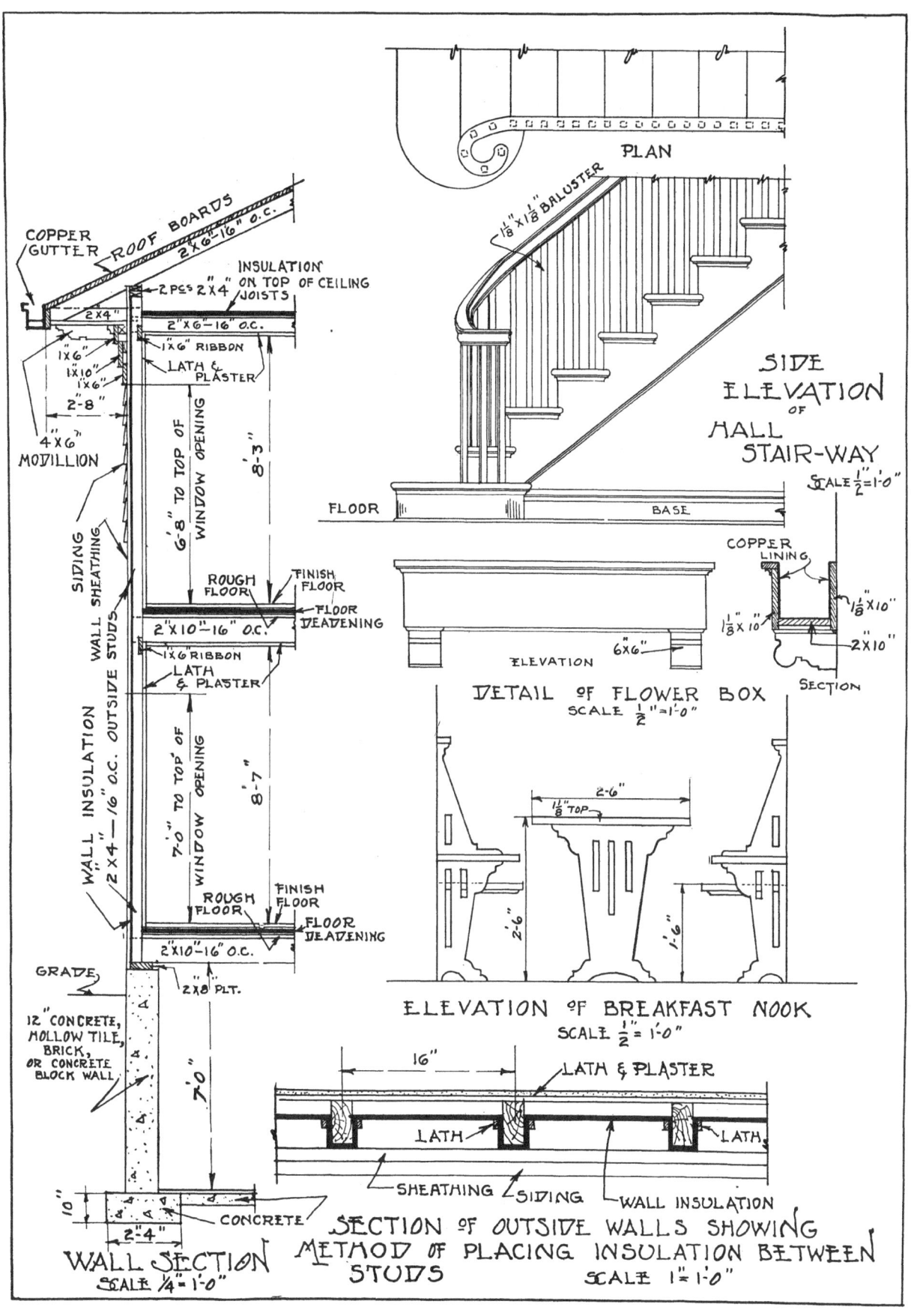

COPPER GUTTER

ROOF BOARDS 2"x6"—16" O.C.

INSULATION ON TOP OF CEILING JOISTS

2 PCS 2"x4"

2"x4"

2"x6"—16" O.C.

1"x6"
1"x10"
1"x6"

1"x6" RIBBON

LATH & PLASTER

2'-8"

4"x6" MODILLION

SIDING

WALL SHEATHING

6'-8" TO TOP OF WINDOW OPENING

8'-3"

ROUGH FLOOR

FINISH FLOOR

FLOOR DEADENING

2"x10"—16" O.C.

1"x6" RIBBON

LATH & PLASTER

WALL INSULATION 2"x4"—16" O.C. OUTSIDE STUDS

7'-0" TO TOP OF WINDOW OPENING

8'-7"

ROUGH FLOOR

FINISH FLOOR

FLOOR DEADENING

2"x10"—16" O.C.

GRADE

2"x8" PLT.

12" CONCRETE, HOLLOW TILE, BRICK, OR CONCRETE BLOCK WALL

7'-0"

10"

2'-4"

CONCRETE

WALL SECTION
SCALE 1/4"=1'-0"

PLAN

1 1/8" x 1 1/8" BALUSTER

SIDE ELEVATION OF HALL STAIR-WAY
SCALE 1/2"=1'-0"

FLOOR

BASE

COPPER LINING

1 1/8" x 10"

1 1/8" x 10"

2" x 10"

SECTION

ELEVATION

6"x6"

DETAIL OF FLOWER BOX
SCALE 1/2"=1'-0"

2'-6"

1 1/8" TOP

2'-6"

1'-6"

ELEVATION OF BREAKFAST NOOK
SCALE 1/2" = 1'-0"

16"

LATH & PLASTER

LATH

LATH

SHEATHING   SIDING   WALL INSULATION

SECTION OF OUTSIDE WALLS SHOWING METHOD OF PLACING INSULATION BETWEEN STUDS
SCALE 1"=1'-0"

THE ALBION; The Walls Are Designed to Give a Summer-Cool and Winter-Warm Interior, Through the Use of Modern Wall Insulating Material. The staircase is an exceptionally graceful design. The breakfast nook design is planned to give plenty of seating room in small space.

Building the Garage

Precautions Necessary in the Design and Construction of the One or Two-Car Residence Lot Garage, or the Garage Semi-Detached or Integral with the House

A TYPICAL construction development of the first 20 years of this twentieth century is the one or two-car garage. The advent of the automobile has caused a shifting of viewpoints, brought a new set of values and uses into our lives. The unsanitary barn or unsightly woodshed is gone from the back lot and the vicinity of most of our city residence and business sections. But the garage which takes its place possesses an inherent danger, unless properly constructed, that far offsets any gain in sanitation or comfort advantage.

If the garage is not properly constructed it is a menace to life and property. A garage should first of all have an incombustible floor. The choice is wide for any type of masonry or wooden wall. If an integral or semi-detached structure, one with the general design of the house, there must be a garage structure of unpierced partitions and ceilings that will meet the 1-hour fire test; the outside walls likewise must be fire-resistant, as well as the outside windows and the garage doors, in order to prevent flames from breaking out and spreading through windows or to the exterior woodwork above. The word "must" here is no legal or ordinance "must;" simply a step dictated by the ordinary standards of safe and sound and profitable construction.

Many materials are acceptable for such garage wall construction from the standpoint of meeting the standard 1-hour fire test recommended by the National Board of Fire Underwriters. Brick, hollow tile, concrete block, or gypsum block 4 inches thick, or reinforced concrete 3 inches thick. The walls may also be constructed of wooden studs, space about 16 inches center to center, with metal lath attached outside and inside. The outer lath could be plastered and back

For the Stucco House this Garage Makes a Pleasing Complement. It is particularly attractive in a setting of foliage.

plastered with Portland cement stucco; the inner lath plastered with ¾-inch Portland cement or gypsum plaster.

Assuming that this would be an integral, or semi-detached garage, the interior partitions separating the garage from the rest of the dwelling, ¾-inch Portland cement or gypsum plaster on metal lath, on both sides of studs spaced 16 inches apart, is satisfactory.

The combined floor and ceiling directly above the integral or semi-detached garage should be unpierced and have a fire resistance of one hour. Ceilings or roofs of reinforced concrete, or some other type of incombustible construction that meets the fire test, are best and most reliable. A good inexpensive overhead construction is obtained by using 2-inch or thicker floor joists, spacing them not more than 16 inches center to center, with proper bridging. The ceiling could be of heavy metal lath weighing

A Sturdy, One-Car Garage of a Pleasing Type Which Will Blend Readily With Almost Any Type of Residence.

not less than 3 pounds per square yard, and Portland cement or gypsum plaster not less than ¾-inch thick. The metal lath to be attached to the joists by 6-penny nails driven nearly home, with the heads turned over against the lath, which in turn is to be bent down 6 inches along the walls on all sides and securely attached to them. The flooring above the ceiling to be double, of ⅞-inch rough and finished floor boards, with a layer of asbestos or other high grade floor felt between.

Where a garage is located beneath a dwelling all outside doors and windows, with their frames and sash, should be of standard fireproof construction, glazed with wire glass. It is important that these have metal frames.

The opening from a dwelling into a garage should be restricted to a single doorway, protected by some standard swinging-self-closing fire door, with approved fire resistive hardware and frame without glass. If the doorway connects directly with a cellar or basement on the same or lower level, in which there is any furnace, boiler, gas fixture or any kind of non-electrical heating device, the door sill should be raised about a foot above the garage floor level, or the doorway should lead into a vestibule which connects with the cellar or basement by a second door.

The reason for this is to prevent the fumes of gasoline which may leak or be spilled upon the floor from reaching a furnace fire or gas light which may be located in the lower part of the building. It is well known that gasoline vapors are heavier than air, and accumulate on a floor like water. They naturally will flow to any lower level. Should they come in contact with fire of any kind—even a spark —there will be ignition and a flash back to the starting point, causing an explosion.

If we consider the garage which is to be situated at some distance from the house, and not connected directly with it in any way, it is natural that many of the structural considerations governing the semi-detached or integral type of garage, considered above, do not apply. With the isolated one or two-car garage the fireproof door and windows are optional; personal likes or dislikes may dictate whether the structure is to be of wood frame, or brick, or of any of the favored types of stucco or concrete walls. But the design is important; it

For the Family With Two Cars or With a Duplex Housing Two Families this Type of Garage Will Prove Its Utility.

should tie up with that of the house.

Within, its concrete floor should be laid so as to drain naturally, and prevent dangerous accumulations of water, oil or grease. There could be a pit, also, to permit working underneath the car as occasion required, and covered at other times by boards that fitted snugly over the aperture in the floor. There should be a sink, with warm water available from the house. In fact, if it is at all practicable, steam or hot water heat piping could also be laid from the house to the garage, making it more comfortable in winter. Connecting to the electric lighting system in the house is both a safety measure and a great help.

In a one or two-car garage a glove-fit is foolish and uneconomical. A spare foot or two saves both nerves and fenders, to say nothing of time.

A shelf of the proper width and height for a workbench will be appreciated by the motorist and a small cabinet for the storage of extra casings and other equipment is a convenience which can be built readily.

Note the Arrangement of the Doors on This Garage for Two Cars. The folding leaves allow either car to be taken out without regard to the position of the other doors.

Garages for Cars of All Types

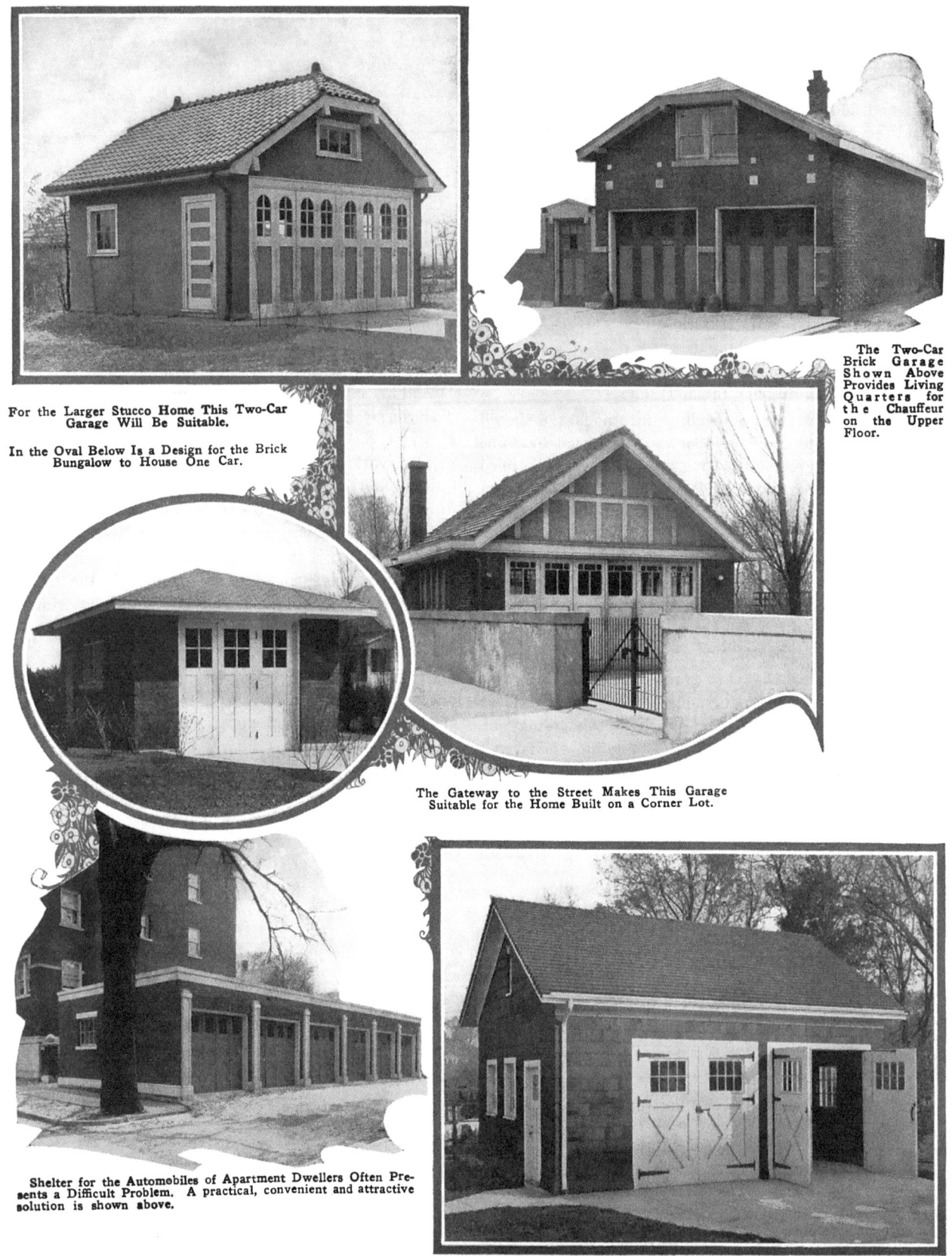

For the Larger Stucco Home This Two-Car Garage Will Be Suitable.

In the Oval Below Is a Design for the Brick Bungalow to House One Car.

The Two-Car Brick Garage Shown Above Provides Living Quarters for the Chauffeur on the Upper Floor.

The Gateway to the Street Makes This Garage Suitable for the Home Built on a Corner Lot.

Shelter for the Automobiles of Apartment Dwellers Often Presents a Difficult Problem. A practical, convenient and attractive solution is shown above.

Ample Space for Two Automobiles and a Well Lighted Workbench Are Provided in This Attractive Shingled Building.

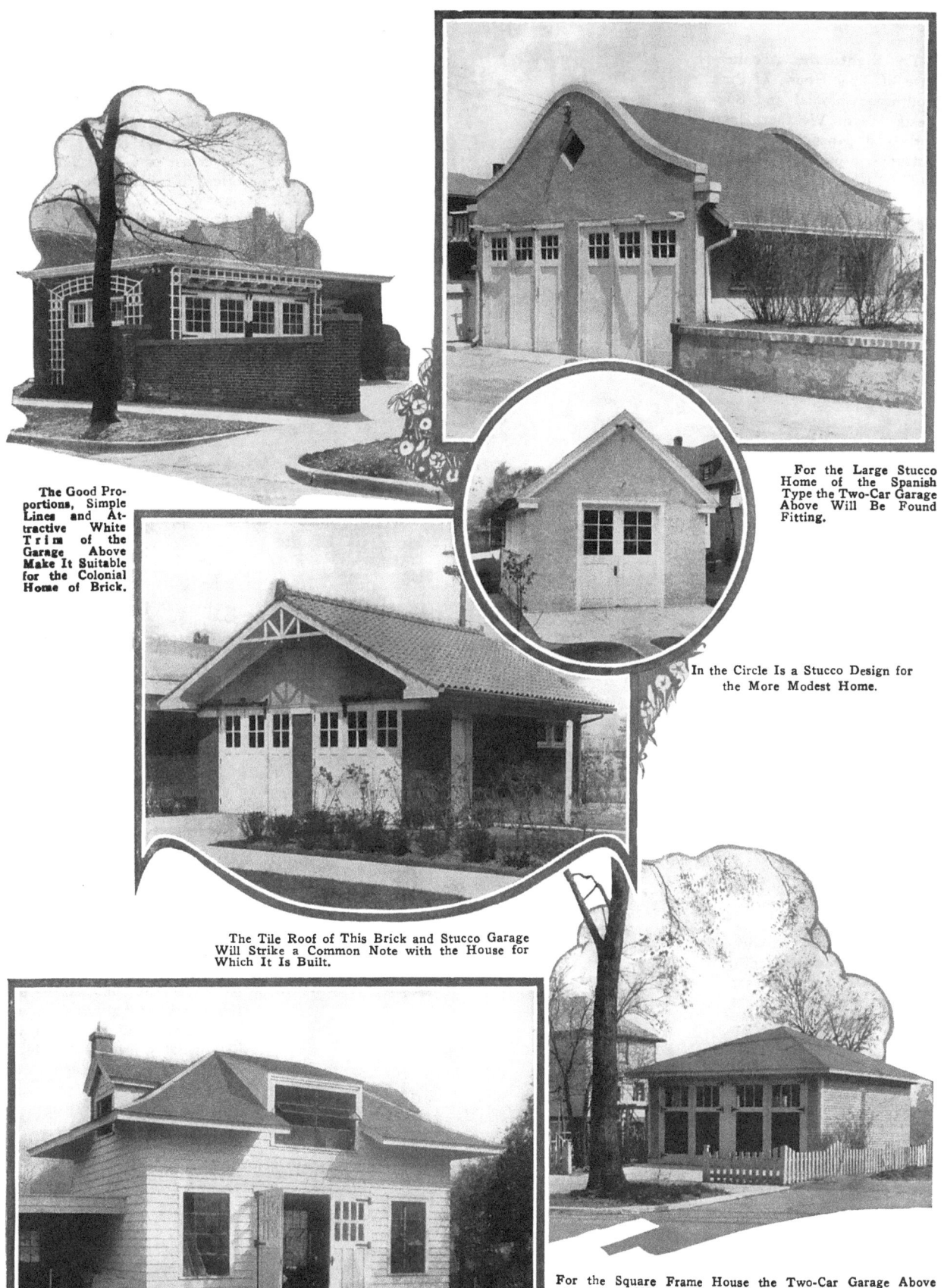

The Good Proportions, Simple Lines and Attractive White Trim of the Garage Above Make It Suitable for the Colonial Home of Brick.

For the Large Stucco Home of the Spanish Type the Two-Car Garage Above Will Be Found Fitting.

In the Circle Is a Stucco Design for the More Modest Home.

The Tile Roof of This Brick and Stucco Garage Will Strike a Common Note with the House for Which It Is Built.

For the Square Frame House the Two-Car Garage Above Will Be Practical and Economical.

Three Automobiles May Be Housed in the Frame Garage Presented Here, with Living Quarters for the Driver on the Second Floor.

To Right; the Architecture of This House Is Pure Southern Colonial and Suggests Warm Weather Comfort and Hospitality. The entrance is particularly inviting.

Below; the Terrace, Brick Walk, Urns, and Portico Add Greatly to the Attractiveness of This Handsome Cleveland Home. Note also the clever use of a belt course of brick to relieve the monotony of the stucco and the square bay with triple windows suggesting a light and airy interior.

Above; This White Painted Doorway, with Its Classic Design, Stands Out in Striking Contrast to the Stained Shingle Siding of the House. The knocker and latch handle of antique design add further distinction.

To Left; Classic Columns Add Grace and Beauty to This Colonial House Design. The recessed entrance is somewhat unusual and the ample sidelights assure a well lighted hall or vestibule. The winding brick walk adds interest to the approach.

Entrances of Beauty Add Greatly to the Attractiveness of these Homes

The Alberhill

A Dutch Colonial of Rare Comfort

A CERTAIN homelike quality is found in a well designed Dutch Colonial house that appeals to many persons. This type of house is quiet and dignified. It allows the owner to give his individual taste full sway in furnishing and decorating.

The service arrangement of the first floor is very good. Here the architects have worked out a scheme that will delight the housewife. At one side of the kitchen is the entry with refrigerator iced from the entry, but with its front in the kitchen, to save steps. On the opposite side of the kitchen is arranged the pantry and the breakfast alcove. Steps to and from the dining room have been reduced to a minimum.

A built-in ironing board is provided in the kitchen. Plenty of cupboard space is provided in both the kitchen and pantry.

A toilet room connects with the rear entry, so it is accessible from the service portion and from the living room.

Four bed rooms, two baths and very generous closets are well laid out on the second floor. The baths are together and are over the first floor toilet room, giving economical plumbing.

A servants' room and bath, and generous storage space are provided on the third floor.

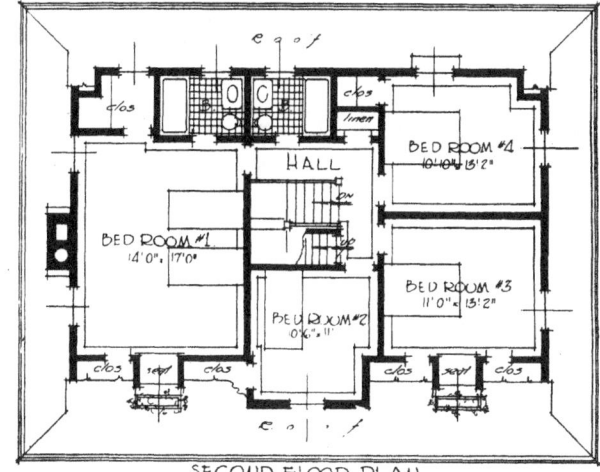

SECOND FLOOR PLAN

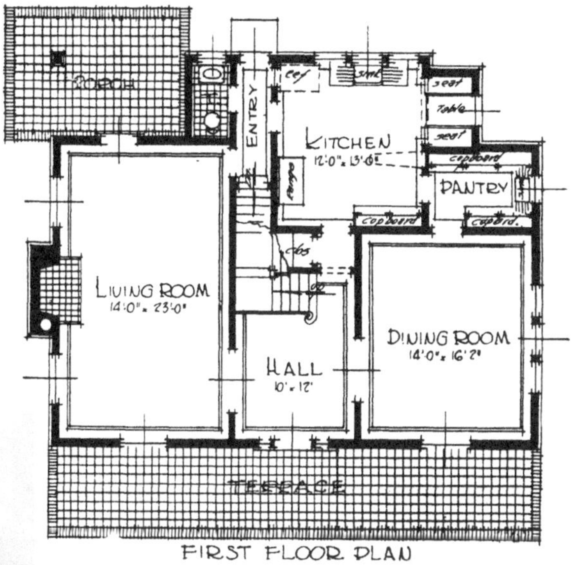

FIRST FLOOR PLAN

THE ALBERHILL: A Terrace Under the Overhanging Second Story Is a Pleasant Feature of This Home.

The Atwood

Dutch Colonial Design Provides Residence of Substantial Beauty with Floor Plans which Insure Efficient Use of Space

For Perspective in Full Colors see page 39

HOMES of the Dutch Colonial type owe much of their popularity to the fact that their general shape allows a most efficient planning of the rooms in a home of moderate size.

The Atwood offers six major rooms of unusually generous proportions and a sun parlor. The dimensions of the home, without considering the sun porch, are 38 by 24½ feet, which will go nicely on a corner. This design is one which is exceptionally attractive in a setting of trees, as shown in the illustration.

A glance at the floor plans, on the opposite page, will show that the attractive entrance leads into a reception hall which houses the stairs. A hall stairway can be made one of the most attractive features of a home with proper design.

The living room, to the left of the reception hall, is one of graceful proportions and well designed lighting.

The location of the fireplace will make for attractive grouping of furniture and the doors to the sun parlor will add much additional space to the room when they are open.

The dining room is of adequate size, made larger by the recess provided for the buffet. The kitchen has a large, well-planned pantry. The lavatory on the first floor is a useful feature.

The large bedroom on the second floor, with its fireplace and the dressing and clothes closet in one end of the room, is one of the attractive features of the home. The two additional bedrooms, one with a lavatory and both with closets, have lighting and ventilation from two sides and are of adequate size.

Working plans to scale with cross sections are presented on the four pages following.

THE ATWOOD; The Attractive Entrance, the Green Wood Shutters and the Placing of the Windows Are Features Which Combine to Make This Home Most Attractive. The wide clapboards used here are well adapted to the Dutch Colonial Design. The working drawings of this home are presented on the four following pages.

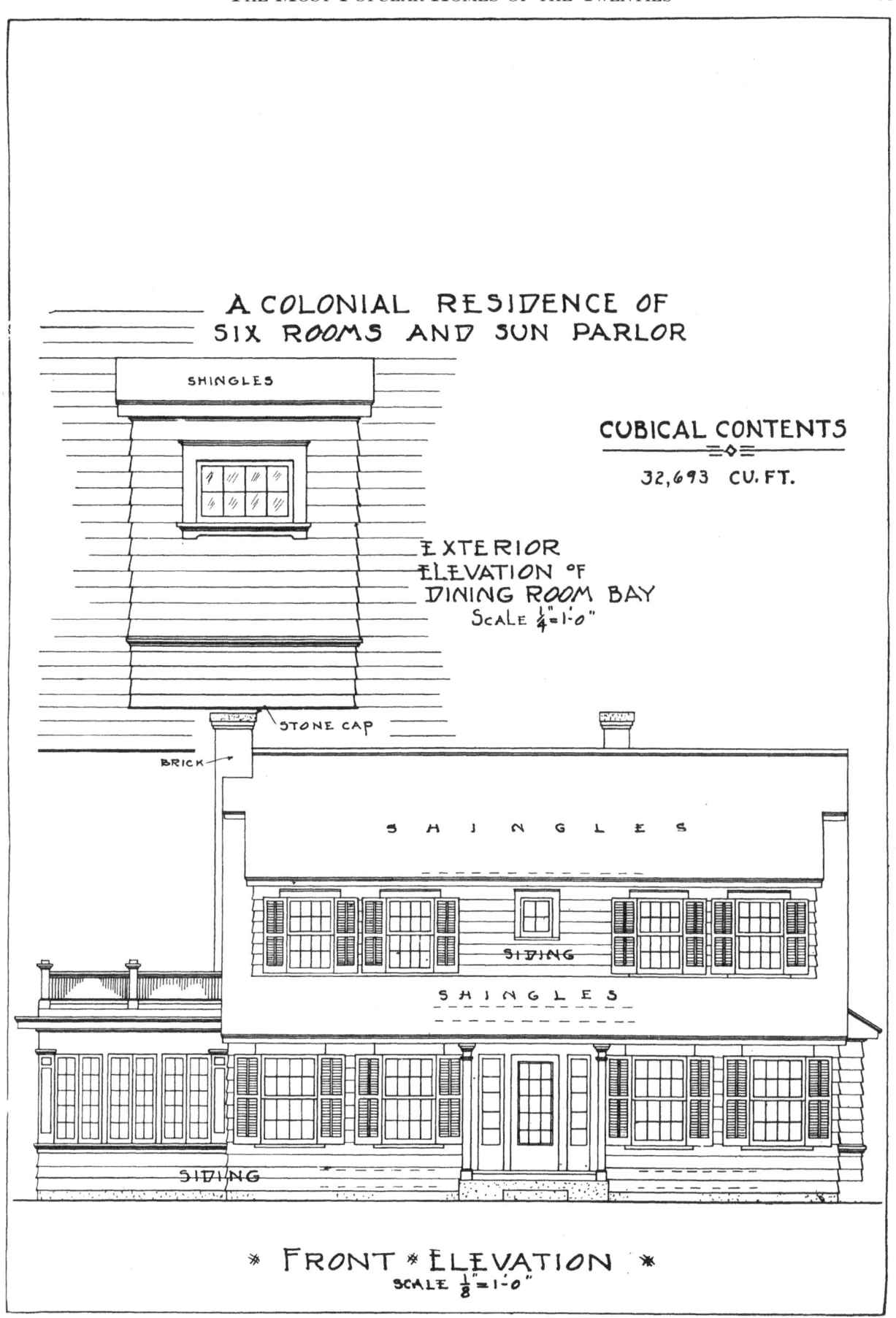

A COLONIAL RESIDENCE OF
SIX ROOMS AND SUN PARLOR

SHINGLES

CUBICAL CONTENTS
32,693 CU. FT.

EXTERIOR
ELEVATION OF
DINING ROOM BAY
Scale ¼"=1'-0"

STONE CAP

BRICK

S H I N G L E S

SIDING

S H I N G L E S

SIDING

✳ FRONT ✳ ELEVATION ✳
SCALE ⅛"=1'-0"

THE ATWOOD; Front Elevation and Exterior Elevation of Dining Room Bay. The relation of this bay to the room may be seen in the floor plan on the following page.

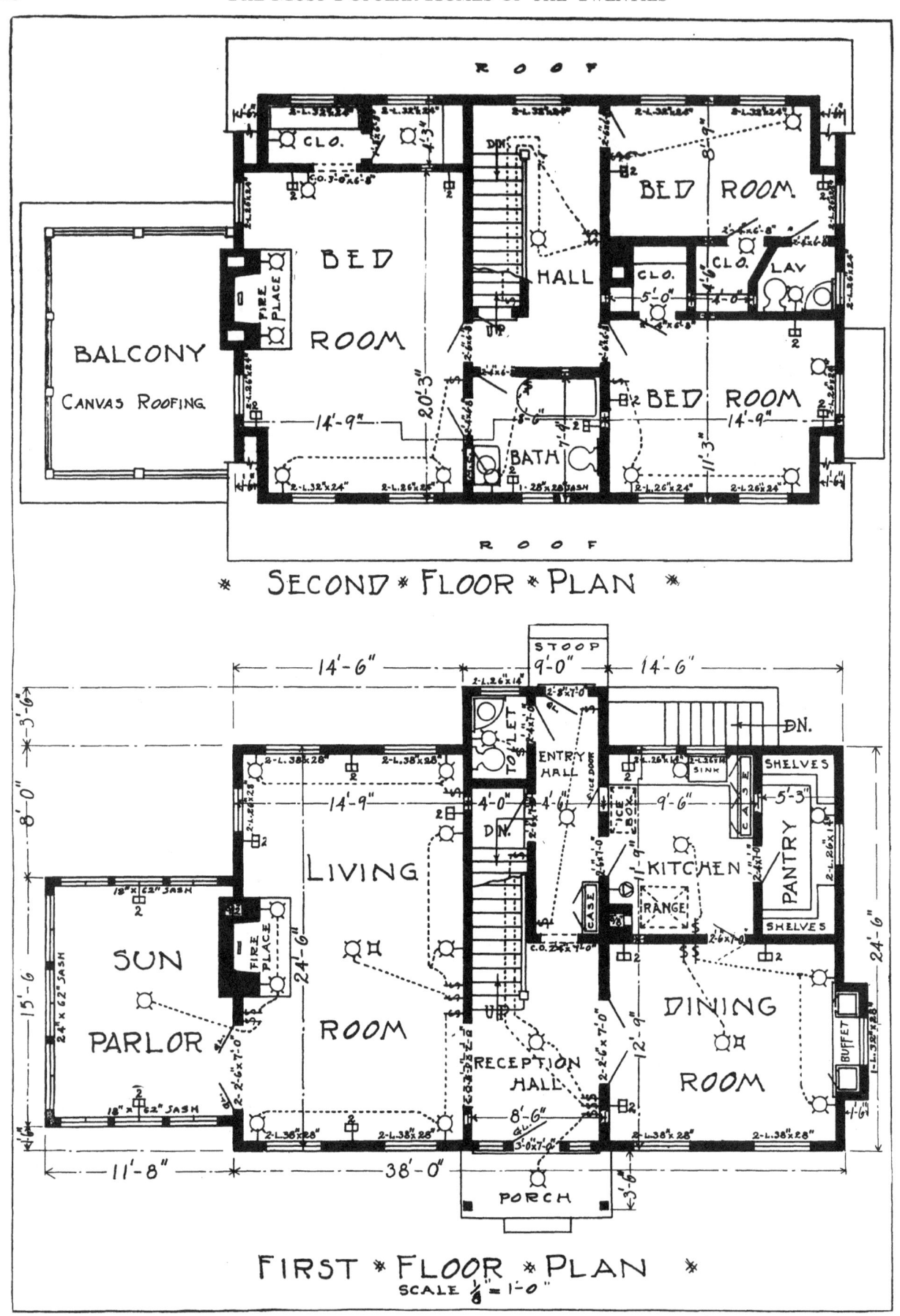

SECOND * FLOOR * PLAN *

FIRST * FLOOR * PLAN *

SCALE ⅛" = 1'-0"

THE ATWOOD; The Spacious Living Room and Pleasant Reception Hall Will Win Many Friends for the Plan.
The floor plan of the basement is shown on the page opposite.

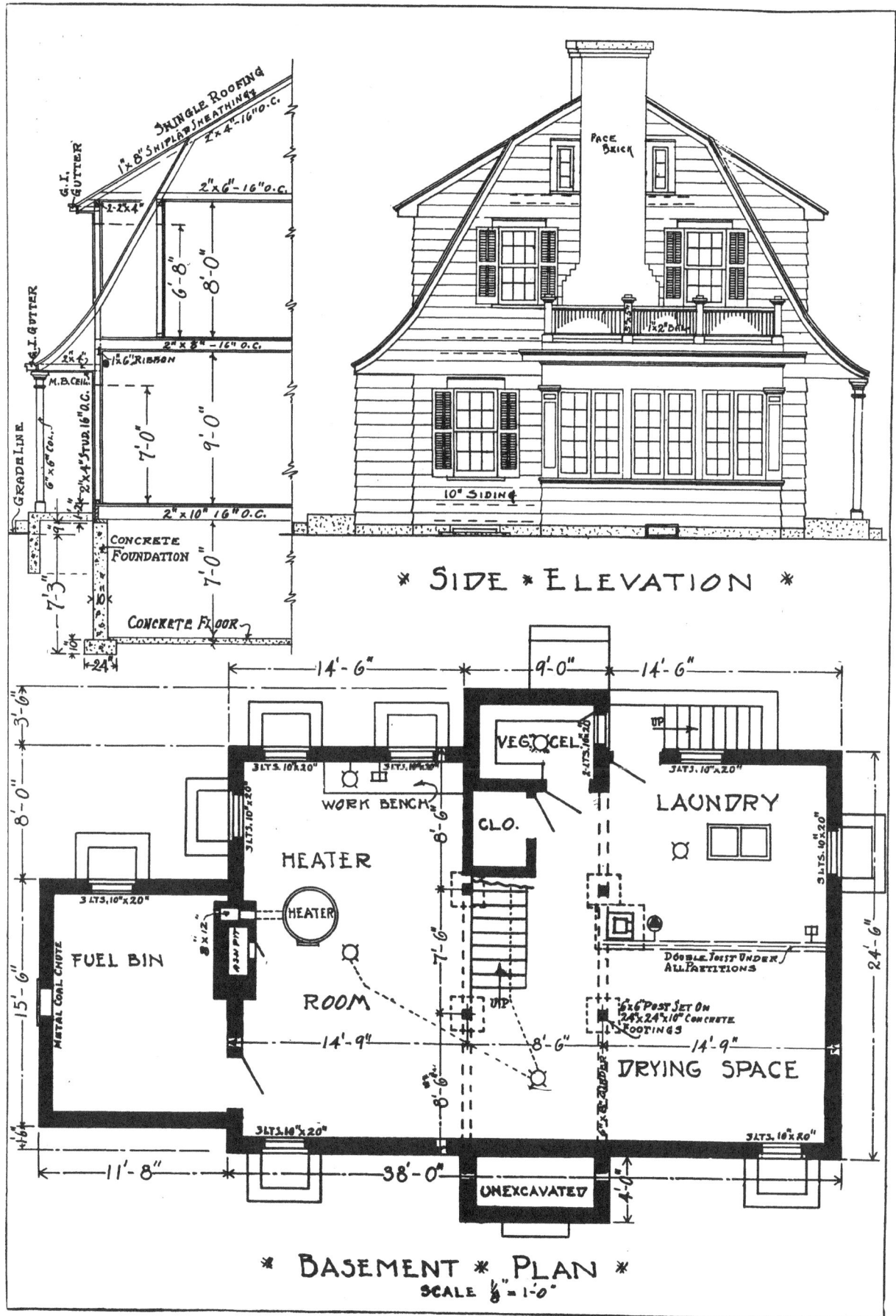

* SIDE * ELEVATION *

* BASEMENT * PLAN *
SCALE ⅛" = 1'-0"

THE ATWOOD; The Basement Plan and Side Elevation, with a Cross Section Giving Many of the Framing and Construction Details. The relation of the basement to the length of the house may be seen in the drawings on the following page.

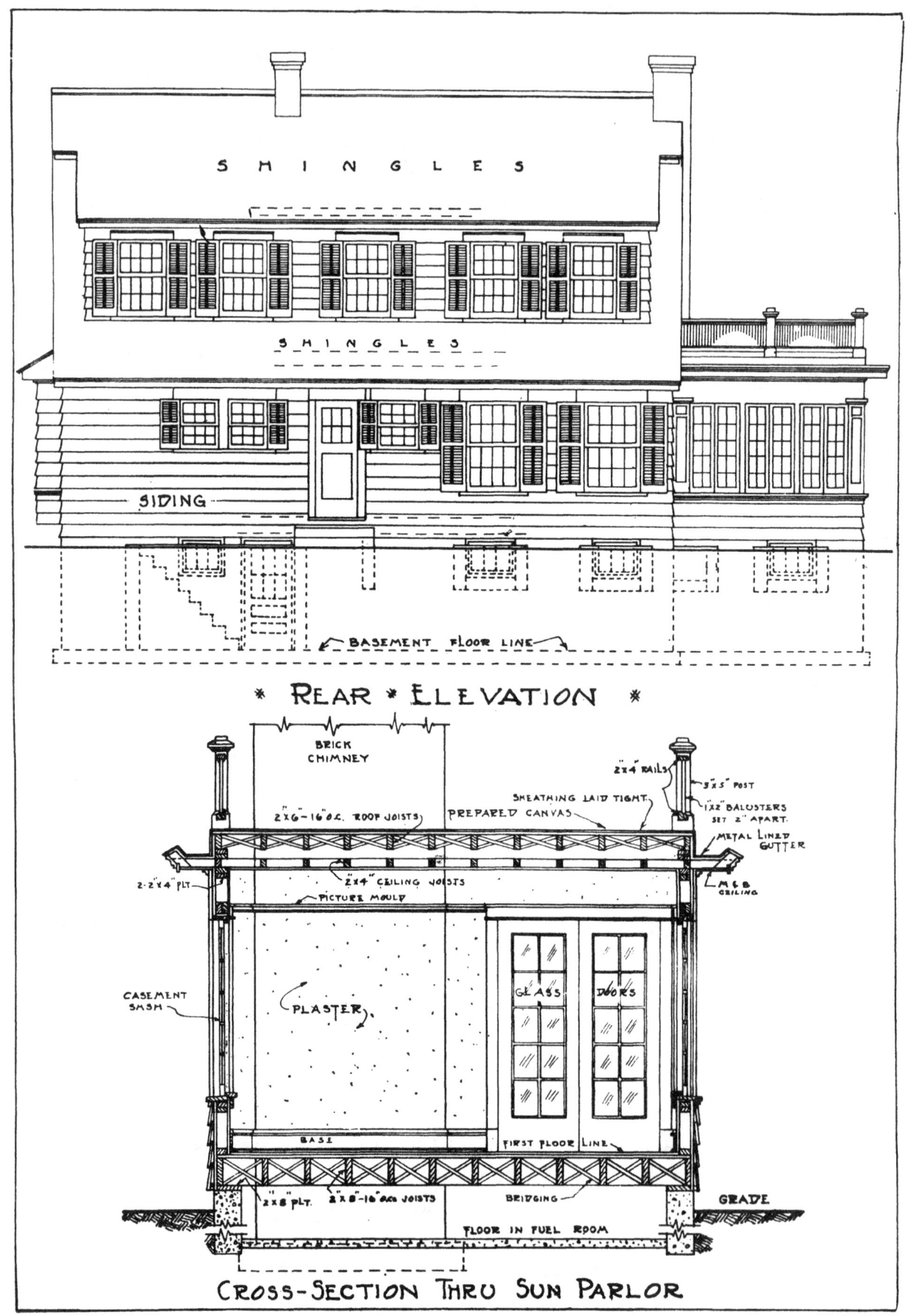

S H I N G L E S

S H I N G L E S

SIDING

BASEMENT FLOOR LINE

* REAR * ELEVATION *

BRICK
CHIMNEY

2"X4" RAILS
2"X6"-16" O.C. ROOF JOISTS   SHEATHING LAID TIGHT   3"X5" POST
PREPARED CANVAS   1"X2" BALUSTERS
                                 SET 2" APART.
                                 METAL LINED
2-2"X4" PLT   GUTTER
              2"X4" CEILING JOISTS   M.G.B
          PICTURE MOULD   CEILING

CASEMENT
SASH

(PLASTER)   GLASS   DOORS

BASE   FIRST FLOOR LINE
                                                              GRADE
2"X8" PLT.   2"X8"-16" O.C. JOISTS   BRIDGING

FLOOR IN FUEL ROOM

CROSS-SECTION THRU SUN PARLOR

THE ATWOOD; The Rear Elevation and a Cross Section Through the Sun Parlor. Note the Efficiency of the
placing of the windows and that provision is made for daylight lighting of the basement.

The ATWOOD

A HOME of Dutch Colonial Design. For Complete Building Plans-Working Drawings to Scale See Pages 35, 36, 37 and 38.

The *ARGYLE*

A FIVE Room Colonial Bungalow. For complete Building Plans-Working Drawings to Scale See Pages 42, 43, 44 and 45.

The Argyle

Five-room Colonial Bungalow Makes Beautiful Home—Alternate Floor Plan Using Space Saving Beds Cuts Out 410 Square Feet

For Perspective in Full Colors see page 40

THE white bungalow with its graceful Colonial elements of design continues to draw new admirers, and to flourish from Coast to Coast. The little five-room home photographed below and pictured so beautifully in colors on the opposite page presents an appeal which few can resist. The exterior is chaste, dignified, inviting; the interior shows an arrangement of rooms both spacious and convenient.

The design is admirably adapted to the terraced lot with its background of fine trees. Entrance and windows present an excellent example of perfect balance and shrubbery has been well placed to break the foundation line of the ground level.

The front is used by the living room, reception hall, dining room group, all generously lighted with French windows in the present-day vogue. At the rear are two fine bedrooms with bath, the kitchen and pantry, a breakfast nook, and an abundance of closets.

An interesting space-saving and money-saving alternate plan is also presented which leaves the front of the house just as it is but eliminates one bedroom, making use instead of disappearing twin beds and a dressing closet. This change saves 410 square feet without hurting the five-room efficiency of this home.

Working drawings to scale are presented on the four pages following; and are full of good suggestions for architects, builders and prospective home owners.

THE ARGYLE; Photo of Five-Room Colonial Bungalow Which Is Shown in Colors on Opposite Page and in Working Plans on the Four Pages Following.

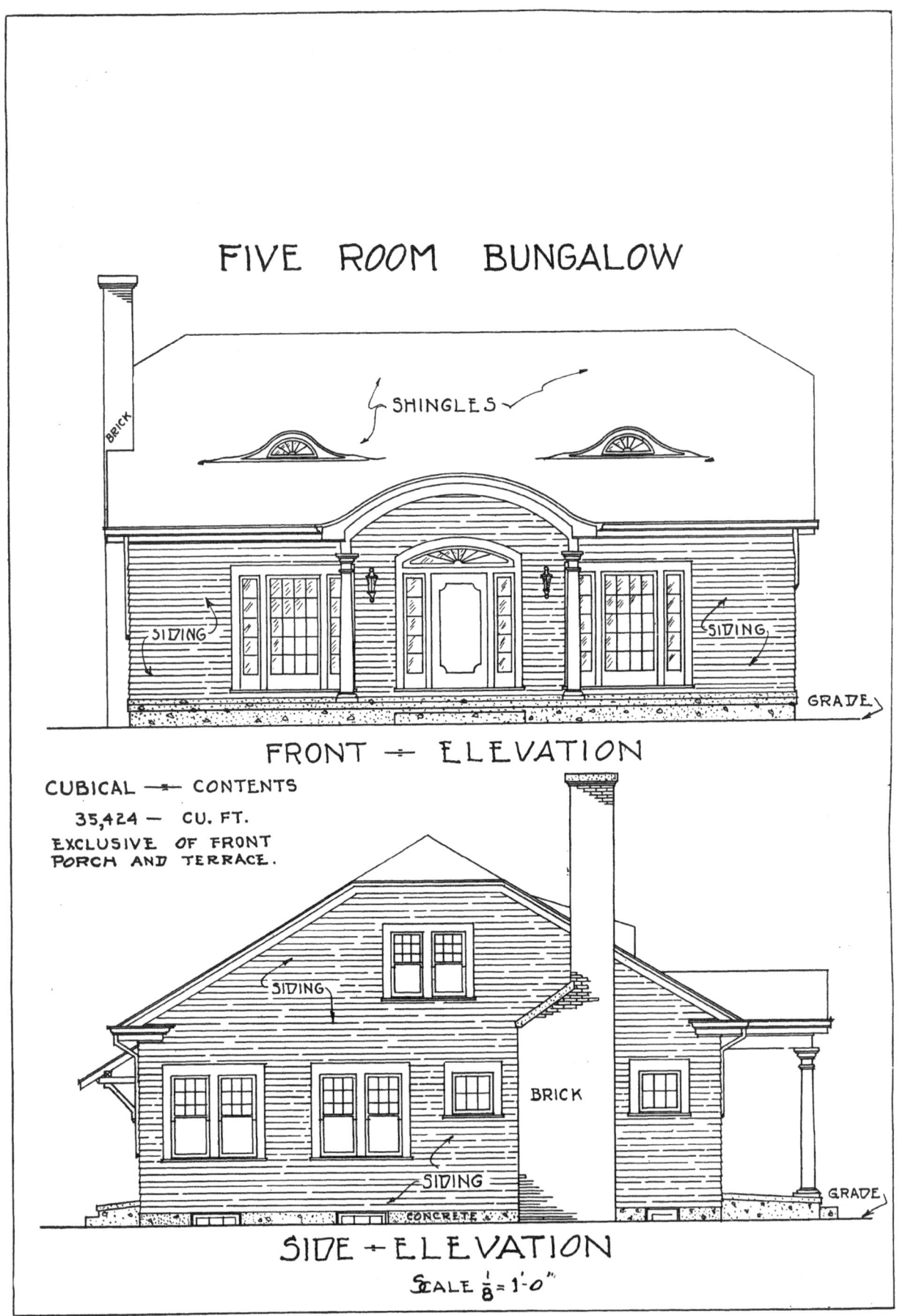

FIVE ROOM BUNGALOW

FRONT ÷ ELEVATION

CUBICAL ÷ CONTENTS
35,424 — CU. FT.
EXCLUSIVE OF FRONT
PORCH AND TERRACE.

SIDE ÷ ELEVATION
SCALE ⅛ = 1'-0"

THE ARGYLE; Eighth-Inch Scale Drawings of Front and Side Elevations.

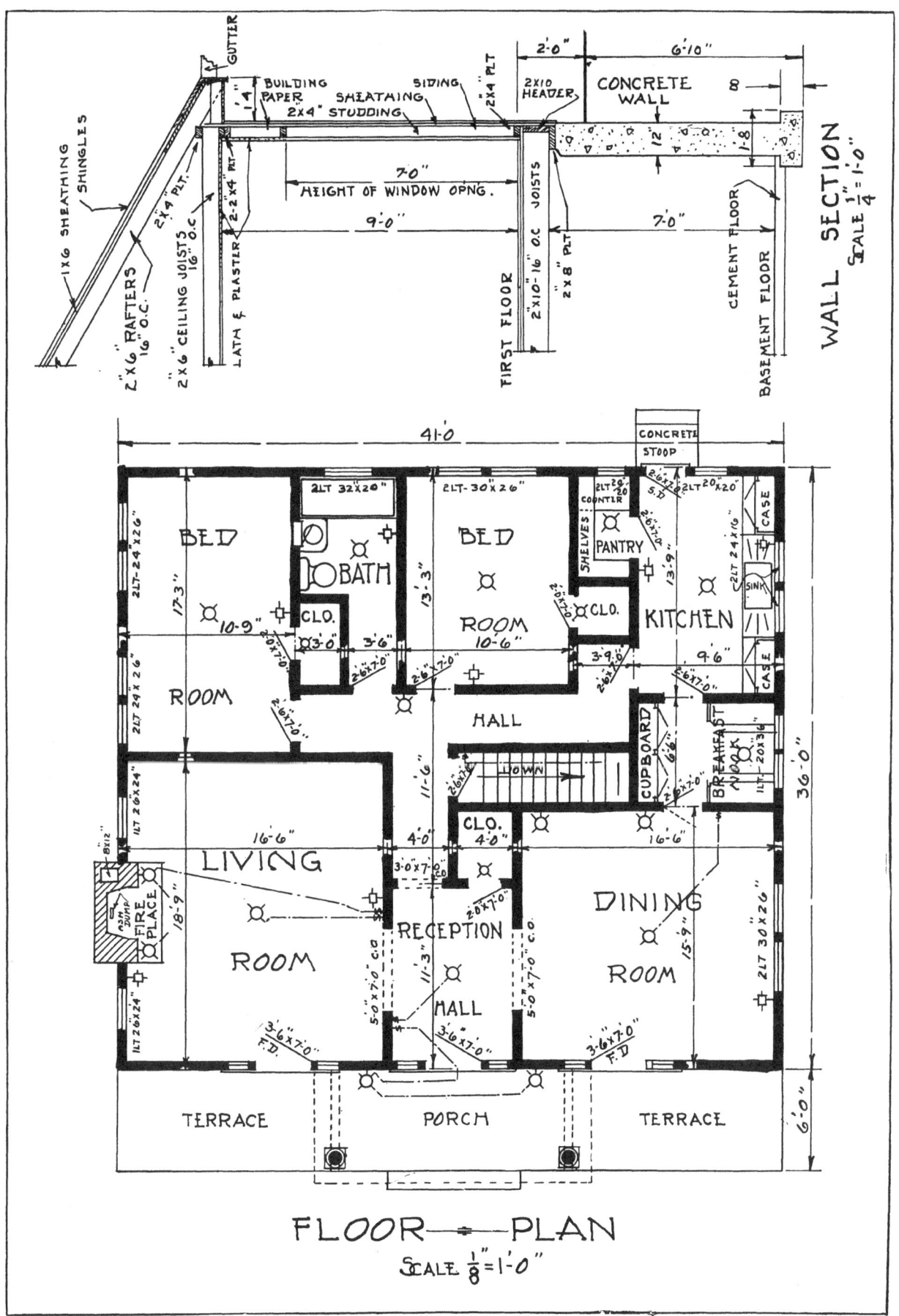

FLOOR ← PLAN

Scale 1/8" = 1'-0"

THE ARGYLE; Main Floor Plan and Detail of Construction. Compare this floor plan with space-saving alternate arrangement on page 44.

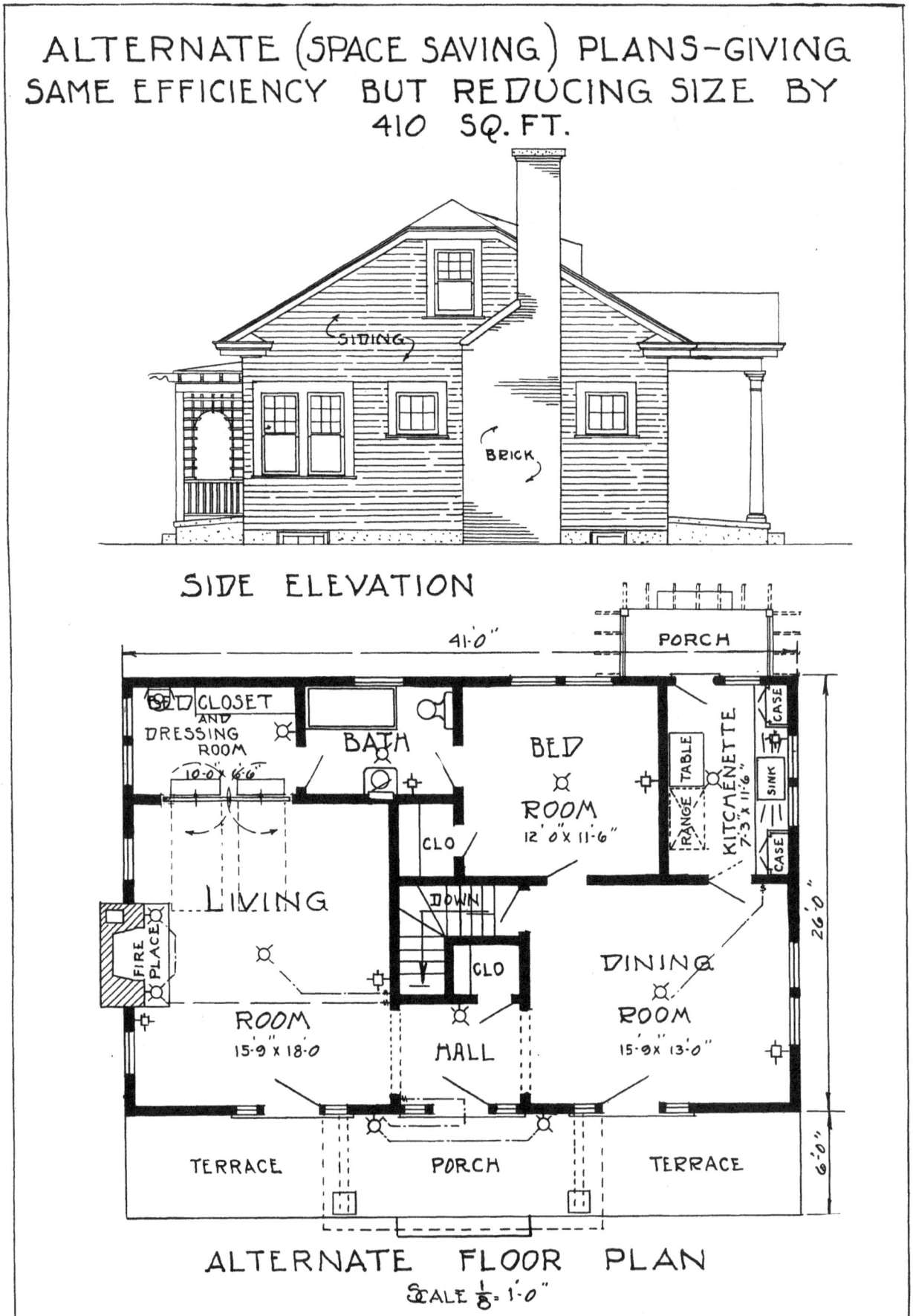

ALTERNATE (SPACE SAVING) PLANS—GIVING SAME EFFICIENCY BUT REDUCING SIZE BY 410 SQ. FT.

SIDE ELEVATION

ALTERNATE FLOOR PLAN

SCALE ⅛ = 1'-0"

THE ARGYLE; These Alternate Plans Save 41 by 10 Feet of Floor Space by Substituting Space-Saving Beds in the Living Room for One of the Bedrooms.

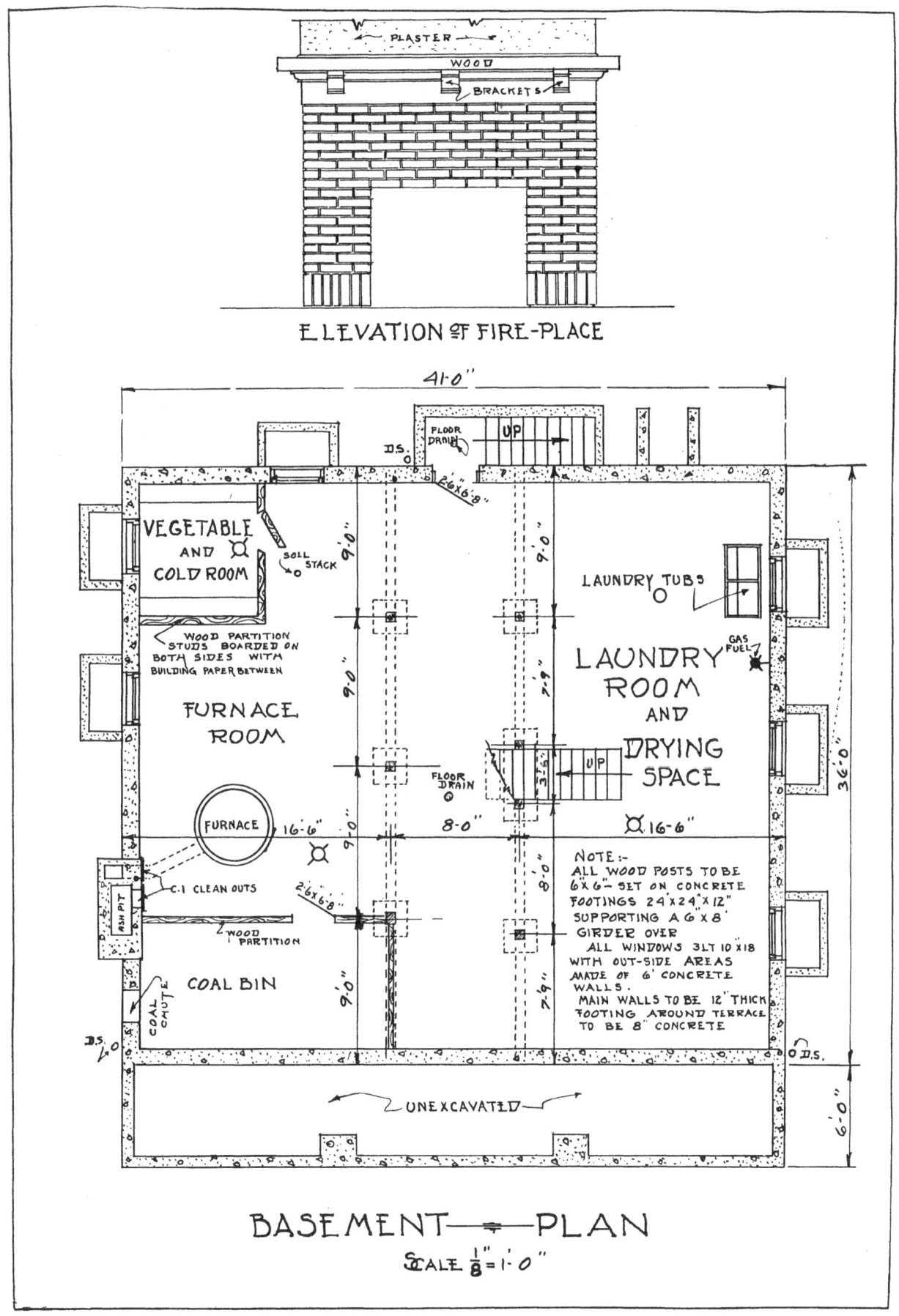

ELEVATION OF FIRE-PLACE

BASEMENT — PLAN

SCALE 1/8" = 1'-0"

NOTE:—
ALL WOOD POSTS TO BE
6"X6" SET ON CONCRETE
FOOTINGS 24"X24"X12"
SUPPORTING A 6"X8"
GIRDER OVER
ALL WINDOWS 3LT 10X18
WITH OUT-SIDE AREAS
MADE OF 6" CONCRETE
WALLS.
MAIN WALLS TO BE 12" THICK
FOOTING AROUND TERRACE
TO BE 8" CONCRETE

THE ARGYLE; The Basement Provides Good Space for Heater, Coal Bin, Laundry and Vegetable Cellar. For the other plans see the three pages preceding.

Attractively Designed Woodwork

Millwork for Porches, Finish and Built-in Conveniences Adds to Appearance, Value and Utility of a Home

THE builder who is on the alert is constantly studying the public taste with a view to supplying those features which will add to the appearance, comfort and utility of a home. And yet very few builders are paying the attention they should to the more effective use of millwork.

It is, of course, natural to cut costs by pruning down the seemingly unnecessary items. The result is often unfortunate, as far as woodwork is concerned, and the owner gains no real economy. Many houses are being built with just enough wood finish to meet the barest standards. Such houses have far less value than those which are embellished by the proper amount of fine woodwork. This does not mean that all should be provided with expensive wood paneling or exposed beamwork. It does not mean that there should be any "gingerbread" carving but rather certain useful features which, at the same time, add that note of distinction so greatly valued by the homeseeker or home builder. And, in the end, these features may also prove an economy.

Quantity production cuts down the cost of millwork. The cost of a door, for instance, is said to be 30 per cent less from the mill than if a single door of that design had to be supplied.

As to the gain in appearance, first let us consider the architectural value of the entrance to a house. Properly designed, the entrance emphasizes the architecture of the whole house, whether it be Colonial, Georgian, Dutch Colonial or any other. It has an even greater influence upon the appearance of a small house than on a large one. A porch which harmonizes with the house design expresses at once the architectural motive, because the entrance is most noticeable and claims the eye.

The architectural beauty of columns may be used as a graceful expression of this architecture. A wide doorway, with symmetrical paneling and sidelights, adds an appearance of hospitality and comfort, just as a narrow doorway without a porch is apt to be plain and forbidding. The wide doorway has also great practical convenience for moving in or out large pieces of equipment or furniture without danger of marring the woodwork.

The design of the door frame is most important. A curved transom light over the door may, with the side lights, give just the arched effect required to harmonize with the porch design. A simple gable over the entrance is most fitting to certain types of architecture.

Millwork entrances may be secured which are splendid examples of New England design, Colonial, Southern Colonial, Empire, Early English design and many others. Simple bench seats at the side of the porch can be used to advantage with some designs and add practical comfort, as well as an expression of hospitality.

The door, itself, should not only be of good design, it should also be of good material, well made, fitted and finished, so that it will resist the weather and retain its serviceable qualities and appearance. The painted door probably re-

Independence Hall, Philadelphia, Offers a Valuable Study in Colonial Stairways. Shown above is the vestibule of Congress Hall. Note the excellent designing of the doorways.

sists sun and rain better than the varnished finish.

Neither the permanent outside doors nor the interior doors should be fitted and hung until the plaster of the house has thoroughly dried out. When the outside doors are first fitted and hung, the freshly cut surfaces at top and bottom should be given a coat of filler and varnish or paint, as the case may be. It is well to treat the interior doors in the same manner. If this is not done, the door will absorb moisture through these surfaces, which is almost sure to result in warping. The resultant swelling will cause the doors to stick. When the house is artificially heated, the doors will dry out and shrink. This is quite apt to crack the veneers. Some mills use a waterproof glue in their veneer work, which gives such exterior doors a longer life and weather resistance. It prevents injury to the doors from storms and wet weather where the water might otherwise weaken the hold of the glue.

Where sidelights are not provided, it is quite common to install exterior doors with a sheet of glass set in as a panel. French doors are popular in better class houses, either as a combined door and window opening on a veranda, a conservatory, a balcony, or between certain interior rooms. Very handsome effects can be secured with glass in doors but the glass itself should be heavy, of extra good quality and well glazed. Most of the mills use special putty with extra lasting quality and set the glass so that the edges are entirely surrounded by an elastic bed of putty, making the door wind and weatherproof.

The man who buys or builds a house soon learns the value of well made doors if he is unfortunate enough to get poor ones. On the other hand, well made and well fitted doors, which do not sag, shrink or swell, but retain their fine appearance and their dependable operation, are a "joy forever." First-class doors from a good mill are skillfully designed and well made. Long, satisfactory service and rich beauty of design and finish are built into them.

Designs are on the market which may be said to set new fashions in doors. Some of these contain but one central panel with a raised moulding which outlines the panel, set in several inches from the stiles and rails. Extra deep moulding effects are gained in some designs by using moulding of extra width along the sides, top and bottom of the panel, producing an effect of extra depth. Glass door knobs add a touch of distinction to these art doors. Flush doors, entirely without panels, produce a novel effect and are coming into more general use.

A wide range of choice in woods and finishes is offered the builder for interior doors. A spruce frame with a sap gum panel, offers a rich effect. Birch makes a particularly handsome door and can be finished in a number of different ways—with paint, stain or natural finish. Plain red oak or brown ash show beautiful grain effects. A white pine frame with a birch or sap gum panel, add variety, and there are other combinations to be had.

The method of assembling doors in a modern mill is interesting. Hardwood dowel pins are used—sometimes a dozen or more to a door. Rails and stiles quite frequently are laminated and dovetailed, making a great many parts to assemble. They are coated with glue at all points of contact and pressed firmly together by powerful machines into a composite whole. Some manufacturers use cleverly designed dowels with

The Dining Room Nook, Breakfast Nook, or "Pullman" Is Now All the Rage. The above Plan and photographic view show a popular example.

wedge ends which expand as the dowels are driven home when the door is pressed together.

The casement window, popular hundreds of years ago, is coming into its own again. While it will probably never supplant entirely the double hung window, there are many places where it will be a decided advantage in most homes. The full window opening which it affords will quickly allow the heated air of a summer day to escape and the cool air of evening to enter a room. Many effective devices are now on the market for securely holding casement sash against the slamming action of the wind, which removes a former objection to the casement window. Another clever method of overcoming the slamming tendency is to pivot casement windows at the top and bottom with center pivots. Where this is done, staggered stops must be provided.

Bay windows are justly popular, both for their appearance and the extra light and air which they afford. The added expense of bay windows is almost always justified by the gain effected, both in appearance and comfort. A two-sided angle bay makes a unique and inexpensive bay. It is usually supported by a bracket on the outer wall.

Double hung windows are a necessity in almost every room and it certainly pays to install windows and frames of the highest possible quality. Any added cost will be more than offset later by the fuel economy gained in heating the house. Even more important will be the added appearance and comfort of high class windows, their longer life and protection to interior wall decorations by leak-proof windows and frames.

Dormer windows will either improve or detract from the appearance of a house, depending upon the character and proportions of the window design. Sash in the sides as well as the front of the dormer, in one novel design, admit extra light. Dormers are proportioned for from one to four windows and casements are quite often used.

There is a wide range of choice in design, moulding and finish, presenting a number of pleasing and varied effects and matching either English or Colonial styles of architecture.

Window shutters can be used in such a way as greatly to improve the architectural appearance of a residence and add to the comfort of those rooms which are exposed to the glare and heat of the sun.

Attic louvres are also to be had in various pleasing designs and are of considerable help in keeping down the temperature, during hot weather, of the rooms on the floor below. They should have solid hinged backs and be equipped with permanent wire screens.

When one enters a home, the staircase is usually the most noticeable feature of the interior. Many superior stairway designs are obtainable in millwork, with a wide range of choice in graceful early Colonial, modern Colonial or in substantial well-balanced modern, mission or other designs. These are furnished complete, including stair string, treads, risers, newels, balusters, mouldings and all other parts. In fact, complete reception hall woodwork is obtainable, which will produce harmonious and pleasing effects.

Wall paneling is said to have begun as a wainscot a few feet high in old Tudor houses. Wainscot adds a durable and attractive finish to any home. Being far from common, it is a most notable feature in better class homes. This paneling is procurable in a number of varying styles and different heights. It is said to have come down to us from the days of Queen Anne.

Every owner should appreciate features of finish which add to the attractiveness and comfort of the living room. The cheeriness of a fireplace appeals to all. Even though the fireplace be of brick, the framing and overmantel are most effective in wood. Here again, millwork is procurable which will harmonize with the doors, windows and trim. Whether in library, "den" or living room, built-in bookcases should be a feature of every home. They are sure to harmonize better with the other woodwork and be more substantial, durable, economical and convenient than when bought at the furniture dealers. Of course, the doors, window and trim will be selected to match in all the main downstairs rooms.

Built-in conveniences are appreciated by the whole

Exterior Millwork Is Apt to Be Colonial in Detail.

family but make a particular appeal to the housewife. Instead of just four bare walls to move into, she is particularly charmed by the convenience and coziness of a breakfast nook, built-in sideboards or buffets, china cases, kitchen cases, linen closets, broom case, ironing board case, hall seats and drawers for overshoes, corner and alcove seats, radiator covers and many similar built-in features—all obtainable in mill work of artistic design. A house equipped with these things, even before the family moves in, has taken on the atmosphere of a home. The speculative builder would find a house with these features readily saleable at a better profit. The builder advising with prospective home owners can give a valuable service by suggesting the installation of these features and the importance and value of good millwork throughout the house.

Building on a Small Site

Residence in Colorado Springs, Shows Successful Meeting of Space Limitations

THE problem of utilizing a residence site only 40 x 90 feet in dimensions is a real one for the conscientious architect. The house here shown, in Colorado Springs, very successfully meets the limitations thus imposed on the architect; the completed structure is both well arranged and so placed on the lot as to afford a bit of room for lawn and garden that is necessary to give real home feeling.

Although the architect was restricted by the smallness of the area, he was favored in that it was a corner lot. As the exposure was with the long side to the north and the shorter to the west, he placed the dwelling right on the north line and as far back from the west frontage as possible, so as to assure on the latter and south sides room for growing things within the privacy of the enclosing wall fence. In this way, too, unob-

The Dining Room in the Colorado Springs Residence Is Exceptionally Pleasant and Well Lighted.

structed lighting was assured, even though there was a two-story house on the adjoining lot to the south. A glance at the plan indicates how by careful arrangement ample sunlight has been insured for every room.

The smallness of the site quite properly suggested simplicity of design and so we have a reliance on carefully studied mass and the substitution of structural emphasis at different points for ornament in the usual sense, together with a careful choice and placing of windows. These elements we discern as the chief sources of the exterior's attractiveness. The windows are mostly casements with fifteen panes, set either in pairs, or strings of four and six as on the same side of the living room and the owner's bedroom. The shingled roof is, appropriately, flat in pitch and wide in overhang.

The material employed was a hard-burned brick, kiln-run, showing a wide variety of color and laid up in a header bond with "raked back" mortar joint. Just below the line of the second-story windows four courses have been set out slightly to give a decorative touch. The unification of the chimney breast projection on the west front with the shallow bay windows on either side and simple

Beautifully Handled Stair Detail in the Colorado Springs Residence.

hood over the front entrance should be noted also as agreeable details.

The entrance hall is finished in a paneled trim painted white. White also is the color of the stairway spindles. The latter has a mahogany handrail and wide treads of the same wood.

From the entrance hall one enters through double-glassed or French doors into the living room on one hand and the dining room on the other. The first is about 20 feet square and is especially well lighted as it has exposure on the south, west and north. The walls are treated with a paneled wainscot of Oregon

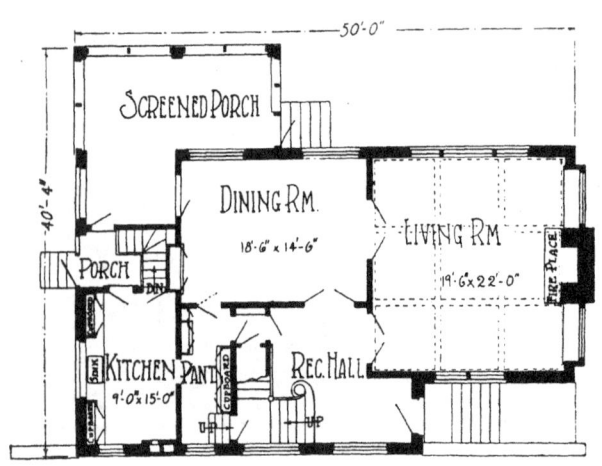
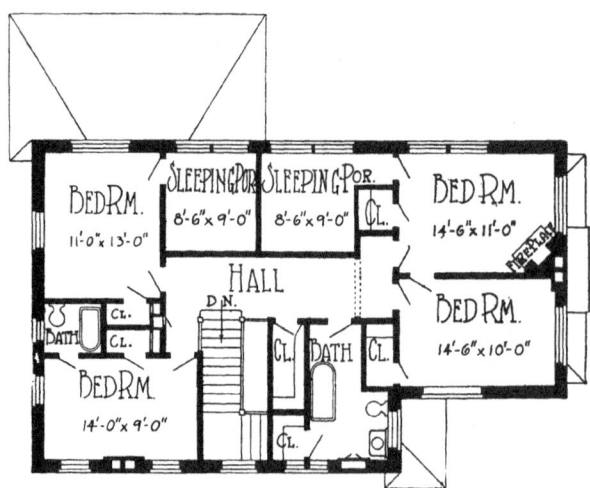

THE ABERDEEN; A Brick House in Colorado Springs Which Utilizes to Excellent Advantage a Corner Lot 40 Feet by 90 Feet, Leaving Room for Lawn and Garden.

fir, stained dark brown. This is carried to a height of six feet with a tinted plaster wall between it and the cornice of the beamed ceiling. The artificial lighting of the room is, in the main, from electric fixtures of iron and frosted glass pendant from the center of the ceiling and the four intersections of the ceiling beams. There is a simply designed brick fireplace with the front carried to the ceiling and with window seats on either side under which there are small radiator coils.

The dining room has wall and ceiling treatment of the same sort as the living room but with lighting fixtures of different design. Like the other, this too is a room of generous proportions, the size being approximately 15 by 18 feet. At the back it opens through French doors into a small room originally planned as a breakfast room but now used as a writing and telephone room. This in turn opens on the south side into a large screened porch which in winter is fitted with glass windows and used as a sun room.

There is a large kitchen—as modern kitchens go—conveniently arranged with ample cupboards and the entire length of one side of the room. Communication with the dining room is had through the pantry. There are no back or special service stairs to the second floor, the maid having access to the front stairs by a short flight from the pantry to the low landing. Front door service is readily afforded from the kitchen by the door opening from the pantry into the front hall. There is a commodious coat closet

The Garage Is Built to Harmonize With the House.

just off the connecting short passage.

The second floor plan shows the arrangement of bedrooms as it was when the house was first built. The present owner has thrown into one large room the two bed rooms on the west front. Off of this and the one guest chamber are sleeping porches under the main roof of the house. This arrangement preserves the integrity of the architect's design by making this adjunct of the modern home an integral part of the plan rather than the unlovely "stuck on" sort of thing we so frequently find.

Every chamber has a good-sized closet and there is a linen closet off the upper hall. The comfort of the maid has been insured by a pleasant room with its own bath and toilet adjoining.

Spacious Living Room in THE ABERDEEN, 19 ft. 6 in. by 22 ft., Looking Through Into the Dining Room and Stair Hall.

The Attica

Shingle Residence of Italian Lines Gives a Pleasing Impression of Hospitality and Happy Home Life

For Perspective in Full Colors, see page 57

THE full meaning of the phrase, "Under your own roof" should be realized by the happy family which builds this home, for the predominating roof of this dwelling seems to hover protectingly over the house beneath it and brings to it a unity which is responsible for much of the pleasing aspect of the exterior. And this unity is further carried out in using shingles both for the roof covering and for the walls, though monotony is avoided by the thatched effect of the roof shingles.

The floor plans, shown to scale on the following pages, present a most pleasing arrangement of seven commodious rooms and three baths, with a large and

well-planned recreation room in the basement in addition. The living room is delightful with its high arched ceiling, its arched window to conform to the arch of the ceiling and its generous proportions. Indirect lighting of the room through lights concealed behind a moulding near the ceiling as shown in the detailed plans on the following pages is an unusual and pleasing feature.

The second floor arrangement provides for one large, well arranged bedroom, with its own bath and two smaller ones, their convenience heightened by careful planning. The recreation room in the basement is a feature which will be appreciated.

THE ATTICA; The Thatched Effect Shingled Roof with Its Pleasing Sweep Over the Living Room and the Shingled Sides of the Walls, with the Wide, Arched Living Room Window and the Carefully Balanced Details of the Doorway Are Charming Features of the Exterior of This Home. Working drawings of the home will be found on the following pages.

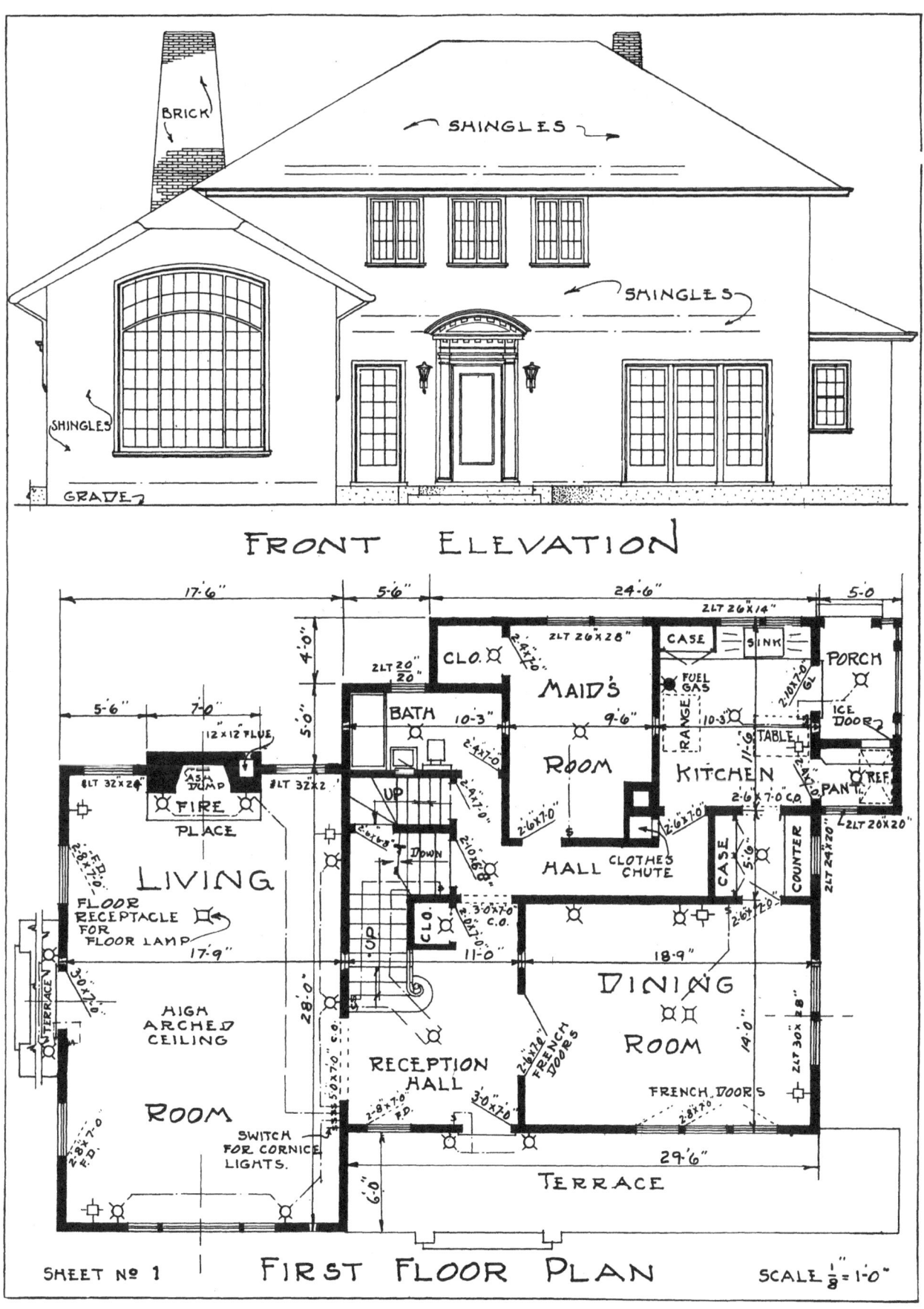

FRONT ELEVATION

FIRST FLOOR PLAN

SHEET Nº 1

SCALE ⅛"=1'-0"

THE ATTICA; The Scale Drawing of the Front Elevation of this Home Shows How Well the Details of Fenestration and the Entrance Have Been Worked Out. The first floor plan is exceptionally efficient, with the high, arched ceilinged living room as a predominating feature. The second floor plans are presented on the next page.

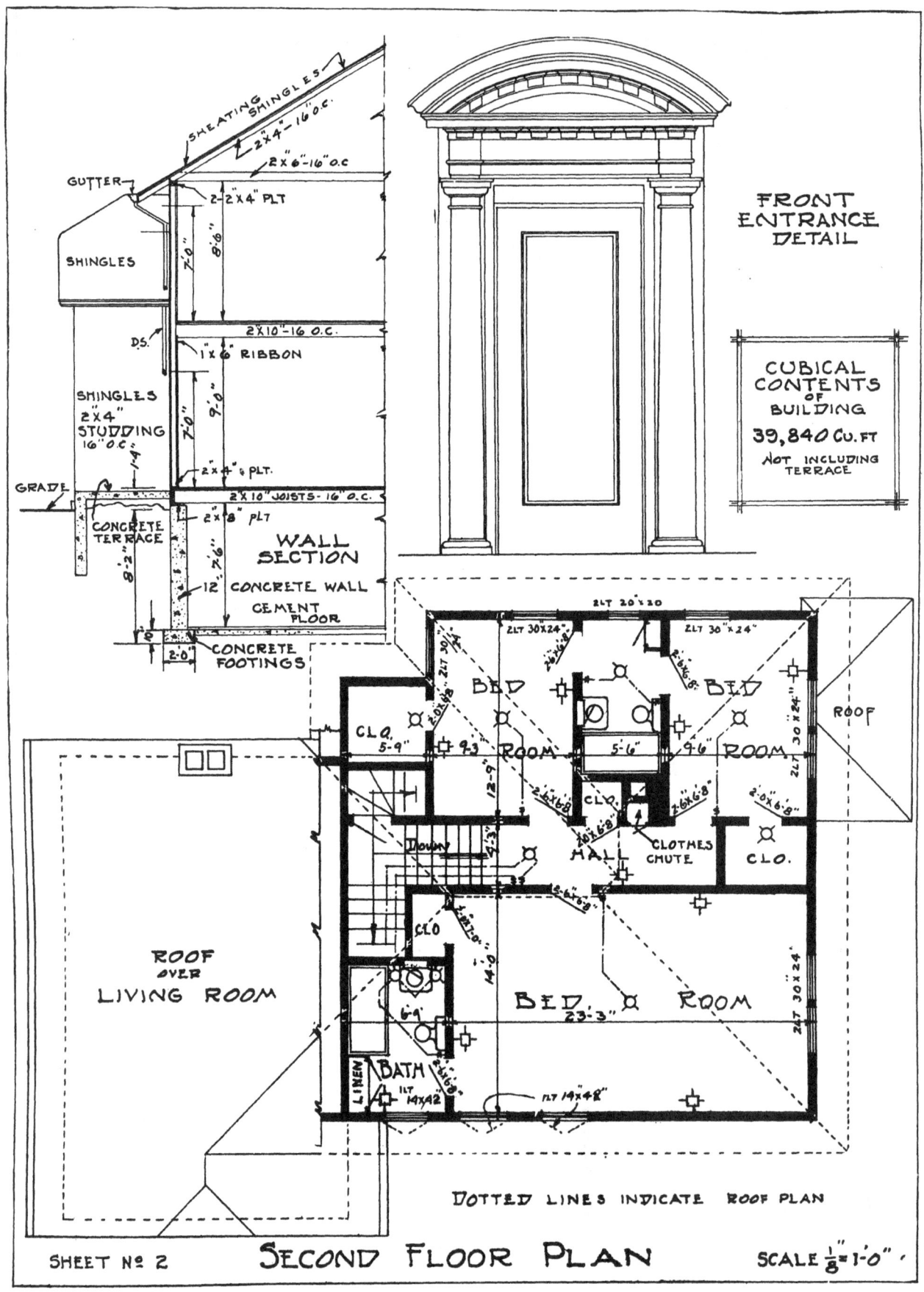

FRONT
ENTRANCE
DETAIL

CUBICAL
CONTENTS
OF
BUILDING
39,840 CU. FT
NOT INCLUDING
TERRACE

WALL
SECTION

SHEET № 2   SECOND FLOOR PLAN   SCALE ⅛"=1'-0"

DOTTED LINES INDICATE ROOF PLAN

THE ATTICA; The Second Floor Plan Shows the Exceptional Quality of the Master Bedroom, with Its Wealth of
Space and Private Bath. The two smaller bedrooms are provided with commodious closets and have a bath accessible
to both. The basement plan and side elevation are presented on the following page.

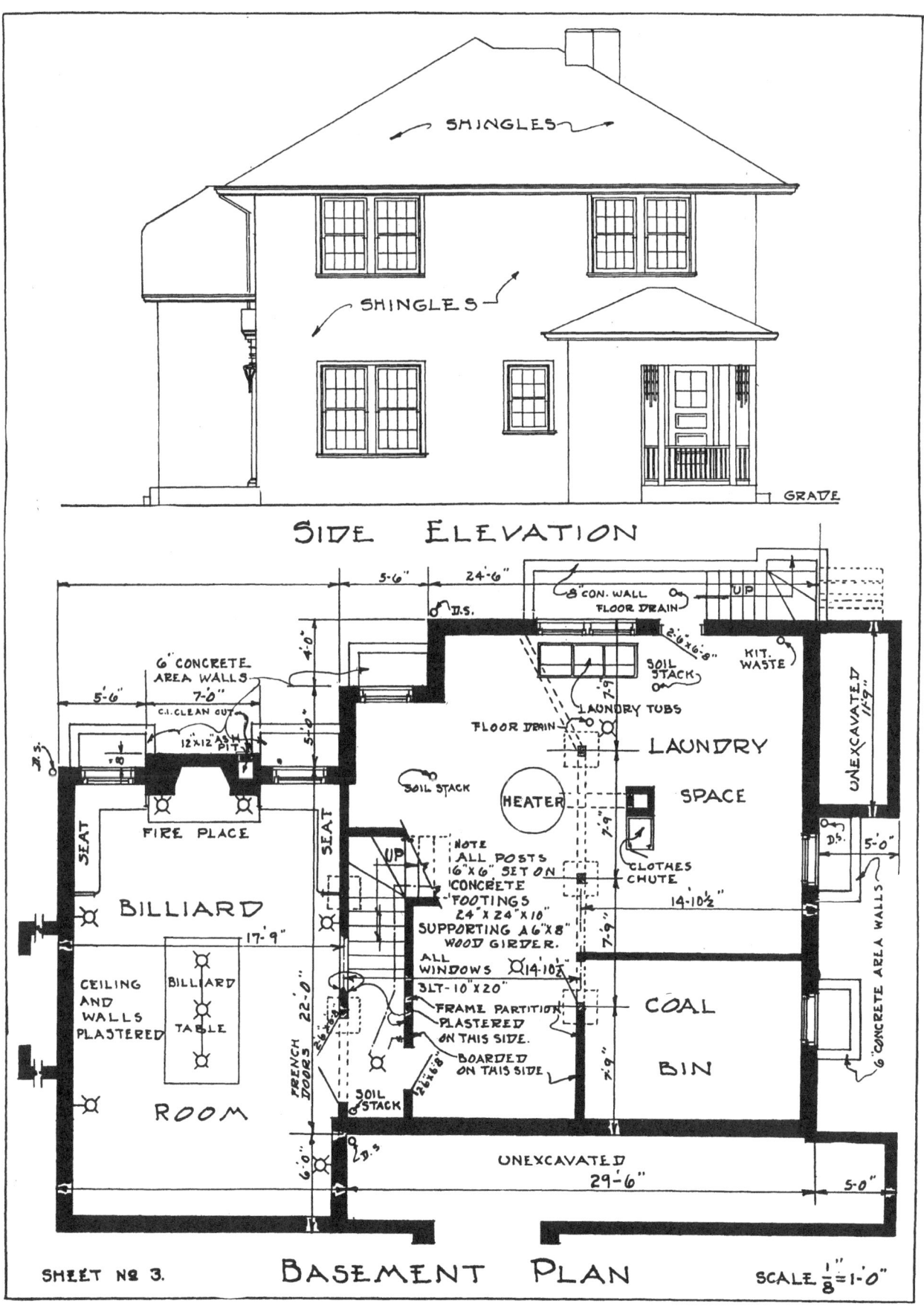

SIDE ELEVATION

SHINGLES

SHINGLES

GRADE

SHEET Nº 3.   BASEMENT PLAN   SCALE $\frac{1}{8}" = 1'-0"$

6" CONCRETE AREA WALLS
7'-0"
C.I. CLEAN OUT
12"X12" ASH PIT
FIRE PLACE
SEAT
BILLIARD
CEILING AND WALLS PLASTERED
BILLIARD TABLE
ROOM
17'-9"
22'-0"
FRENCH DOORS
SOIL STACK
UP
NOTE ALL POSTS 16"X6" SET ON CONCRETE FOOTINGS 24"X24"X10" SUPPORTING A 6"X8" WOOD GIRDER.
ALL WINDOWS 3 LT-10"X20"
FRAME PARTITION PLASTERED ON THIS SIDE. BOARDED ON THIS SIDE
SOIL STACK
HEATER
FLOOR DRAIN
8" CON. WALL FLOOR DRAIN
UP
SOIL STACK
LAUNDRY TUBS
LAUNDRY
SPACE
CLOTHES CHUTE
KIT. WASTE
UNEXCAVATED 1'-9"
D.S.
5'-0"
6" CONCRETE AREA WALLS
COAL BIN
14-10½"
14-10½
UNEXCAVATED 29'-6"
5'-0"
5'-6"   24'-6"
4'-0"
5'-6"
6'-0"
7'-9"
7'-9"
7'-9"
7'-9"

THE ATTICA; The Basement, Through Careful Attention to Detail, Is an Important and Usable Portion of the House Which Adds Much to Its Convenience. The billiard room is an inviting one and the rest of the basement area is utilized to good advantage. A cross-section of the billiard room and the living room above is presented on the following page.

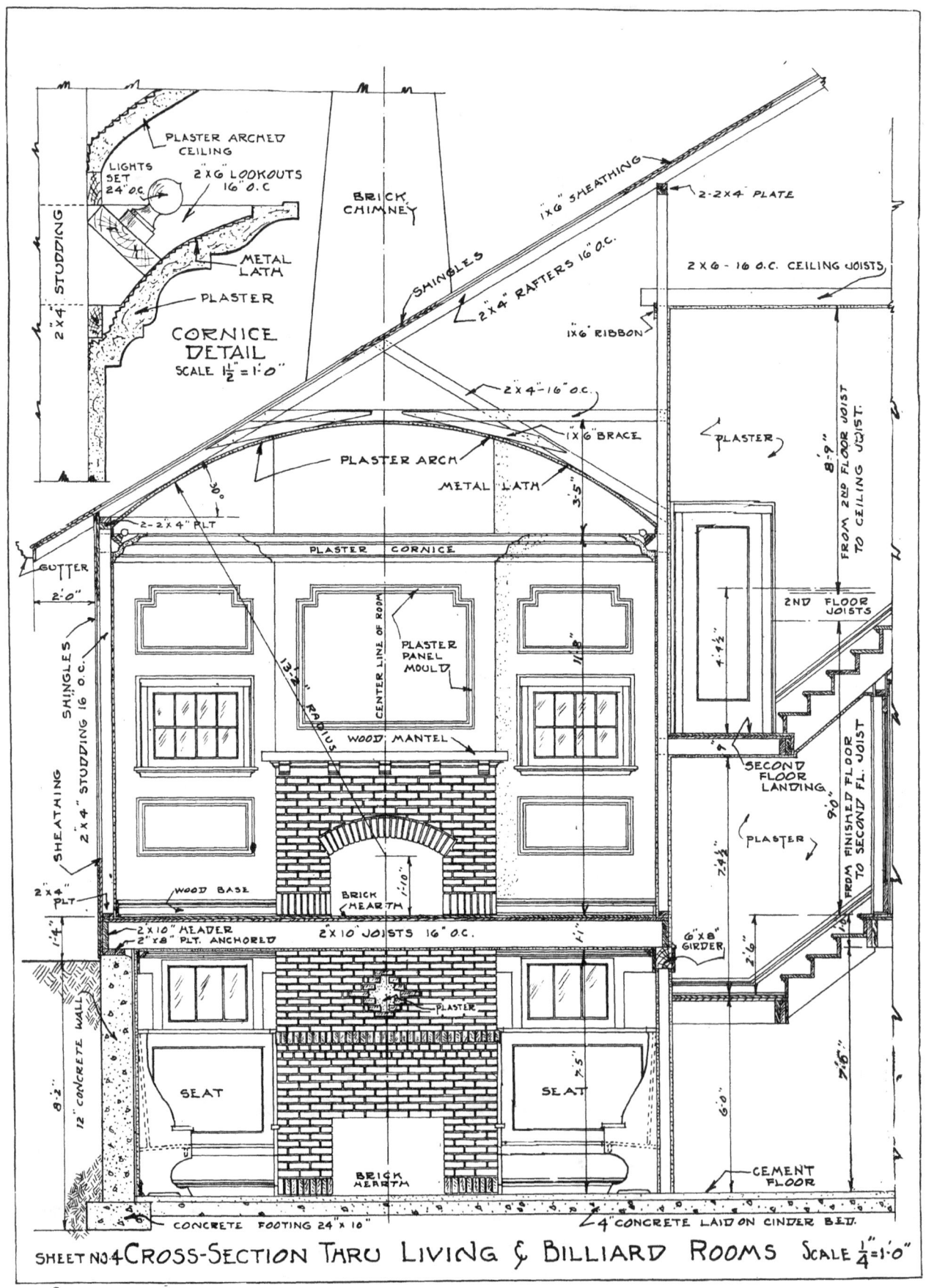

PLASTER ARCHED CEILING

LIGHTS SET 24" O.C

2"x6" LOOKOUTS 16" O.C

BRICK CHIMNEY

2"x4" STUDDING

METAL LATH

PLASTER

CORNICE DETAIL
SCALE 1½"=1'-0"

1"x6" SHEATHING

2-2"x4" PLATE

SHINGLES

2"x4" RAFTERS 16" O.C.

2"x6"-16" O.C. CEILING JOISTS

1"x6" RIBBON

2"x4"-16" O.C.

1"x6" BRACE

PLASTER

PLASTER ARCH

METAL LATH

3'-5"

8'-9"   FROM 2ND FLOOR JOIST TO CEILING JOIST

30°

2-2"x4" PLT

PLASTER CORNICE

GUTTER

2'-0"

SHEATHING

SHINGLES

2"x4" STUDDING 16" O.C.

CENTER LINE OF ROOM

PLASTER PANEL MOULD

11'-8"

2ND FLOOR JOISTS

4'-1½"

13'-2" RADIUS

WOOD MANTEL

SECOND FLOOR LANDING

PLASTER

2"x4" PLT

WOOD BASE

BRICK HEARTH

1'-10"

7'-4½"

FROM FINISHED FLOOR TO SECOND FL. JOIST

9'-0"

2"x10" HEADER
2"x8" PLT. ANCHORED

2"x10" JOISTS 16" O.C.

1'-4"

1'-1"

6"x8" GIRDER

2'-6"

8'-2"

12" CONCRETE WALL

SEAT

PLASTER

SEAT

7'-5"

6'-0"

7'-6"

CEMENT FLOOR

CONCRETE FOOTING 24"x10"

4" CONCRETE LAID ON CINDER BED.

SHEET NO. 4 CROSS-SECTION THRU LIVING & BILLIARD ROOMS   SCALE ¼"=1'-0"

THE ATTICA; Details of the Construction of the High Arched Ceiling of the Living Room with the Placement of the Indirect Lights Are Shown in the Cross-Section. The fireplace of the basement room, with its built-in seats gives an idea of its attractiveness. If the nature of the building site permits this basement ceiling height should be increased.

The ATTICA

A SHINGLED Residence of Italian Lines. For Complete Building Plans Working Drawings to Scale See Pages 53, 54, 55 and 56.

The AUBURN

A SHINGLED English Cottage. For Complete Building Plans-Working Drawings to Scale See Pages 60, 61, 62 and 63.

The Auburn

A Shingled English Cottage; the Shingles Rounded at the Eaves in Thatch Effect are the finishing touch for this Pretty Home

For Perspective in Full Colors see page 58

A HOME that quickly gives the effect of being lived in, of really being a home instead of maintaining the "new and for sale" aspect indefinitely, is presented for this Home. The long sweep of the roof lines, the inviting doorway under its arch and the soft tone of the shingles, laid wide to the weather on the sidewalls, all add to the attractiveness of this dwelling for real home lovers.

The entrance, with its attractive side lights, admits one to a pleasant central hall, with open stairs to the second floor. This hall separates the dining room and kitchen from the living room and sun parlor. The living room is rather large and has an interesting feature in the grouping of the fireplace and the built-in bookcase. Folding French doors make the large sun parlor, with its separate entrance, virtually a part of the larger room.

The dining room is well planned to receive a maxi-

mum amount of sunlight and is conveniently arranged with reference to the kitchen and the serving pantry, which will be found to save many steps. The breakfast porch, opening directly from the kitchen, is a pleasant feature of the home.

On the second floor are three bedrooms and two baths. The unusual amount of closet space shows at once that the wishes of the women who have to care for the home have been considered. The master's bedroom is roomy and its angles permit interesting arrangements of furniture. The large closet and individual bath are commendable.

The two additional bedrooms are of an adequate size and permit the convenient arrangement of the furnishings.

It will be noticed that the plans for the home, as shown in detail on the four pages following, call for adequate lighting equipment.

THE AUBURN; Shingles Rounded at the Eaves and Over the Arch of the Doorways Give to This Home a Delightful Air of Old World Snugness, Decidedly in Keeping With the Soft Tones of the Shingled Sidewalls. Full working details of this home will be found in the drawings on the four following pages.

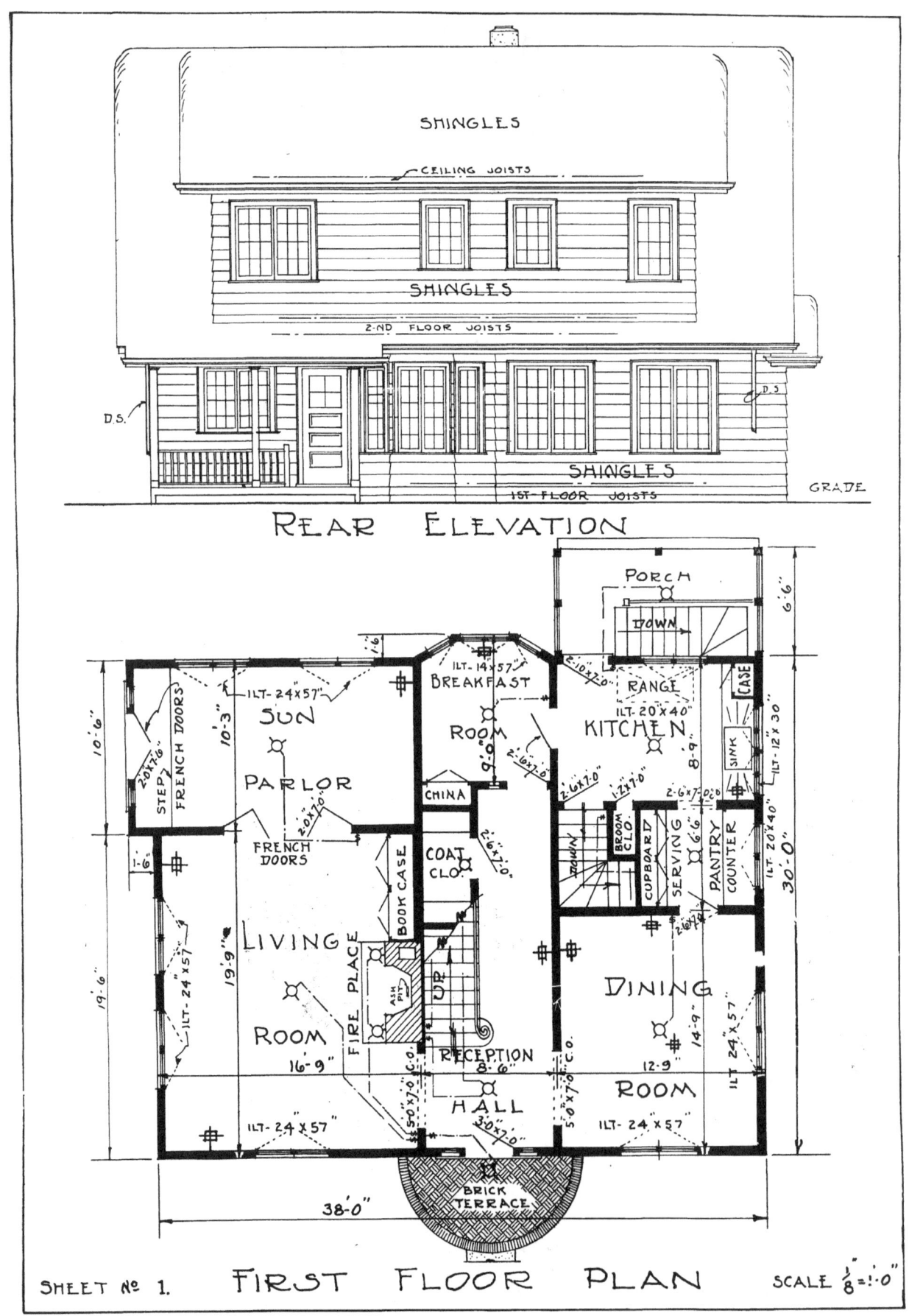

REAR ELEVATION

FIRST FLOOR PLAN

SHEET № 1.

SCALE ⅛"=1'·0"

THE AUBURN; The Living Quarters of this cottage Home are Well Separated from the Noise and Bustle of the Preparation of Meals by a Central Reception Hall, as Shown in the First Floor Plan. The plan for the second floor and the cross section of the home are shown on the page opposite.

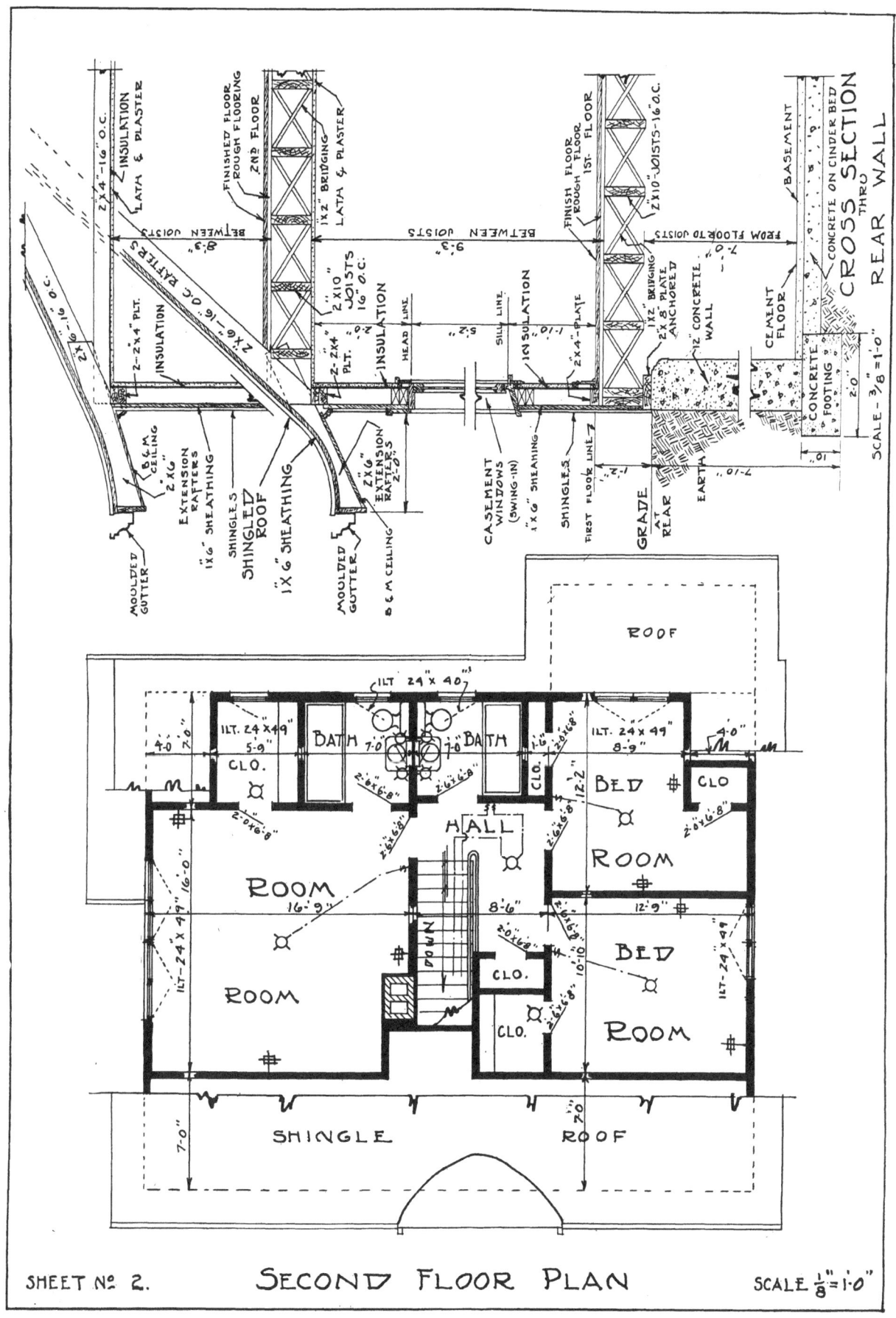

SHEET Nº 2. SECOND FLOOR PLAN SCALE $\frac{1}{8}$"=1'·0"

THE AUBURN; Three Bedrooms with Two Baths Are Shown in the Plans for the Second Floor. The wealth of closet space will prove an attractive feature to feminine home seekers. The cross section detail is worthy of study.

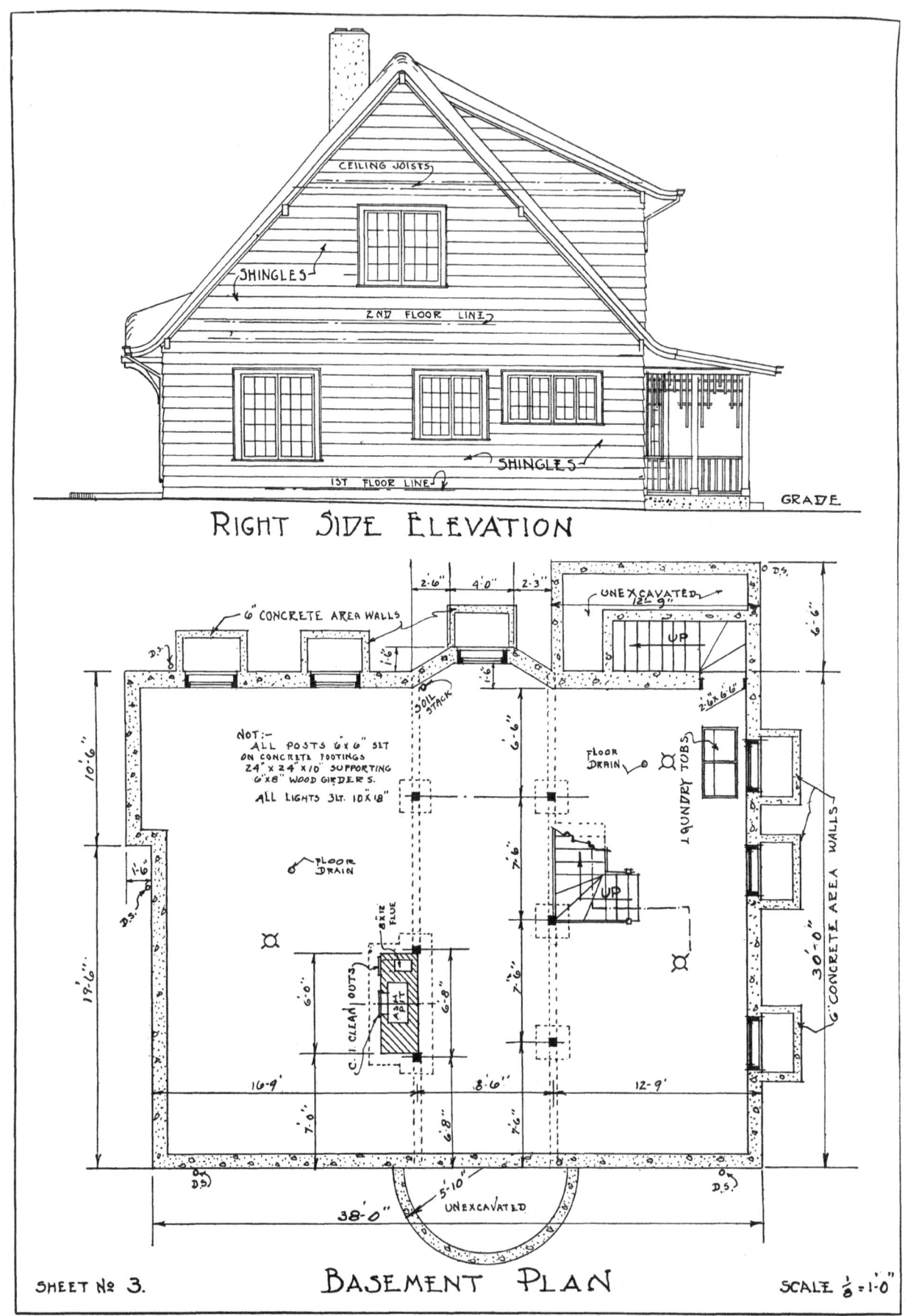

RIGHT SIDE ELEVATION

BASEMENT PLAN

SHEET Nº 3.   SCALE ⅛ = 1'-0"

THE AUBURN; The Plan Provides for Laundry Tubs in the Basement, Which Is Excavated Under the Main Portion of the Home and the Areaways Provide Light for This Portion of the Home, Despite Its Apperance of Setting Close to the Ground. The right side elevation is shown above, the left side and front elevations on the opposite page.

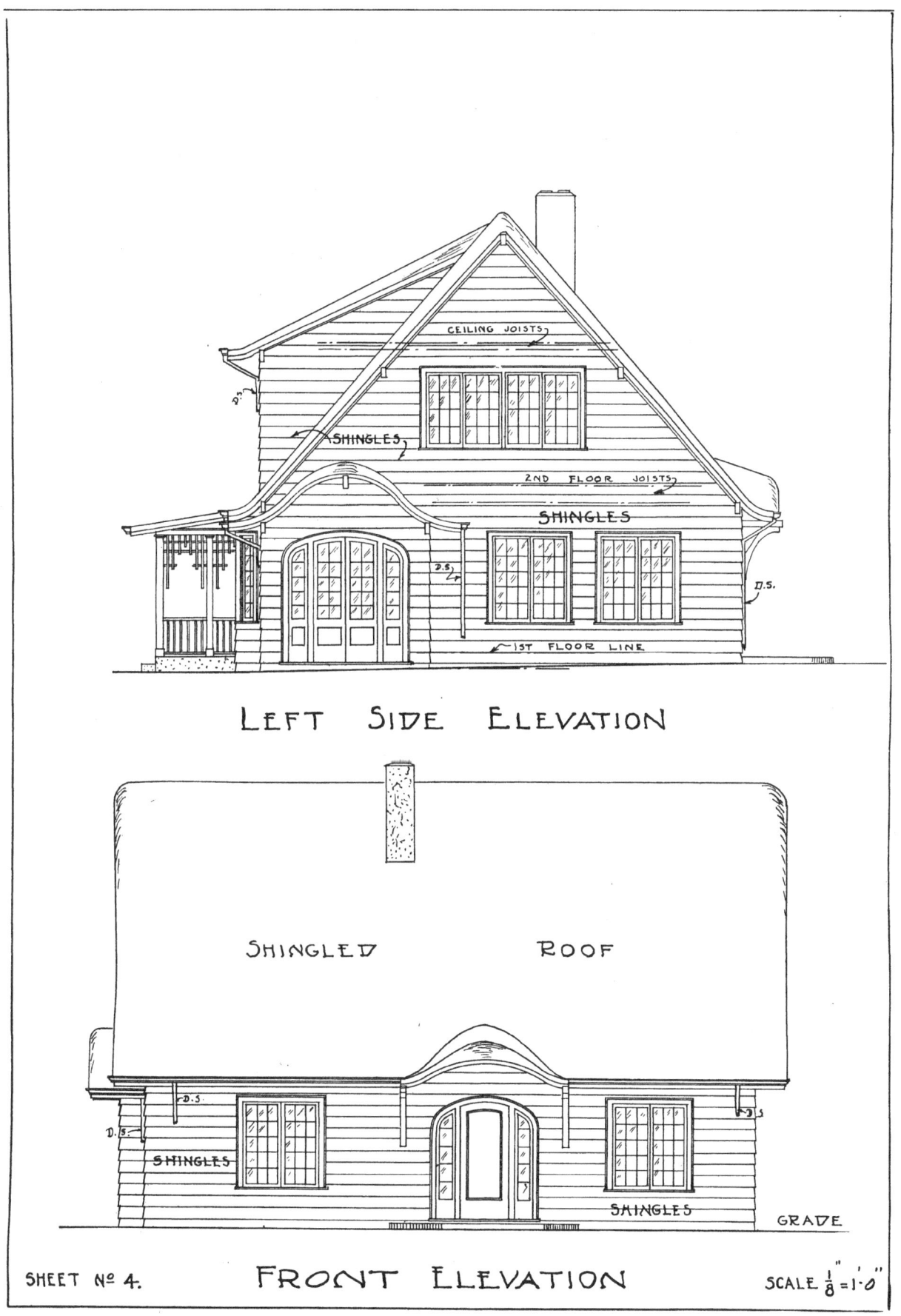

LEFT SIDE ELEVATION

FRONT ELEVATION

SHEET № 4.

SCALE ⅛" = 1'-0"

THE AUBURN; The Dormer on the Rear of the Home, as Shown in the Side Elevation Above, Presents an interesting Study in Roof Lines as Well as Providing Much Additional Space in the Second Story.

The Ajax

An Electrical Home Efficient

Charming White Colonial Bungalow is Example of How Careful Planning of Electrical Equipment Increases Comfort

THE quiet dignity of the distinguished Colonial bungalow shown on page 65 surely deserves nothing less than the best equipment to make the interior as comfortable and as livable as the charming exterior seems to promise that it will be. And no single item of the equipment of such a house, so plainly meant to be a home of charm, is more important than the wiring and the electrical equipment.

All who have given any thought to building a home are aware of the charm that the proper fixtures add to a correctly lighted home and many know of the wealth of conveniences and labor-saving devices which electricity can bring to the help of the housewife. But few know the extent to which the success of the electrical equipment is dependent on the manner in which the house is wired.

Perhaps the test of the efficiency of the wiring in any home is the amount of thought which is given to this major detail of construction both before and after the house is built.

Queer though it may seem, if the wiring is given due consideration and intelligent attention before the home is erected, it will be forgotten when the house is occupied. On the other hand, if the house is wired, with cheapness as the most important consideration, as so often happens, the wiring never can be forgotten while the house is occupied.

Unpleasant things, like inadequate lighting, lack of facilities for utilizing electrical conveniences and all sorts of limitations will recall the hidden wiring.

Of course, these limitations can be overcome in a home after it is built, just as it is being remedied now in thousands of homes built only a short time ago. But the proper time for the builder to assure himself of the best in electrical equipment is at the time when the home is constructed.

In the Dining Room of this Electrical Home Efficient, Illustrated with an Exterior View and Floor Plan on page 65, the Engineers Have Fixed the Height of the Central Fixture at Just 24 Inches Above the Table Top. Notice the utility of the floor outlet.

Even though the installation of some of the fixtures must be delayed to a later date, on account of the requirements of economy, the complete wiring of the new house should be done right at the start. Whatever additional investment this may require will be amply justified and it will more than pay for itself by the saving which it will afford when the time comes to install the additional fixtures. Nor is this the only saving for if the wiring is properly done at the start it will eliminate the need of service costs which are bound to occur wherever this work is slighted.

The wiring of the home shown on these pages is diagramed in the accompanying floor plan and if the instructions are followed a wiring system will be obtained which will meet every present and future need both for lighting and for supplying the many electrical appliances which are rapidly becoming a necessary part of the convenient modern home.

The porch of the charming and practical home illustrated on this page is one made to be used. And to make the welcome of the home especially appealing to the after-dinner guests and the late homecomer, a luminaire of type "L" is placed on the porch ceiling, equipped with a 40-watt Mazda B clear lamp.

A convenience outlet is provided under the window so that a pleasant grouping about the subdued light of a floor lamp will be most natural on summer evenings. A fan might be pleasant attached to this outlet on a hot, breathless afternoon.

The living room, with its excellent daylight illumination from two sides and its wall spaces well suited to attractive arrangement of furniture, is a room too attractive to be spoiled by improper lighting.

For this room the engineers have specified as the central fixture a luminaire of the type "B" equipped with

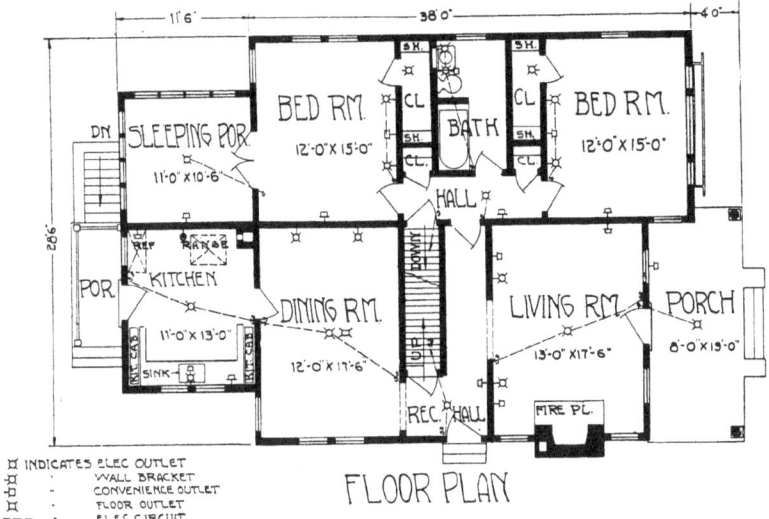

FLOOR PLAN

⊠ INDICATES ELEC OUTLET
WALL BRACKET
CONVENIENCE OUTLET
FLOOR OUTLET
ELEC CIRCUIT
S SWITCH

THE AJAX; This Beautiful White Colonial Bungalow is an Electrical Home Efficient. The floor plan, shown above, gives a diagrammatic presentation of the electrical wiring as described in the following pages, where the different types of luminaires are illustrated.

four 25-watt Mazda B all-frosted lamps. This is to be hung directly from the ceiling as indicated in the diagram. Three-way switches, one just inside the entrance from the porch and the other adjacent to the opening from the reception hall, allow this light to be controlled from either point, without the necessity for crossing the room in the dark, either before the light is turned on or after it is turned off.

On both sides of the door leading from the living room to the reception hall is placed a luminaire, illustrated here as type "A," equipped with a Mazda B all-frosted 25-watt lamp. These fixtures are to be mounted six feet above the floor, the proper height to insure efficient lighting, and with the type of light and fixture specified, to avoid any eyestrain.

Three convenience outlets are provided in the baseboard of the living room for stand and table lights. Note that these outlets are placed so that they are available for lamps in all positions in the room where such a light might be desired. It is necessary that the wiring should allow such lamps to be placed where they are wanted without the inconvenient and dangerous trailing of cords over long expanses.

The architect who designed this house did so with the idea that additional space would be made available on the second floor if it were desirable. You will notice a stairway to the second floor in the reception hall.

This hall is lighted with luminaire "H," unobtrusive but efficient. The light is a 25-watt, round bulb, all-frosted Mazda B lamp. But you will note that the switch just inside the door is part of a three-way circuit, so that the light may be controlled either from the switch indicated in the floor plan or another installed on the second floor.

The convenience outlet in this hall is placed waist high, where it will be most convenient for use with a vacuum cleaner or in a proper place for attaching a table lamp which might be placed on a console table in the hallway.

The designer of this home has been particularly fortunate in the proportions of the dining room, which is too often considered as the room which may take the left-over space or be adjusted to make the rest of the rooms adequate. This room, 12 by 17½ feet, is one for real entertainment

Luminaire "B" Is Specified for the Central Lighting Fixture in the Living Room. It is attached directly to the ceiling.

This Pendant Lamp, Luminaire "G," Is Placed in the Dining Room. It is shown in place on page 64.

or family gatherings.

The central light for the dining room is a charming one suspended directly above the dining room table. The lighting engineers have specified luminaire "G" for this position and insist that the lower edge of the shade shall be exactly 24 inches above the surface of the table. This insures a pleasant light that will not allow any direct rays to attack the eyes of the company gathered about. The light specified is one 75-watt, all-frosted Mazda C. This is controlled from switches both at the kitchen and hallway entrances.

On the inner wall of the room, two luminaires "D" are placed. These are equipped with 15-watt Mazda C clear lamps. It is almost inevitable that the buffet will occupy a position between these lamps.

One of the features of this room is the floor outlet, placed in the floor below the position which will be occupied by the dining room table. This outlet allows a connection to come up directly under the table which may be attached to a multiple outlet built into the table itself. And this equipment would allow the number of electrical conveniences which are aids in preparing breakfasts and other meals to be connected at the same time.

The attachment for the dining room table is quite simple. It is merely an oblong box, attached out of sight, under the top of the table where it is convenient. One cord brings the current to the fixture and outlets such as are known to every housewife are available for the toaster, percolator and other devices.

Kitchens, as is proper, are receiving more attention. This is where a major portion of the housework is done and it should be made more than an efficient workshop; it should be a room where work may be enjoyed. And very recently lighting experts have recognized the demand for efficient and shadowless lighting housewives desire for spotless kitchens.

In the kitchen planned in this house the major part of the lighting responsibility is placed on a central fixture, luminaire "K" mounted on the ceiling and equipped with a 100-watt Mazda C clear lamp. Over the sink is a Mazda B all-frosted 40-watt light mounted in luminaire "J" with a pull

Luminaire "L" for Illuminating the Porch.

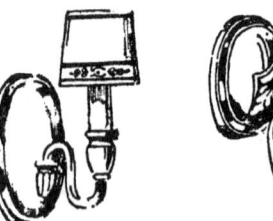

The Sidewall Fixture, Luminaire "D" Is for the Dining Room, Above the Buffet.

Luminaire "A" Is for the Walls of the Living Room. It is made to fit well with central fixture.

Luminaire "F" Is to Be Attached to the Ceiling of the Sleeping Porch.

chain switch.

In no place in the home can electricity be of as much service as in the kitchen if the wiring is planned properly. In this plan the engineers have designated a 30-ampere power outlet for the electric range. An outlet is supplied for the electric refrigerator also.

One of the features of this kitchen which will appeal to all cooks is the provision made for the installation of the exhaust fan above the sink. This outlet is placed high enough so that the connection to the fan is short. Such a device insures a cool kitchen and a home free from the odors of cooking. Another outlet, just above the kitchen cabinet level, provides a place where the utility kitchen motor, cooking appliances and an electric iron may be attached.

The bedroom group in this home is particularly happy in its arrangement. It is cut off from the rest of the house to a large extent and insures a privacy which is always desirable in this portion of the house and is not always attained in a house with bedrooms on the first floor.

The bath, while conveniently adjacent to both of the bedrooms, still is isolated from them by means of closets which will prove effective in sound insulation.

The hallway of the bedroom group is illuminated by a 25-watt Mazda B all-frosted lamp, mounted in luminaire "H" and controlled by a switch at the entrance from the reception hall. The convenience outlet here is waist high to make for convenience in attaching the vacuum cleaner.

Each bedroom has two luminaires, type "C," one mounted on either side of the space which naturally will be occupied by the beds or dressers. These fixtures are to be mounted six feet from the floor and equipped with Mazda B clear bulb lamps of 40 watts capacity. Notice that a switch for these lights is provided at the door to prevent unnecessary searches in the dark. The convenience outlets provided in the bedrooms will find their uses in providing current for curling irons, hair dryers, massage vibrators, heating pads, electrical heaters, boudoir lamps and electric fans.

Closets off both of the bedrooms are illuminated

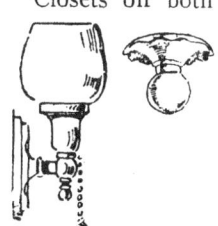

Two Luminaires "E," to the Right, Are Used to Light the Bathroom Mirror. Luminaire "H" Is for the Hallways.

with 25-watt Mazda B clear lamps in pull sockets. These are to be hung directly above the center of the closet floor.

In the bathroom two luminaires of type "E" are mounted on the sides of the mirror. They are equipped with 25-watt Mazda B clear lamps and are five and a half feet from the floor. This insures that the head of the

house will have adequate illumination when he shaves. No arrangement which throws one side of the face in bold light and the other in a shadow correspondingly deep can be considered at all satisfactory.

A convenience outlet in this room is located above the wash bowl, where it will be found useful for the operation of the immersion heater, sterilizer, milk warmer, massage vibrator and other devices.

A sleeping porch of the type shown in the plan for this home virtually adds another bedroom to the home if it is planned and built properly. This room, with its rather generous size, opens from the bedroom with French doors, which often will be thrown open on warm days and nights for ventilation.

The lighting equipment specified for this room is a 75-watt Mazda lamp, mounted in luminaire "F" on the ceiling. A convenience outlet is provided in the baseboard for a reading lamp and for mechanical devices. It is possible that such a room would be used often as a sewing room, when a connection for the electrical sewing machine will be found most desirable.

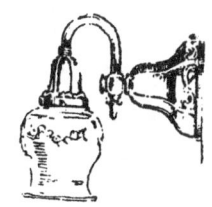

Two Fixtures of This Type, Luminaire "C," Illuminate Each of the Bedrooms.

The Kitchen Is Lighted with Luminaire "K," Shown Here, to Insure Diffused Shadowless Light.

Home Light Standards

J. W. Lofts, distinguished illuminating engineer, has recently completed a detailed study of light required for human comfort and health.

The intrinsic brilliancies of the more common forms of artificial light in terms of candle power to the square inch are used as follows:

Modern candle	2	Incandescent mantle	40
Flat gas flame	4	Electric light	40
Flat wick oil lamp	4	Acetylene flame	100

The use of globes, which is recommended to reduce glare and sharp lighting contrasts, was found to reduce the brilliancy of the light source from 5 per cent for clear glass to 40 per cent for heavy frosted glass.

Indirect illumination, the avoidance of glare and of deep shadows and the installation of diffused lighting systems are advocated for the home. The standards of illumination found desirable, as given below, are given in foot-candles; i. e., in multiples of the amount of light thrown upon an object one foot distant by a standard sperm-oil candle. The illumination levels for various rooms are:

This Fixture, Luminaire "J," Is Placed Over the Kitchen Sink.

	Foot Candles
Dining tables	6-8
Drawing rooms	4-6
Library or study	5-8

The Ainsworth

A Modern Home of English Type

HERE is a thoroughly modern American home of English adaptation.

The many gables of the exterior give interest and variety, their steep pitch and low eaves are characteristic of the English cottage, in fact, the entire exterior is true to this type.

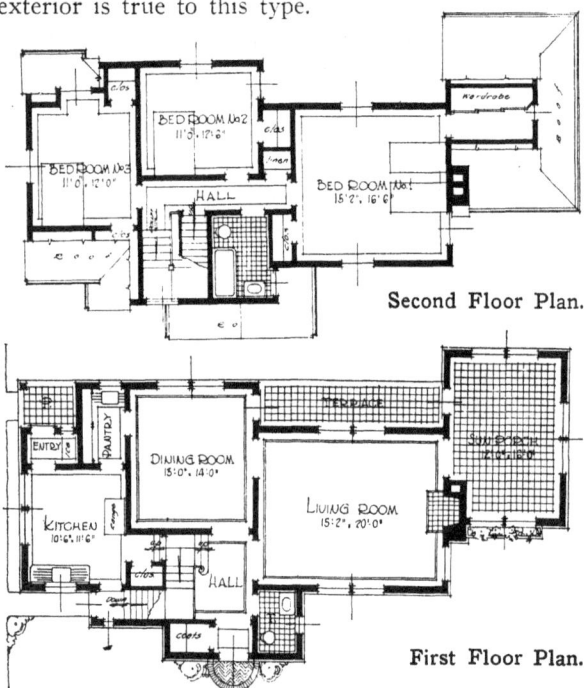

Second Floor Plan.

First Floor Plan.

A Charming Feature of this Home is the Entrance, Shown Above. The second floor plan, above to the left, shows the effective bedroom arrangement. The first floor plan shows a careful separation of living room and kitchen.

THE AINSWORTH; The Interesting Treatment of the Gables in this Home, with the Idea Developed Even in the Garden Wall, Forms a Motif of Unusual Interest. The one timbered gable makes an interesting contrast while the attractive, shuttered small window and the details of the entrance and door all do their part in adding attractiveness to the house.

The entry, with its distinctive door, the fitting lamp above and the brick stoop, are inviting and carry out well the English atmosphere. The sun porch of generous size and the recessed terrace are features which will insure the comfort of the owners of the home.

The interiors have been carried out in a later period, they are well furnished, are thoroughly livable and distinctly American. The simplicity of these interiors lends strong character, no fussy decorations, no overcrowding of furnishings, they are open, spacious and cheerful.

The plan arrangement of this house is good. The toilet off the entrance hall affords a real convenience for the owners and their guests. The kitchen and adjoining service portions are well arranged.

On the second floor are three bedrooms and a bath. There is plenty of closet space. A very generous wardrobe opens from the master's bedroom.

Looking From the Living Room of the Ainsworth Into the Sun Porch. The pleasing simplicity of the fireplace and mantel design and the general atmosphere of the room make the Windsor chair in the corner of the room seem peculiarly fitting.

The Hallway and Dining Room of the Ainsworth as Seen from the Living Room Give an Adequate Idea of the Roominess of the House. The stairs are interesting. Note how the living room is given a large appearance through keeping the center of the room free from furniture and avoiding over-crowding.

The Altamonte

This Five-Room House Follows the Spanish Style with High Arched Ceilings and Arched Doorways

For Perspective in Full Colors see page 75

THE Altamonte is a five-room house with the rooms well grouped for comfort and convenience. The general style of the building is Spanish, this effect being most apparent in the high arched ceilings of the living and dining room and the arched doorways.

Externally it presents a most pleasing appearance with its stucco walls, tiled roof, French windows and striped awnings. The awning on the front of the house is especially valuable in balancing the larger French doors at the other end of the house. These doors are ornamental as well as supplying ample light for the dining room from which they open.

The small porch, over which the main roof extends, has two openings in which the arched effect has been used and this same arching is seen at the tops of the windows. The porch gives access directly into the living room. This is a large room, 19 feet by 26 feet 4 inches, with a fireplace at one side. The arched ceiling of this room, as well as of the dining room, is 14 feet 2 inches above the floor. From the living room arched doorways open into a hall at the rear and the dining room at the right.

The dining room is also large and well lighted by the French doors at the front and two windows at the side. Like all the rooms it is equipped with numerous light fixtures and a floor receptacle. Directly behind it is a small but well-arranged kitchen. This kitchen is equipped with built-in cases and fixtures. Off of the kitchen opens a grade entry and a third door leads into the hall.

This hall also gives entry to the two bedrooms and bathroom as well as by the arched doorway to the living room. It is provided with a linen closet and each of the bedrooms also has its closet. The ceilings in this part of the house are 9 feet from the floor.

On the pages following this are shown complete floor plan, basement plan, front and side elevations and details.

The sections give details of construction and here special attention is called to the construction of the arched ceilings which are such an important feature of this house. It will be noticed that these arches are plastered over metal lath and rise from a plaster cornice and metal picture mould. Above the ceiling is an ample air space for insulation.

THE ALTAMONTE; Is a Five-Room House of Spanish Style, Finished in Stucco and with Tile Roof, Ornamental French Windows and Striped Awnings. On the next four pages working plans for this house are shown.

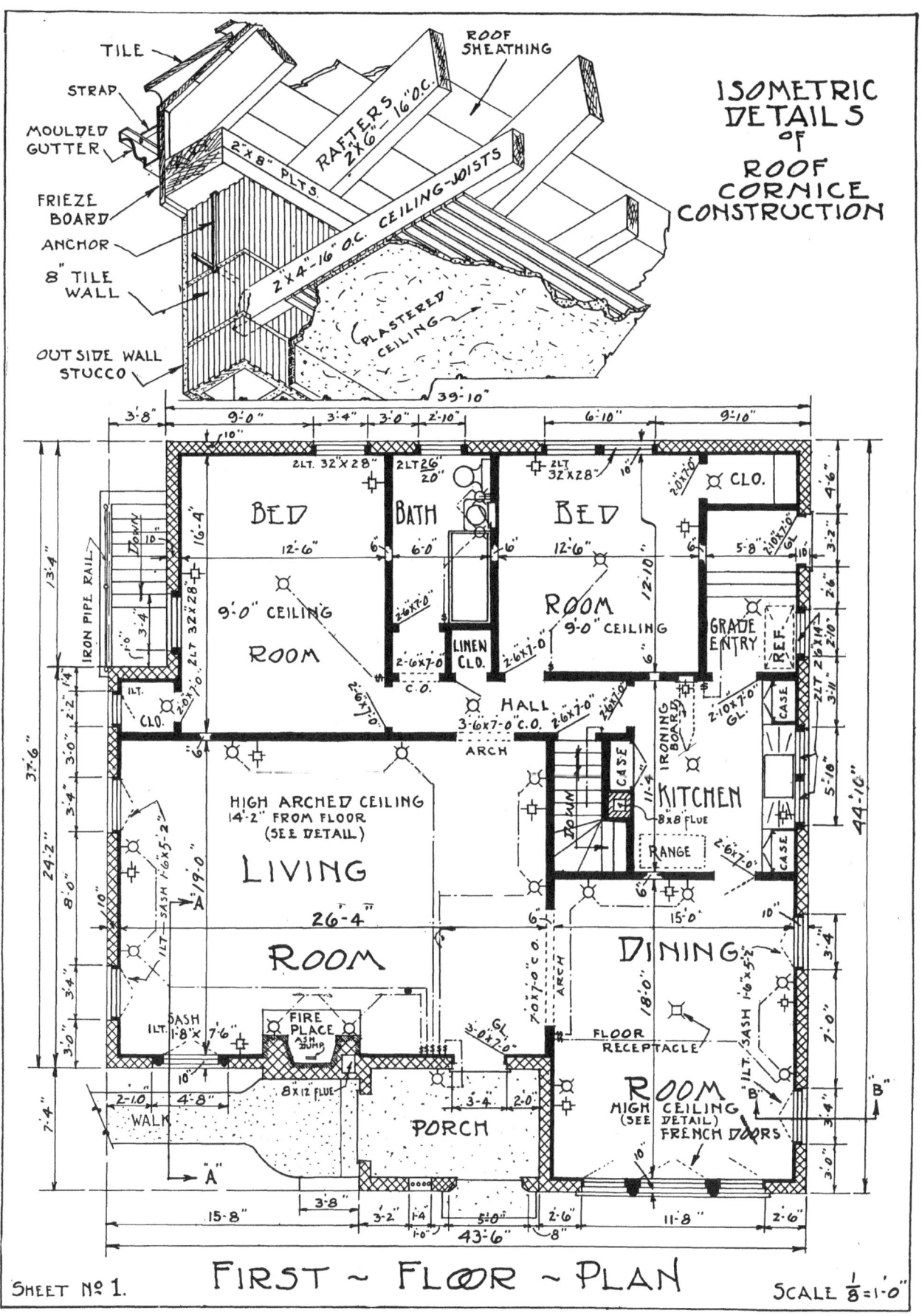

ISOMETRIC DETAILS of ROOF CORNICE CONSTRUCTION

TILE
STRAP
MOULDED GUTTER
FRIEZE BOARD
ANCHOR
8" TILE WALL
OUTSIDE WALL STUCCO

ROOF SHEATHING
RAFTERS 2×6—16"0.C.
2×8" PLTS.
2×4—16" O.C. CEILING-JOISTS
PLASTERED CEILING

FIRST ~ FLOOR ~ PLAN

SHEET Nº 1.   SCALE ⅛=1'-0"

THE ALTAMONTE; The First Floor Plan Shows the Convenient Arrangement of Its Five Rooms with the Large Living Room and Dining Room Extending Across the Entire Front. Above is a detail drawing of the roof construction while on the next page will be found the basement plan and fireplace elevation.

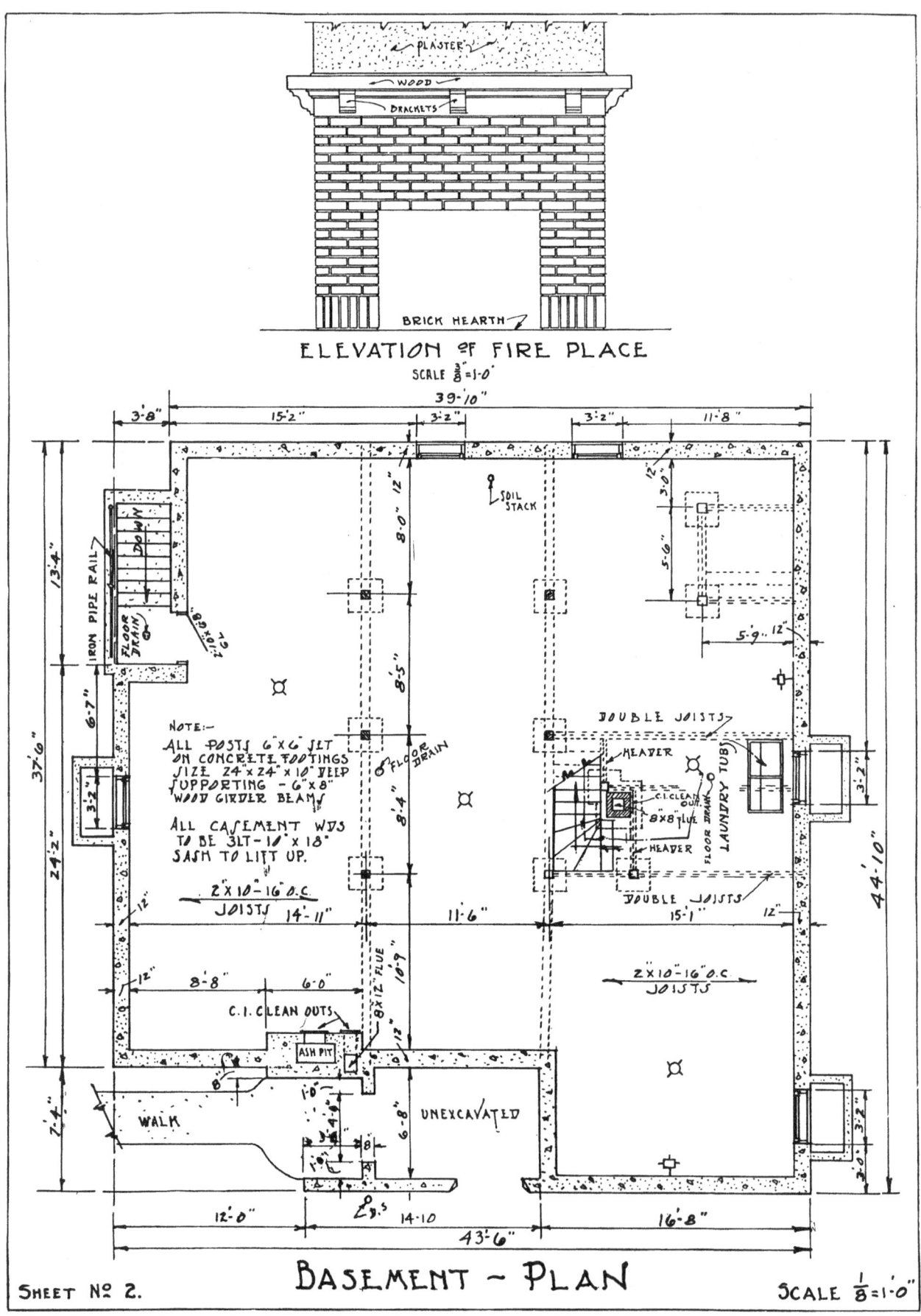

ELEVATION OF FIRE PLACE

SCALE 3/8"=1-0'

BASEMENT - PLAN

SHEET Nº 2.   SCALE 1/8=1-0"

**THE ALTAMONTE; In the Basement Plan Full Data on Supports, Partitions and Lighting Arrangement Are Given.
Above is an elevation of the fireplace and on the opposite page the front and side elevations of this house.**

LEFT ~ SIDE ~ ELEVATION

FRONT ~ ELEVATION

ELEVATIONS

SHEET Nº 3   SCALE ⅛=1′-0″

THE ALTAMONTE; Front and Left Side Elevations Show, Besides the Placement of Windows and Doors, the Relative Lines of Grade, Floor and the Arched Ceilings Which Are Features of the Living Room and Dining Room. For section details see the next page.

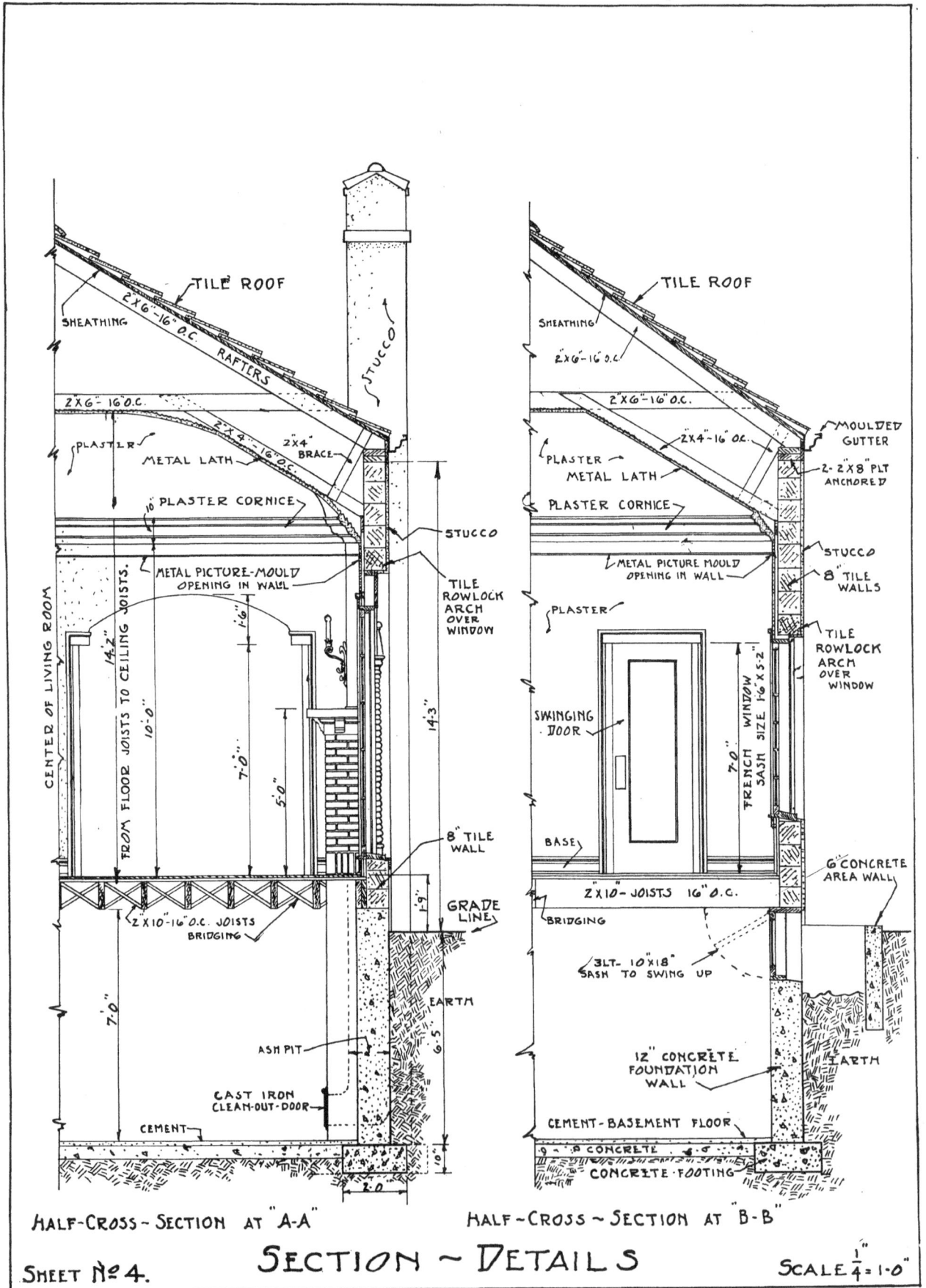

TILE ROOF

SHEATHING

2"X6"-16" O.C. RAFTERS

STUCCO

2"X6"-16" O.C.

PLASTER

2"X4"-16" O.C.   2"X4" BRACE

METAL LATH

PLASTER CORNICE

STUCCO

METAL PICTURE-MOULD OPENING IN WALL

TILE ROWLOCK ARCH OVER WINDOW

CENTER OF LIVING ROOM

FROM FLOOR JOISTS TO CEILING JOISTS.

14'-2"

1'-6"

10'-0"

7'-0"

5'-0"

14'-3"

8" TILE WALL

1'-9"

GRADE LINE

2"X10"-16" O.C. JOISTS BRIDGING

7'-0"

EARTH

6'-5"

ASH PIT

CAST IRON CLEAN-OUT-DOOR

CEMENT

10"

2'-0"

HALF-CROSS-SECTION AT "A-A"

TILE ROOF

SHEATHING

2"X6"-16" O.C.

2"X6"-16" O.C.

2"X4"-16" O.C.

PLASTER METAL LATH

PLASTER CORNICE

MOULDED GUTTER

2-2"X8" PLT ANCHORED

STUCCO

8" TILE WALLS

TILE ROWLOCK ARCH OVER WINDOW

METAL PICTURE MOULD OPENING IN WALL

PLASTER

SWINGING DOOR

FRENCH WINDOW SASH SIZE 1'6"X5'-2"

7'-0"

BASE

2"X10"-JOISTS 16" O.C.

BRIDGING

6" CONCRETE AREA WALL

3LT-10"X18" SASH TO SWING UP

12" CONCRETE FOUNDATION WALL

EARTH

CEMENT-BASEMENT FLOOR

8" CONCRETE

CONCRETE FOOTING

HALF-CROSS-SECTION AT "B-B"

SECTION ~ DETAILS

SCALE $\frac{1}{4}$" = 1'-0"

THE ALTAMONTE; Construction Details Are Shown in These Two Sectional Views. Particular attention is called to method of construction of the arched ceilings.

The *ALTAMONTE*

A DELIGHTFUL Spanish Bungalow. For Complete Building Plans-Working Drawings to Scale See Pages 71, 72, 73 and 74.

The AKRON

BRICK and Timbered Stucco Home of Distinction. For Complete Building Plans-Working Drawings to Scale See Pages 78, 79, 80 and 81.

The Akron

Brick and Timbered Stucco and a Roof of Tile Combine to Make a Pleasant Exterior for this Seven Room Home

For Perspective in Full Colors see page 76

THE inspiration for the design of this comfortable cottage, may well have come from Old England, where brick, timbers and stucco often are the means of effecting happy exteriors for homes.

The windows are arranged nicely and the long, horizontal lines of their groupings carry out the effect of low snugness which the house gives the passer. The arched and recessed entry is particularly interesting, with its white keystone and friendly lanterns.

The interior of the home is so planned that it will appeal to any number of American families, particularly where there are children and elderly folks who make downstairs bedrooms a real convenience.

The entry leads directly into the reception hall where the stairs allow access to the second floor. To the left, the reception hall is open to the roomy living room with its charming and unusual corner fireplace. The sun parlor, equipped with casement windows, adds much to the space in the room.

The dining room is separated from the reception hall by French doors. It is adequate in size and the interior wall is such that it allows the convenient placing of a buffet or other large piece of furniture.

The arrangement of the kitchen and pantry is particularly good. Two swinging doors allow one to come to the dining room directly from the kitchen or through the pantry, where cases and shelves are built in for the convenience of the housewife. The kitchen allows the refrigerator to be iced from the outside and has a number of other interesting features.

The downstairs bedroom group, reached through the reception hall, is well isolated from the rest of the home and has its bath well placed. Both of the bedrooms on the second floor are pleasant rooms with large closets and casement windows.

THE AKRON; Pleasant and Substantial, This Residence Will Prove a Most Attractive Home for the Average American Family. While it is distinctly individual, it is not freakish. Detailed drawings of the home are presented on the four pages following, and a perspective view in full colors appears on page 76.

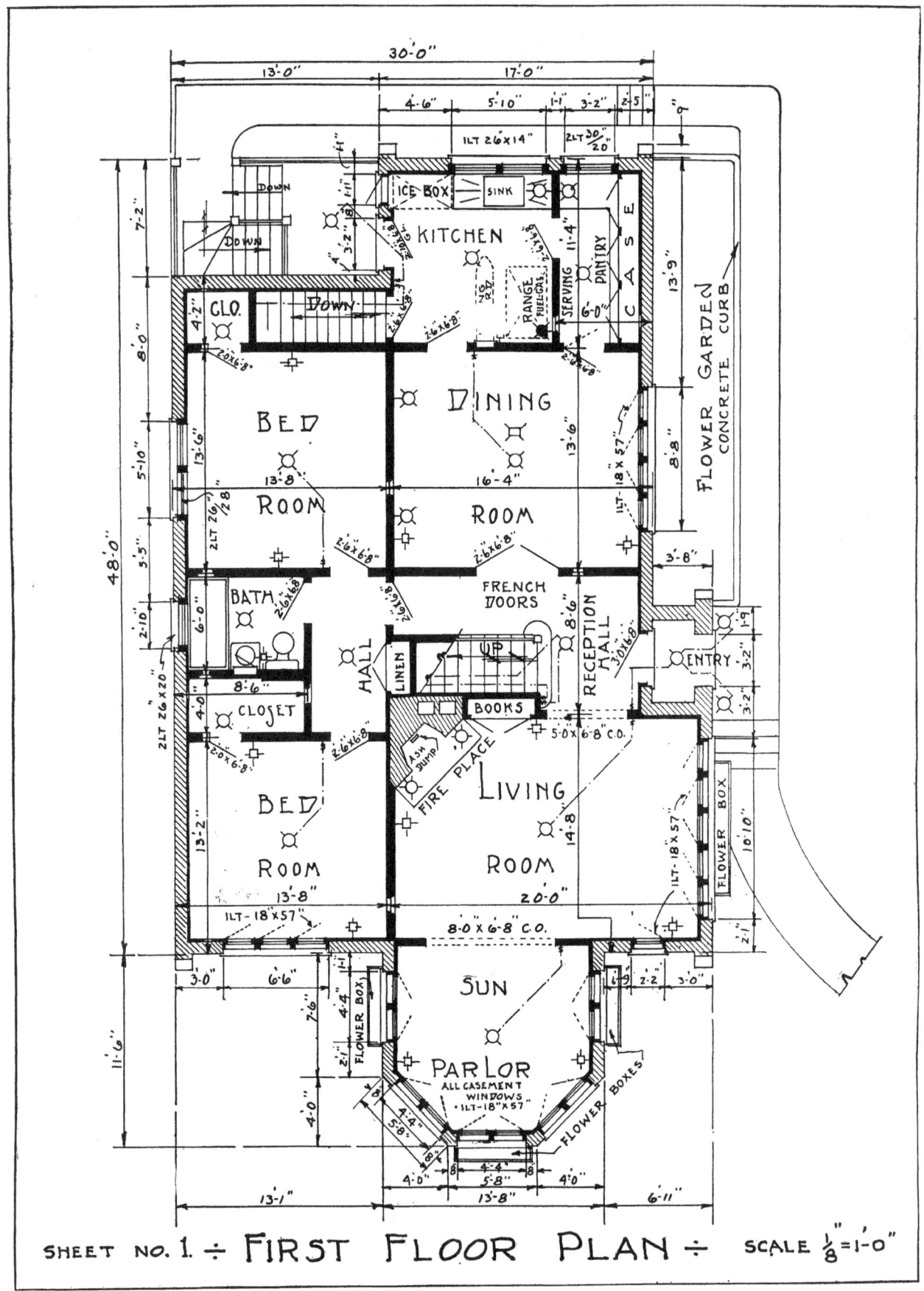

SHEET NO. 1. ÷ FIRST FLOOR PLAN ÷ SCALE ⅛"=1'-0"

THE AKRON; The First Floor Plan Shows the Interesting Manner in Which the Fireplace Has Been Built in One Corner of the Living Room. Another interesting detail is the built-in bookcase. The second floor plan is shown on the opposite page.

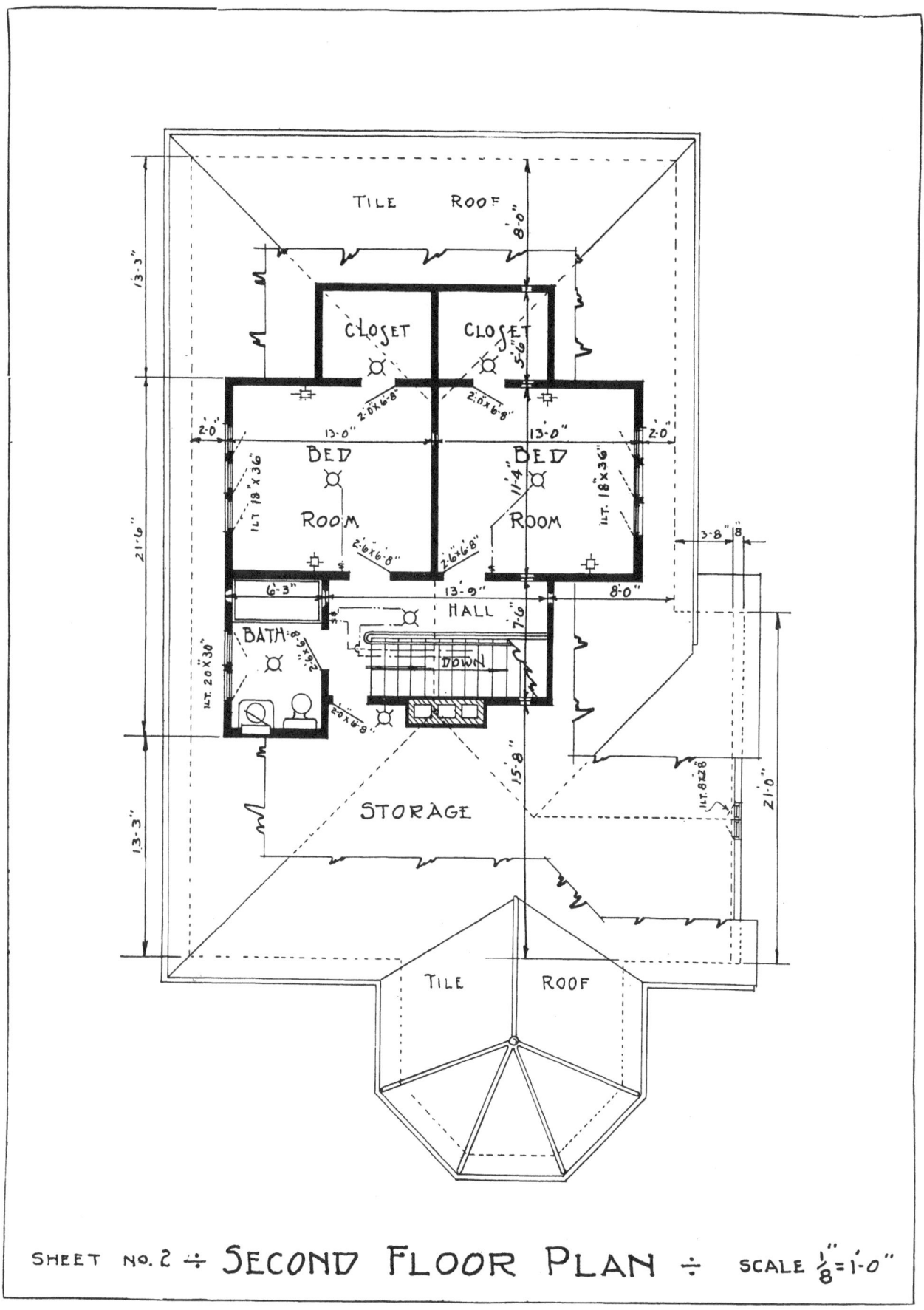

TILE ROOF

CLOSET CLOSET

BED BED

ROOM ROOM

BATH

HALL

DOWN

STORAGE

TILE ROOF

SHEET NO. 2 ÷ SECOND FLOOR PLAN ÷ SCALE $\frac{1}{8}$"=1'-0"

THE AKRON; Two Well Proportioned Bedrooms with Commodious Closets and a Bath are Provided for in the Plans
for the Second Floor. The storage space, reached through a door in the stair hall, is a convenient feature. Plans for
the basement are given on the page following.

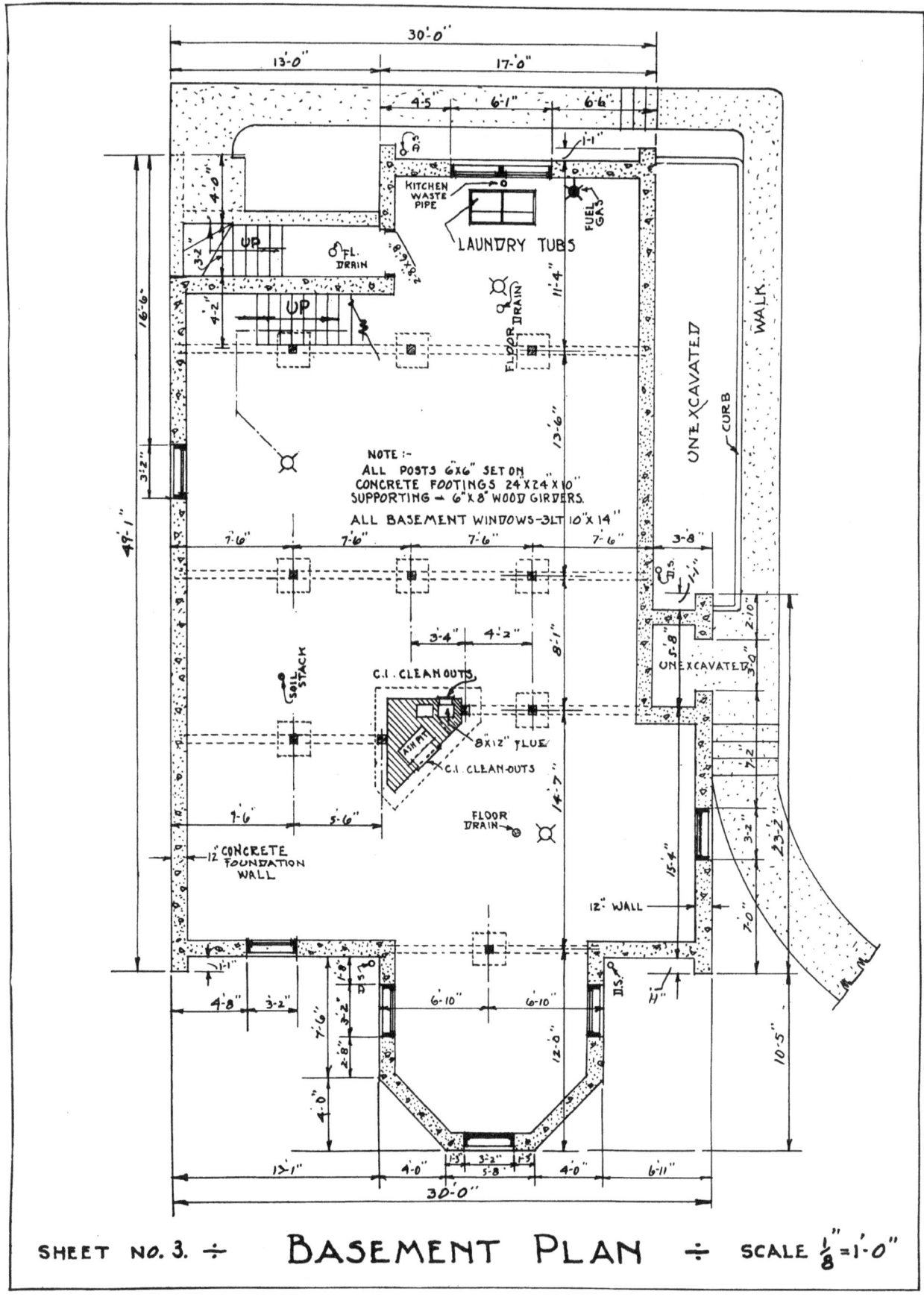

SHEET NO. 3. ÷ BASEMENT PLAN ÷ SCALE $\frac{1}{8}$"=1'-0"

THE AKRON; The Details of the Excavation, Cement Work, Floor Supports and Other Features of the Basement Are Shown in This Plan. The front and side elevations and cross section of the home are presented on the following page.

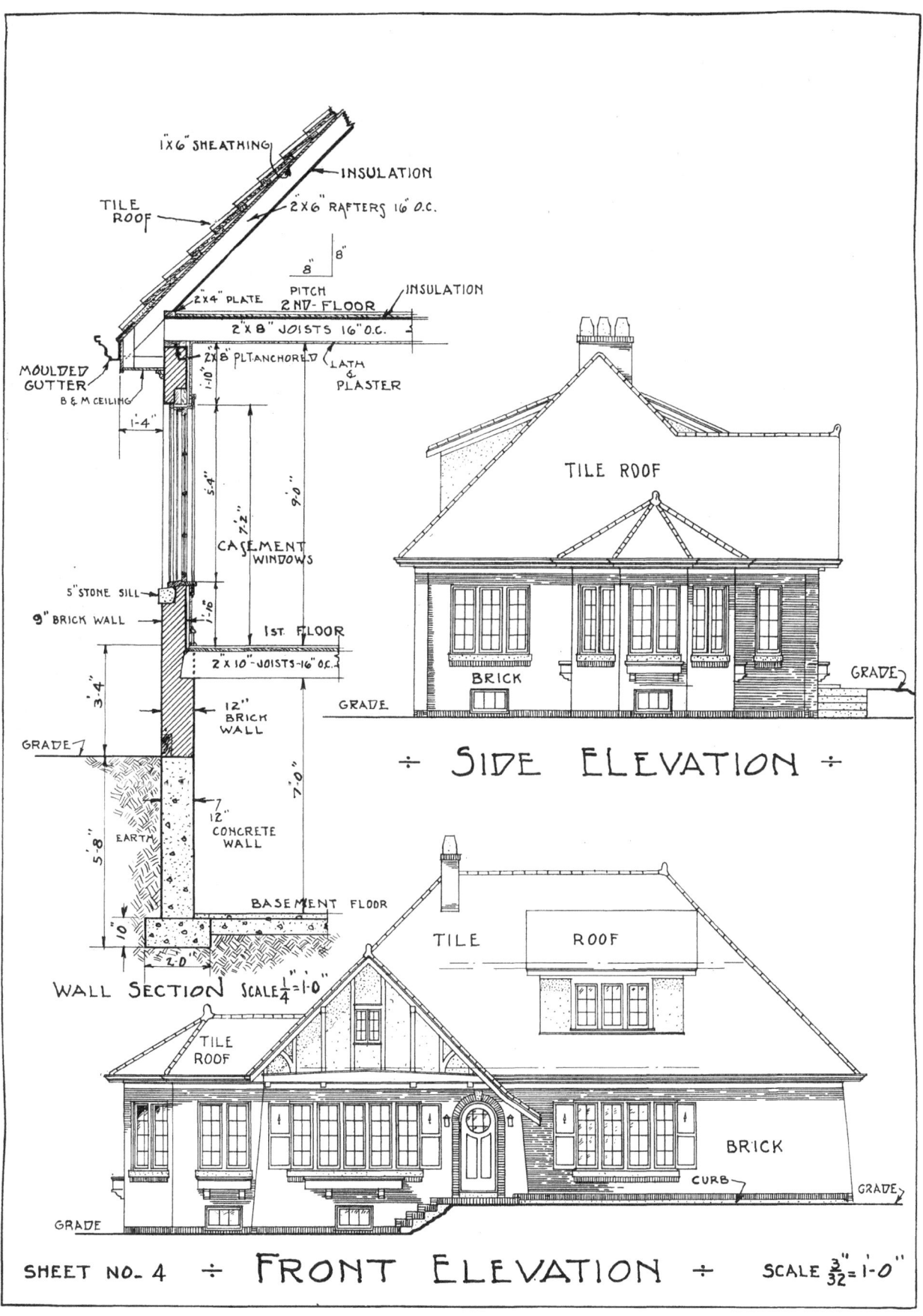

1"X6" SHEATHING

INSULATION

TILE ROOF

2"X6" RAFTERS 16" O.C.

8" 8"

2"X4" PLATE

PITCH 2ND-FLOOR

INSULATION

2"X8" JOISTS 16" O.C.

MOULDED GUTTER

2"X8" PL.T ANCHORED

LATH & PLASTER

B & M CEILING

1-4"

1-10"

5'-4"

9'-0"

7'-2"

CASEMENT WINDOWS

5" STONE SILL

9" BRICK WALL

1-6"

1ST. FLOOR

2"X10" JOISTS-16" O.C.

3'-4"

GRADE

12" BRICK WALL

7'-0"

5'-8"

EARTH

7"

12" CONCRETE WALL

BASEMENT FLOOR

10"

2'-0"

WALL SECTION SCALE ¼"=1'-0"

÷ SIDE ELEVATION ÷

TILE ROOF

BRICK

GRADE

GRADE

TILE ROOF

TILE ROOF

BRICK

GRADE

CURB

GRADE

SHEET NO. 4 ÷ FRONT ELEVATION ÷ SCALE 3/32"=1'-0"

THE AKRON; Details of the Construction Are Presented in the Cross Section Shown Here. Note the insulation under the roof and under the second story floor. This will stop much heat loss through the roof.

Some Day We All Hope We shall Have a Home Porch with a View Like This. In the meantime, let us make the best of what we have and consider the home porch and its pleasurable possibilities to the full.

The Porch as a Living Room

THE real purpose of porches is utilitarian. We build them with the expectation that we will use them. Yet how often do we permit them to become but ornaments, and scarcely creditable ones at that! And when we do actually make use of the porch which we have gone to the work and expense of building, how prone, usually, are we to let it serve its purpose only indifferently!

The porch should, of course, afford pleasure, enjoyment. It should constitute a retreat, moreover, that will potently entice, allure to frequent use. It ought to comprise, in short, a real summer living room —a living room of the semi-outdoors, permeated by healthful breezes and perfumed from adjacent gardens. Quite naturally, therefore, it should be furnished both for comfort and for attractiveness. The matter of furniture is particularly important; but the porch that is to be a true, all-round delight must also, it is equally apparent, receive thoughtful consideration from various other angles. In making the porch into a genuinely inviting summer living room, there are

innumerable interesting and charming possibilities. Perhaps the accompanying illustrations will help in stressing these as well as offer some suggestions.

The first illustration shows a porch of the very charming home, in southern California, of Julian Eltinge. The house is of old Italian architecture, and the porch is naturally designed to conform to this style. It possesses an arch and column treatment which, in conjunction with the enclosing iron railing, gives it, structurally, an especially attractive appearance. It is floored with cement and carpeted with a great oval-shaped, weather-proof rug. Its furniture consists of comfortable hickory chairs and an Italian-style iron table. The house is situated on a commanding eminence overlooking a lake, and the outlook is particularly interesting.

The other illustration shows what is actually both a sun room and a porch in one. Originally it was a quite ordinary porch, but subsequently it was equipped with French windows and doors on its exposed sides and thus made into a closed room. It, however, has this distinct advantage, that all the glass doors and windows may be thrown open, with true porch-like results, or any or all of them may be closed, as desired. The floor is of tile, covered with an attractive fibre rug, and the furniture consists of reed, with chairs possessing comfortable cushions. This is, indeed, a particularly enjoyable summer living room, governable to all kinds of weather.

A well-planned porch comfortably and attractively furnished is unquestionably capable of affording much real pleasure.

Whether it is to be protected from the elements by permanent windows, or left open to the winds and weather, the porch deserves attention on its own account as an individual part of the house. The floor may be of cement, tile, or brick, in preference to wood, if desired. Weather-proof fibre rugs are always preferable to other rugs, since if wet they dry out more easily, to say nothing of remaining undamaged. Reed furniture, together with child's swing and a hammock, capable of being used as a bed on occasion, give all the required furniture. Tubs and hanging baskets of ferns, flowers or decorative palms lend a charming touch of greenery to the porch retreat.

Properly furnished, the porch makes a delightful summer room in every way—comfortable and invitingly furnished for the retreat and the meeting place of all the members of the family.

There is another reason for the popularity of the porch, not often kept sight of in the midst of planning, but present nevertheless. In the past 10 years human society as we know it has changed its habits and its methods of living. There was a time when the porch was a point of vantage, wherefrom to view the passersby and draw conclusions, flattering or otherwise, about their general appearance and what might be the business which drew them forth.

Now, however, the housewife uses the porch as a therapeutic agent. It is her retiring room; her rest room, in whose attractive surroundings and suggestion of flowers and ferns and the great outdoors she can escape from the reality of housework at intervals during the day, and gain a rest that is recuperative in the extreme.

A nice touch for the porch is the presence of a bowl of goldfish, with an electric light, conveniently placed; it can turn into a great fascinating globe of light in the evenings. Care should be taken that the water in the bowl is not changed too frequently, and that the bowl is brought inside on chilly nights.

A Porch Like This Belongs to a Home Where Father and Mother Never Need Worry Over the Absence of Son and Daughter at Questionable Amusements. Ten to one, all the young folks of the neighborhood will congregate right here for the dances that mean so much to the young.

When We A-Gardening Go

Mother Nature is a Wonderful Helper of Those Who Help Themselves to Her Treasury of Earth and Air and Water. She Even Furnishes the Seeds

WHO would be without a garden, when a packet of seeds costing less than a dollar can transform black earth into that magical carpet—a flower garden!

In this case we can paraphrase an old axiom. Mother Nature surely helps willingly all who help themselves. It is, paradoxically, not a case of helping ourselves and ending there; it is a case of helping ourselves to what she has to offer. And she is never so lavish of her treasure as when she begins with us to make a garden.

No Lot Too Small

Suppose we begin with the small lot. I have seen a perfect little garden in a space five feet by five feet. But this was in Japan, where finesse in gardening goes to microscopic degrees. I would say that on a typical narrow city lot a thoroughly practical and perfect small garden could be obtainable within an area twenty feet by twenty feet square.

Suppose we consider such a garden. Let us raise part of it—about six feet of it—making the raised portion about a foot higher than the other level of the garden. See what we have done? We have created a false horizon; already our garden seems deeper than it is.

Elements of Garden Architecture

There are three elements of garden architecture all know—beds, paths and ornament. The fourth element, equally important, is often neglected—water. A pool of water in a small garden does for it what a mirror does for a small room—its reflecting capacity makes the garden seem larger, to say nothing of the continual play of color and light and shadow from the foliage, the flowers, and the wind, and the clouds and the sky above.

In a small garden it is best to keep the height of all the plantings low. Buy your shrubs of a good tree nursery and let them grow well, then trim low. The barberry makes a good hedge; the dwarf forms of the broad-leaved evergreens, the azalea, the rhododendron, the Japanese holly, and catoneasters help to keep the

A Good Example of the Formal Garden Layout, But With Informal Plantings. Observe how ornamental stone is used to good effect. The flagstone walk opposite the pool has in-between plantings of moss pink and saxifrage.

A Garden Is An Intimate Affair. Size is not an essential, but proper arrangement is. This is what one householder did with the rear of a narrow lot.

plan on bringing back from autumn Sunday journeyings sufficient of the wild deciduous shrubs and ferns to make the planting of a shady wall spot an easy problem.

Color Harmony

Perhaps you have considered Mr. Bullfrog as good for nothing but pickerel bait; or, if he is larger, for a nice mess of frog legs. Study him well the next time you catch his slippery majesty. His green and mauve and brown and pearly white give you the most gorgeous and cool interior decorating suggestion you ever saw.

No yellow satin can equal the cowslip; no green is quite like its green leaves. Combine the two and you have the proper caper for summer porch in wicker. Look at the flowers in your own garden; at the butterflies above them. See the use Nature makes of blues and purples to enrich shadows. Try to study her scheme of things and you will never want for a color scheme or idea.

beds from having too scrawny an appearance. The smallest garden should have a seat, a sun dial or a fountain figure, and in the latter case you give yourself an opportunity for having water lilies. The yellow pond lily, or Spatter Dock; the Star Maiden, or white lotus; or, in the South and extreme West, the fragrant yellow hybrids developed from the Mexican variety fit in excellently here. Do not, please, put gold fish in your garden pool. They are decorative, but some prowling Thomas cat will work to their disaster.

In the small garden, as in the large, one tries to plan a complete change of plants throughout the blooming season. Thus, one begins with bulbs, followed with such an early bloomer as the columbine. July can see the small garden a vision of blue from ageratum, heliotrope, verbena, bachelor's button, blue sage, larkspur, Veronica, blue bells and forget-me-not.

The Walks Make the Border

Gone are the days—we hope beyond recall—when broken bricks and clam shells or bottles bordered the garden. Now we use flagstones, or brick, patching them together loosely, and planting the in-between places with moss pink or saxifrage. If our lot ends against another building, or against an unsightly alley, we have an opportunity to silhouette our tiny garden against lattices or a wall on which ivy has been let grow. And the advent of the motor car permits us to travel so conveniently it is a poor tourist who cannot

A Garden Pool, Like a Mirror in a Room, Makes the Garden Seem Larger. Aquatic plants give a riot of flowers and foliage, anywhere, with little effort.

The Abbeville

Architectural Excellence Applied to a Home of Moderate Size

The Sunny Dining Room of the Abbeville.

THE advantages of excellent architecture as applied to the smaller home are demonstrated forcefully in this home.

The dignity and careful restraint of the exterior make it especially attractive, with the ideal well carried out in the wide, white painted clapboards and the graceful balustrade utilized to finish the roof. The recessed entrance, with its pilasters and columns is particularly interesting. The door, with its sidelights, is true to the Colonial sources from which the architects have drawn for the entire home.

The floor plan, although containing many features which might not be practicable for the purse of the builder of the usual five-room home, has a number of unusual and attractive features. To the right of the entrance hall is the living room, of unusually large size and with the fireplace placed between the two outside windows. To the left is the dining room, with a bay for a buffet and with shell closets in two of the corners. The kitchen is reached through an exceptionally

The Details of the Mantel and the Fireplace in the Abbeville, Are in Keeping with the Colonial Exterior.

roomy closet and to the rear of the kitchen is a ground floor laundry.

The two bedrooms open off a second hall. It will be noted that one is supplied with a firepace, while the other has a sleeping porch which varies from the usual square or rectangular shape. One bath, directly between the two bedrooms, can be reached from either, while a second, accessible from the one bedroom or from the hall, is equipped with a shower.

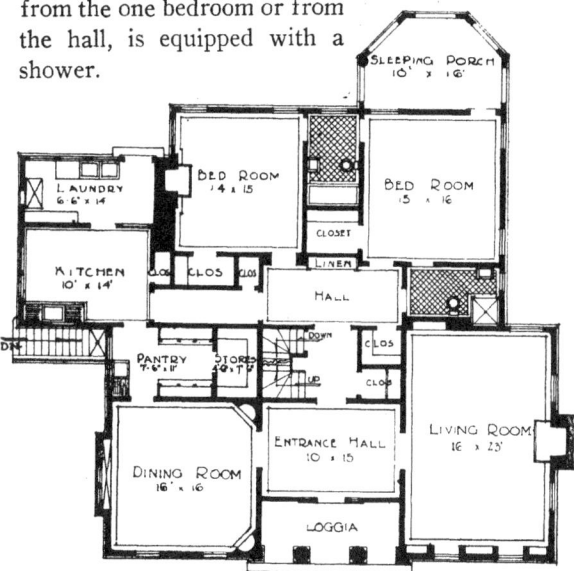

The Floor Plan of the Abbeville Shows an Interesting Room Grouping.

Pilasters and Columns Add Interest to the Entrance.

THE ABBEVILLE; A Colonial Type Home.

The Alton

A Pennsylvania Dutch Design With Overhanging Roof and Massive Porch Columns Features This Low Cost Six-Room Home

For Perspective in Full Colors, see page 93

HERE is a good narrow-lot house requiring only 26 feet in width, while the depth is 35 feet. The overhanging roof at the front, supported by three massive columns in the Pennsylvania Colonial manner, give this house a look of solid stability.

The space inside is arranged in a straightforward, convenient way, giving the cheerful side of the house to the living room and dining room which open together, and providing easy access from the front door and reception hall through to the kitchen as well as to the grade entrance, and the basement. The cozy and cheerful breakfast nook adjacent to the kitchen will be appreciated.

Notice the convenient placing of the refrigerator in this kitchen. It can be conveniently iced from the outside through the icing door indicated or if this is to be a truly modern home, the refrigerator will be an electrically operated ice machine, and its placing as indicated will prove most convenient.

Entering the front door from the imposing, columned porch, you step into a reception hall of good size with attractive open stair going up to the left. It starts with two steps to a square landing, just the place for a grandfather's hall clock. Then the stairs continue up eleven steps to a second landing, then turning back again to land in the central upstairs hall. This makes a convenient, easy stair, well placed with reference to both floors.

On the four pages following you will find working drawings made to ⅛-inch scale, showing the floor plans and the principal elevations of this house.

THE ALTON; Photograph of This Popular Type Home. Working drawings made to ⅛-inch scale are presented on the four pages following.

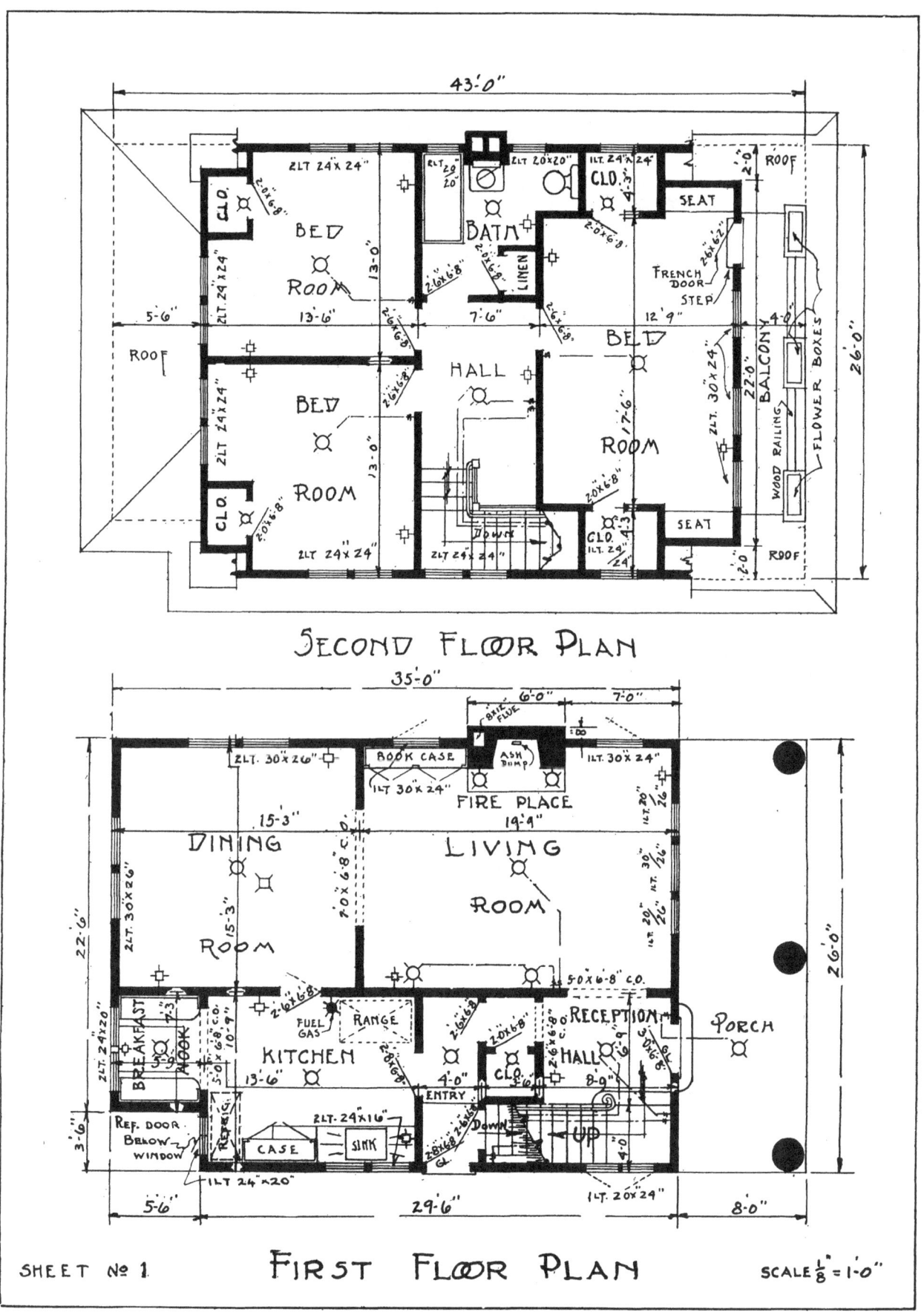

SECOND FLOOR PLAN

FIRST FLOOR PLAN

SHEET № 1   SCALE ⅛" = 1'-0"

THE ALTON; The First and Second Floor Plans Show a House 26 by 35 Feet, Conveniently Arranged into Six Fine
Rooms. Elevations and construction details are on the pages following.

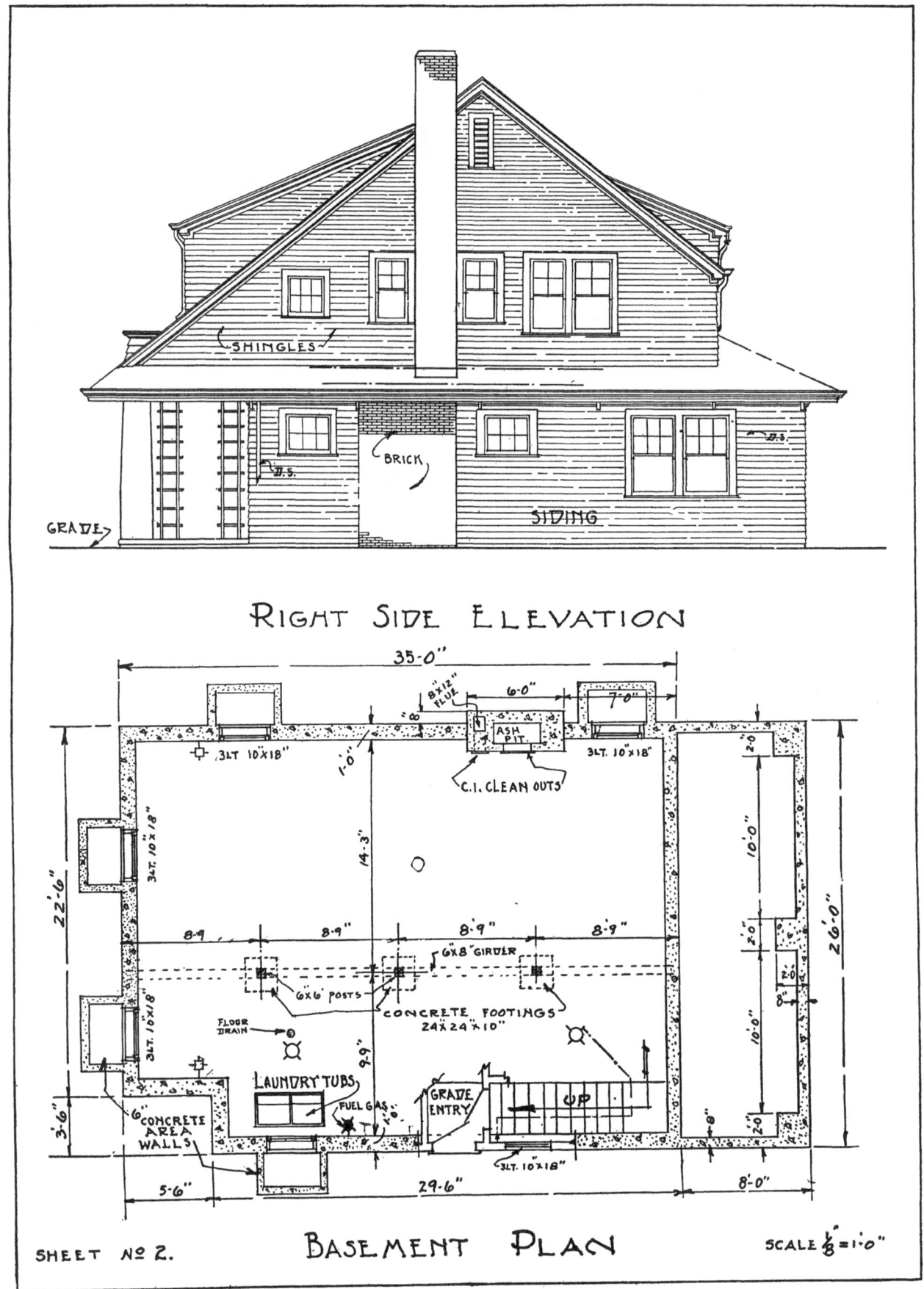

RIGHT SIDE ELEVATION

BASEMENT PLAN

SHEET N○ 2.

SCALE ⅛"=1'0"

THE ALTON; The Basement Plan Has Been Left Undivided by Partitions. Storage space for either coal or oil should be provided. For additional elevations and details of construction see next two pages.

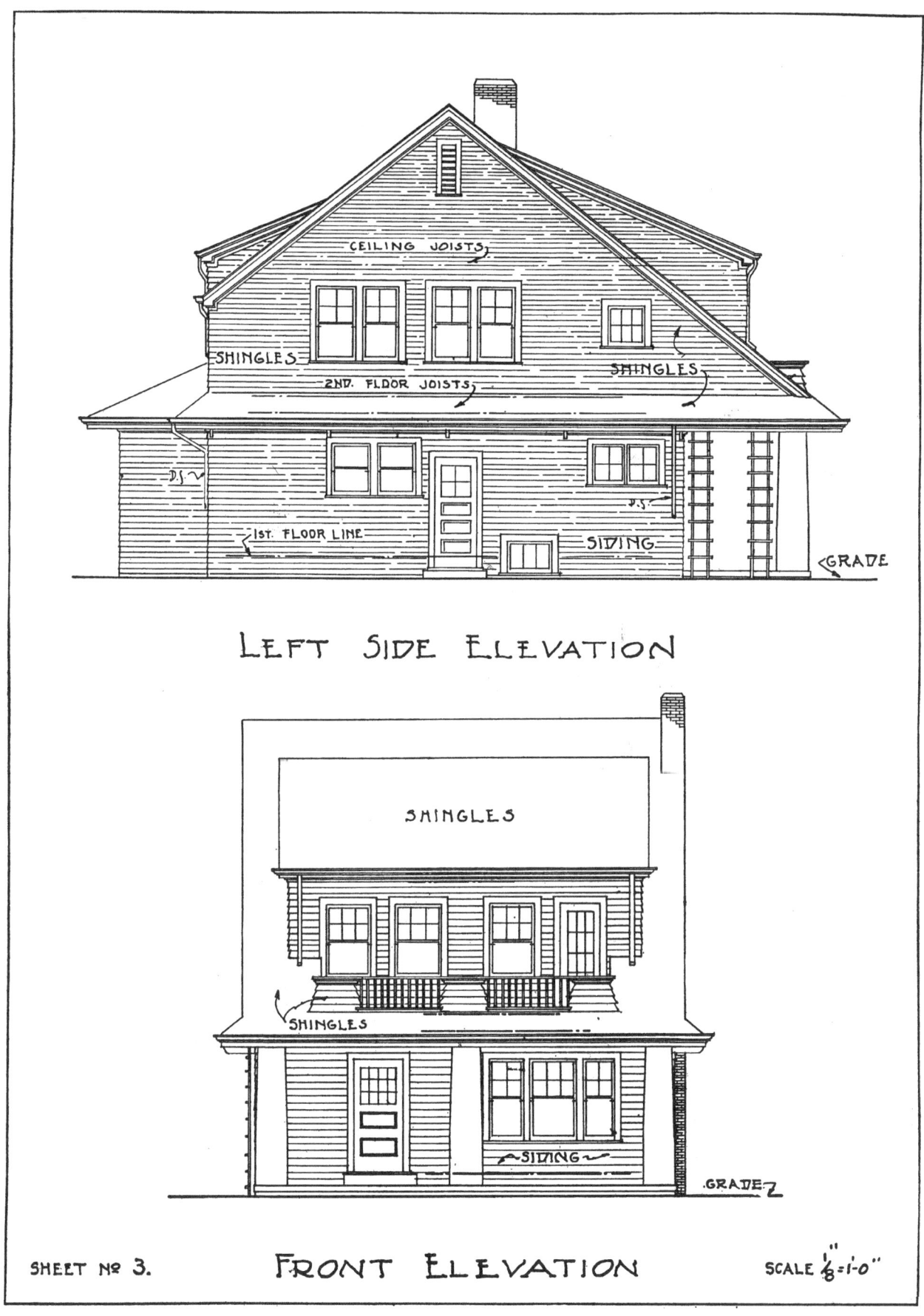

CEILING JOISTS

SHINGLES

2ND. FLOOR JOISTS

SHINGLES

D.S.

D.S.

IST. FLOOR LINE

SIDING

GRADE

LEFT SIDE ELEVATION

SHINGLES

SHINGLES

SIDING

GRADE

SHEET № 3.   FRONT ELEVATION   SCALE ⅛"=1'-0"

THE ALTON; The Elevations Show a Pennsylvania Colonial Design of Substantial Charm.   See details of construction
on next page.

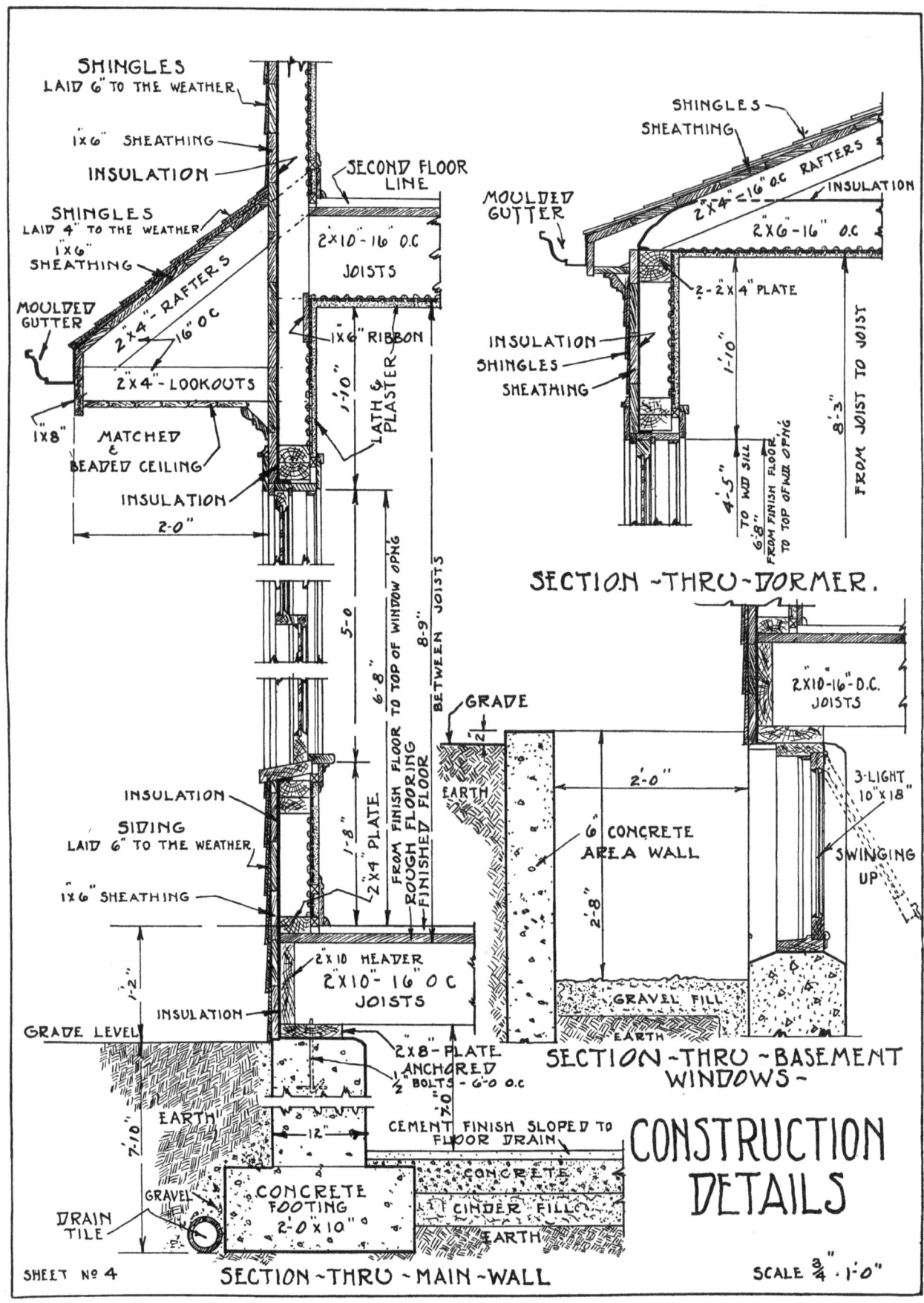

SHINGLES
LAID 6" TO THE WEATHER

1X6" SHEATHING

INSULATION

SHINGLES
LAID 4" TO THE WEATHER

1X6" SHEATHING

MOULDED GUTTER

2"X4" RAFTERS 16" O.C.

2"X4" LOOKOUTS

1X8"

MATCHED & BEADED CEILING

INSULATION

2'-0"

SECOND FLOOR LINE

2"X10"-16" O.C. JOISTS

1X6" RIBBON

LATH & PLASTER

INSULATION

SIDING
LAID 6" TO THE WEATHER

1X6" SHEATHING

INSULATION

GRADE LEVEL

1'-2"

7'-10"

EARTH

GRAVEL

DRAIN TILE

CONCRETE FOOTING
2'-0"X10"

12"

2"X4" PLATE

2"X10 HEADER
2"X10"-16" O.C. JOISTS

2"X8" PLATE ANCHORED BOLTS-6'-0 O.C.

1'-10"

5'-0"

6'-8" FROM FINISH FLOOR TO TOP OF WINDOW OPNG

8'-9" BETWEEN JOISTS

1'-8"

FROM FINISH FLOOR TO TOP OF WINDOW OPNG

ROUGH FLOORING
FINISHED FLOOR

GRADE

2"

EARTH

CEMENT FINISH SLOPED TO FLOOR DRAIN

CONCRETE

CINDER FILL

EARTH

SECTION - THRU - MAIN - WALL

SHEET Nº 4

SHINGLES
SHEATHING

MOULDED GUTTER

2"X4"-16" O.C. RAFTERS

INSULATION

2"X6"-16" O.C.

2-2"X4" PLATE

INSULATION
SHINGLES
SHEATHING

1'-10"

4'-5" TO WD SILL

6'-8" FROM FINISH FLOOR, TO TOP OF WNDW OPNG

8'-3" FROM JOIST TO JOIST

SECTION - THRU - DORMER.

2"X10"-16" O.C. JOISTS

2'-0"

6" CONCRETE AREA WALL

2'-8"

3-LIGHT 10"X18"

SWINGING UP

GRAVEL FILL
EARTH

SECTION - THRU - BASEMENT WINDOWS -

CONSTRUCTION DETAILS

SCALE 3/4" = 1'-0"

THE ALTON; Details of Construction. Side walls and attic space are thoroughly insulated. For additional working plans see the three preceding pages.

The ALTON

A PENNSYLVANIA Dutch Design. For Complete Building Plans-Working Drawings to Scale See Pages 89, 90, 91 and 92.

The *AMBOY*

A HOME of English Georgian Design. For Complete Building Plans Working Drawings to Scale See Pages 96, 97, 98 and 99.

The Amboy
A Home of English Georgian Design

Quiet Charm Is Dominating Quality of Sturdy Seven-Room Home of Concrete Blocks Finished With Stucco

THE well-arranged floor plan, which must be the basis for architectural worth in any residence, is reflected in the pleasant exterior of The Amboy. Entirely without any one dominating or blatant feature, it has an atmosphere of hospitality and comfort which cannot fail, in its unobtrusive way, to impress even the casual passer.

The fenestration is simple but particularly happy in its relation to the door, sharply outlined by the brickwork of the doorway.

The floor plans, shown to scale on the four pages following, reveal the central reception hall as the pivotal point about which the house has been planned.

To the left is the living room, 15 by 25 feet, with the fireplace as its center of interest. The sun parlor virtually is an integral part of this long, well-proportioned room.

The dining room, of pleasing and efficient size, is reached from the kitchen through a well-designed pantry, which has built-in cases and is designed to house the refrigerator, so placed as to permit outside icing. The garage can be reached from the rear door of the central hall.

The second floor has three bedrooms of remarkable convenience, though the plan of the floor is not complicated. The house is 42 feet wide, including the garage, and 29 feet deep.

THE AMBOY; The Lines of the Roof as It Sweeps Over the Sun Parlor Give an Air of Hospitality to This Home of Seven Rooms and Two Baths. The floor plans and details of the stucco over concrete type of construction are presented on the following pages.

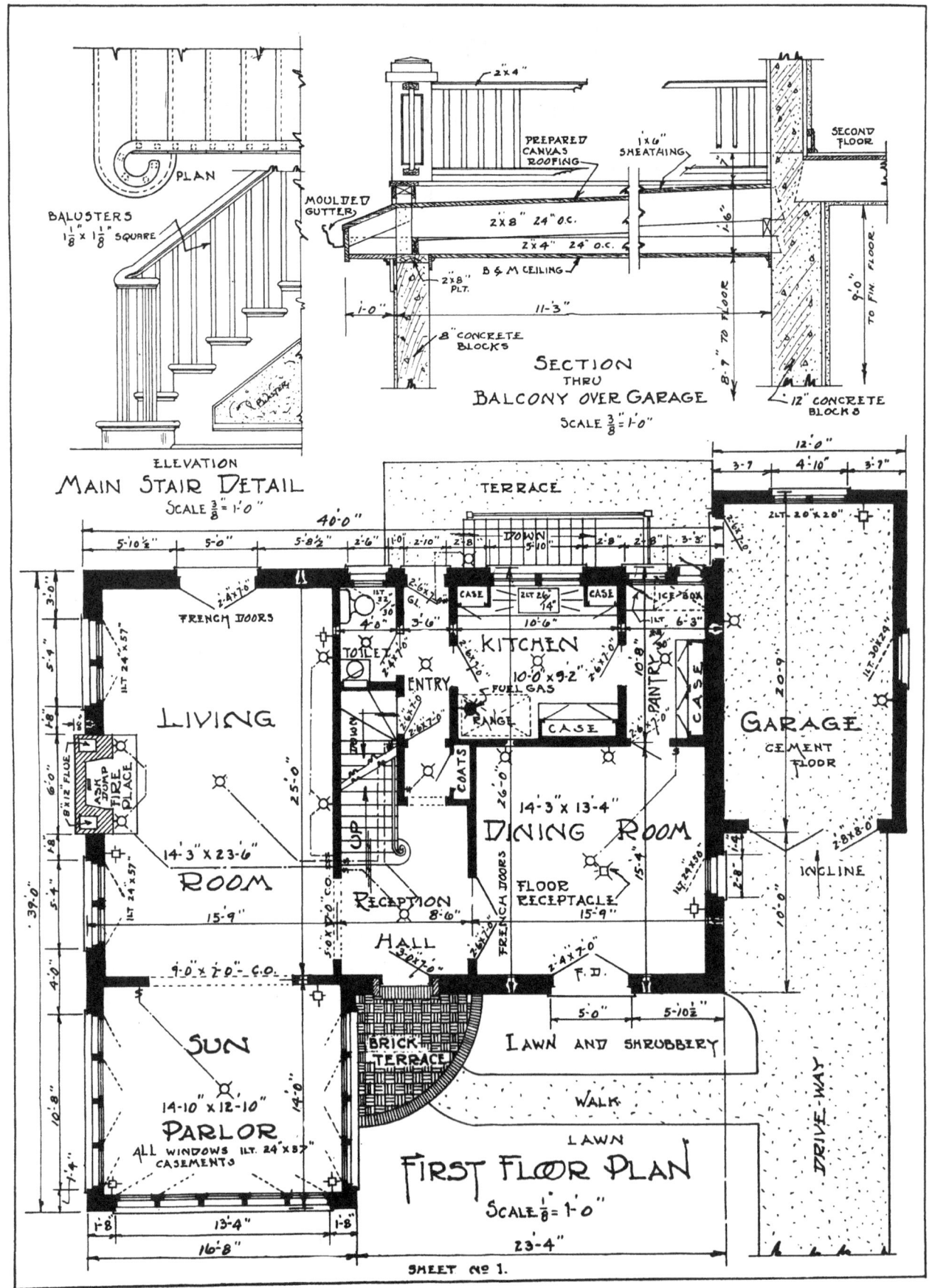

MAIN STAIR DETAIL
SCALE 3/8" = 1'-0"

SECTION
THRU
BALCONY OVER GARAGE
SCALE 3/8" = 1'-0"

FIRST FLOOR PLAN
SCALE 1/8" = 1'-0"

SHEET No. 1.

THE AMBOY; The First Floor, Shown Here, Is Notable for Its Simplicity and Convenience. Working drawings of the main stair and of the balcony over the garage are shown here. The second floor plan and a cross section of the wall are shown on the following page.

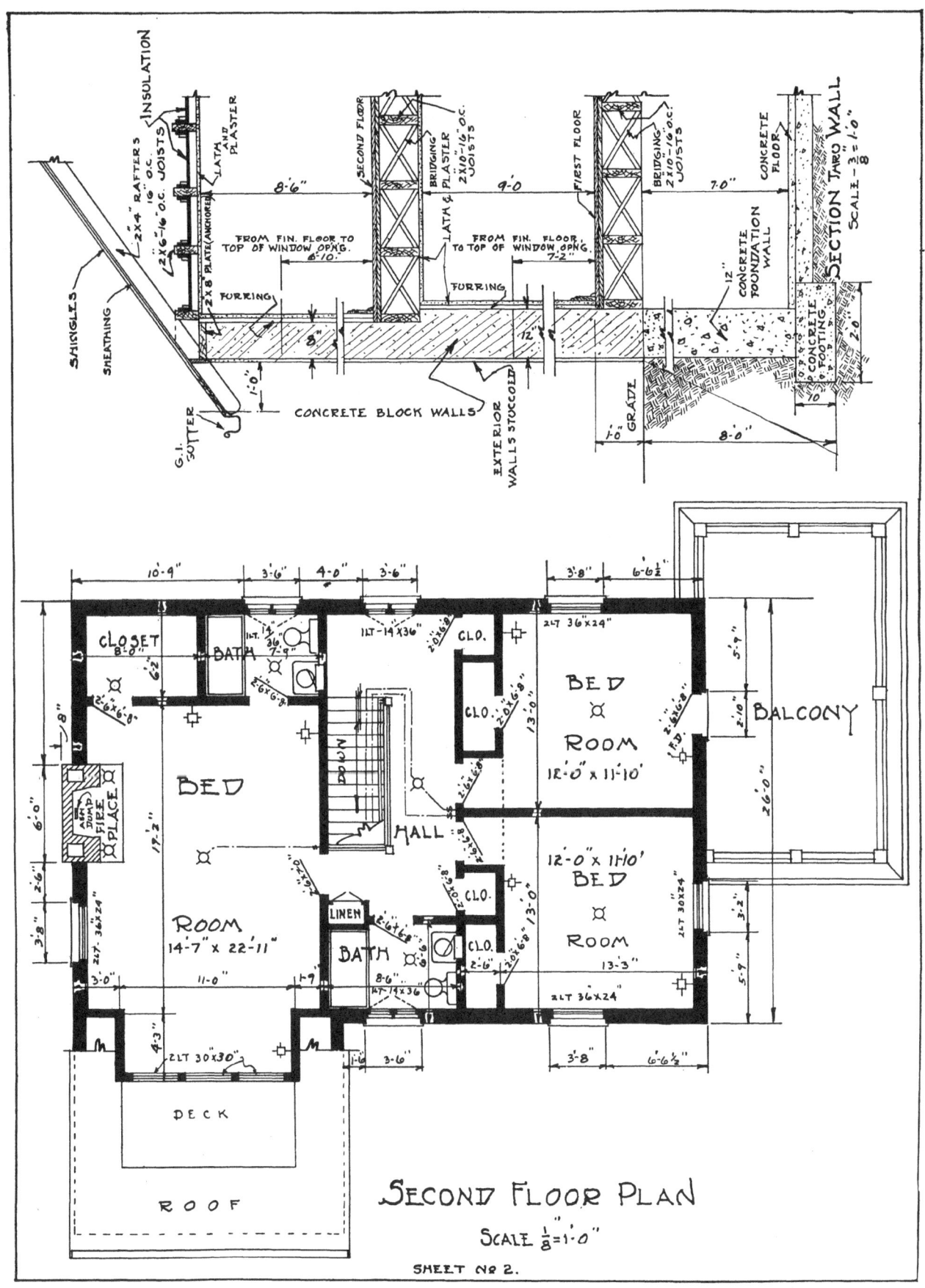

SECTION THRU WALL
SCALE - 3/8 = 1'-0"

SECOND FLOOR PLAN

SCALE 1/8" = 1'-0"

SHEET № 2.

THE AMBOY; Three Commodious Bedrooms Are Provided for on the Second Floor. Their arrangement allows for cross ventilation of all three. Two bedrooms and a wealth of closet room are features of the plan. The cross section of the wall shows construction details. The front and side elevations of the home are shown to scale on the next page.

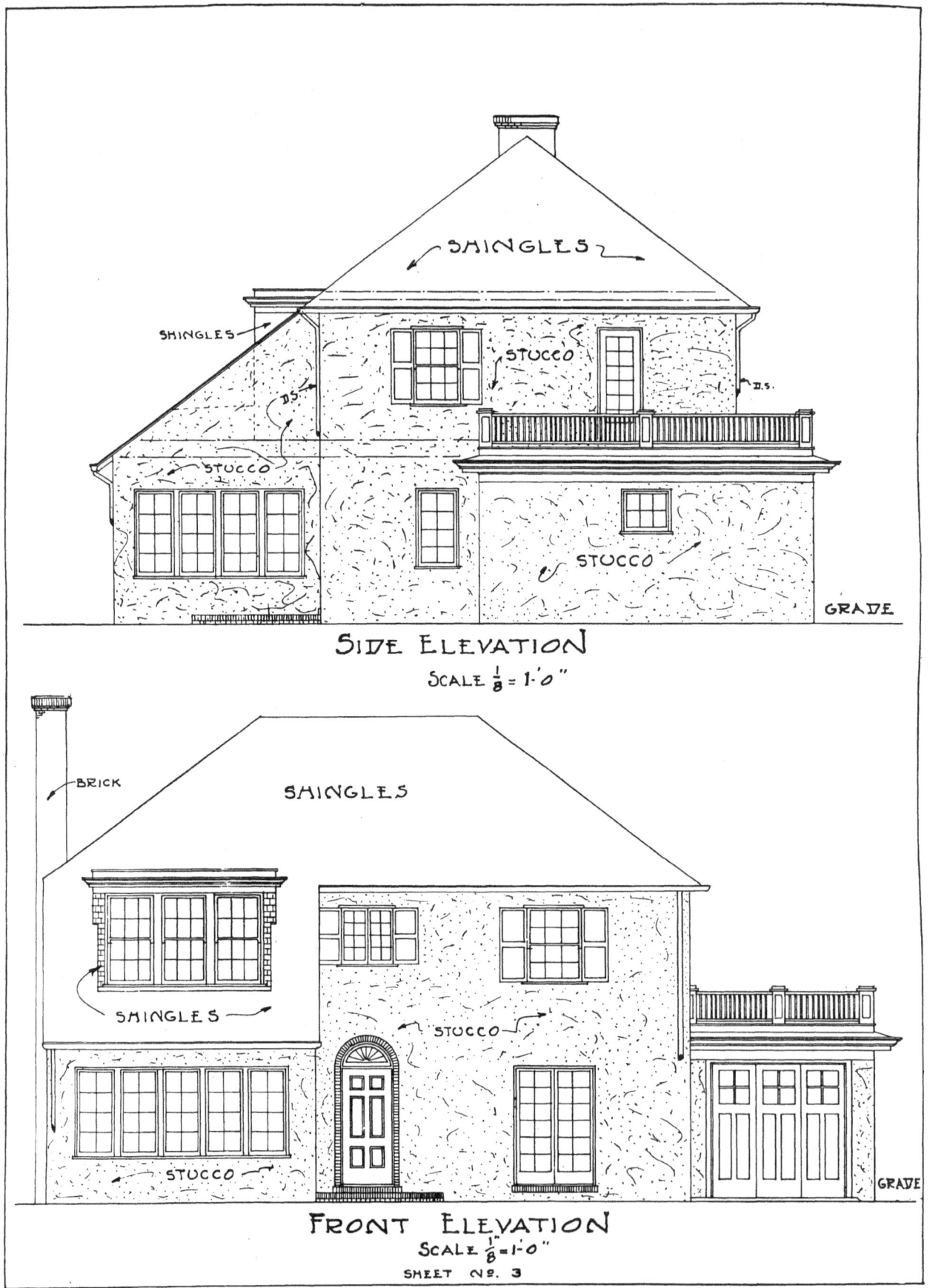

SIDE ELEVATION
SCALE ⅛ = 1'·0"

FRONT ELEVATION
SCALE ⅛ = 1'·0"
SHEET № 3

THE AMBOY; The Front Elevation Shows the Excellent Placing of the Windows and the Manner in Which the Dormer is Handled. The side elevation presents the details of the balustrade about the garage roof and the lighting of the garage. The basement plan and the detail of the fireplace design are shown on the next page.

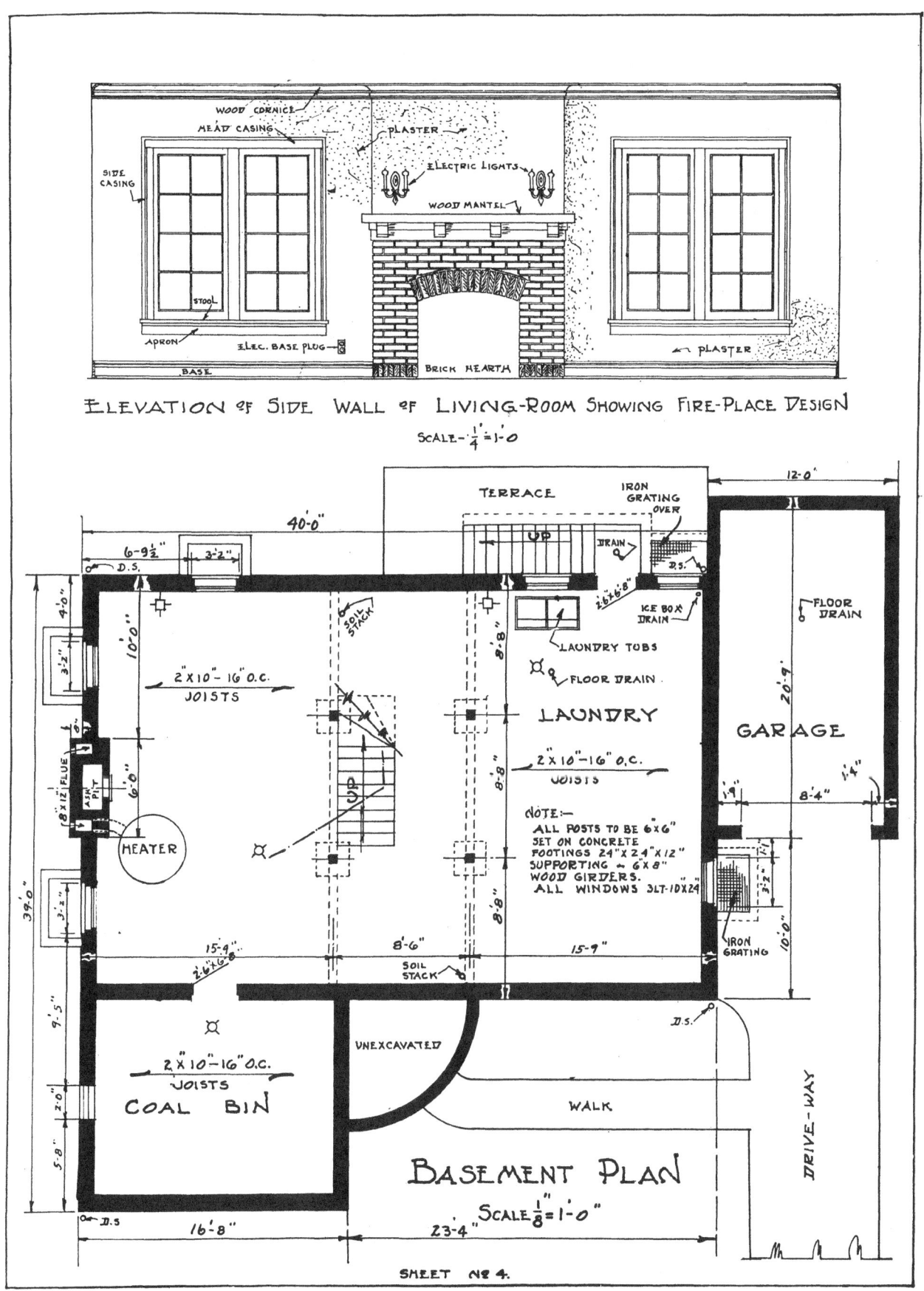

ELEVATION of SIDE WALL of LIVING-ROOM SHOWING FIRE-PLACE DESIGN

SCALE—¼"=1-0

BASEMENT PLAN

SCALE ⅛"=1-0"

SHEET № 4.

THE AMBOY; The Basement Plan Shows the Coal Bin Carefully Separated from the Rest of the Room and Excellent Planning of Household Facilities. The fireplace and its relation to the windows are shown above.

Make the Garage Attractive

Harmonious Surroundings Add to the Attractiveness of a Garage That Has Plain But Neat Lines.

TOO often only slight attention is given to making the residential garage attractive. Located on the rear of the lot, the garage frequently constitutes a decided blemish to the property, although it usually could and should add materially to the appearance of the surroundings. From a strictly utilitarian point of view, the private garage is admittedly a homely affair—merely a container for an automobile; but when considered as a part of the modern residential establishment, entitled to as much architectural and landscaping attention as the dwelling, possibilities loom up. The garage may be made so attractive that it actually will beautify its surroundings, creating a harmonious atmosphere and adding to a pretty home picture.

The small garage has been unattractive because it has been

thought of as a necessary evil—one of these unavoidable expenses which a property owner has to put up with if he must have the comforts and pleasures of a car. Consequently, garages have been built very plain, with the wall materials conforming to those used in the house, or, perhaps, stucco; as a foregone conclusion there has been a door large enough to let the car in and out, a smaller door, two or three windows and a simply framed roof. The desire usually has been to build the garage as inexpensively as possible.

Builders may at least be partly to blame for many of the unattractive garages which so often adjoin good residences, for they have willingly put up such garages without raising

A Plain But Well Built Garage Is Made More Attractive and Substantial Looking by a Heavy Roof Conforming to That of the Residence.

A Pretty Planting Will Add Much to the Appearance of Any Garage.

an argument for something more appropriate and refined in appearance. This is a very serious mistake from the builder's own point of view. It frequently costs very little more to build in the attractive features and these are sure to retain the good will of the purchaser and induce him to recommend his builder to others.

In designing a garage that will have an attractive exterior and advantageous location, one must start it with consideration of the floor plan. Plenty of space within the garage is a very desirable feature which is usually inexpensive and often saves money eventually. Many car owners have built the garage so small that when disposing of the old car for a larger one they find the space inadequate. Where a single car is to be stored, a width of 12 feet or more is satisfactory, and for a two-car garage the corresponding dimension should be 20 or 22 feet. The length may vary from 20 to 24 feet. These figures are for clear space within.

The best time to build the garage is when the house is built, making architecture and color scheme conform, or, at least, harmonize. In building the garage in connection with a house already built, a good "match" as to architecture and construction details is very desirable, but perhaps less important than to give the garage proper setting.

If the garage is an outstanding, massive or ponderous appearing structure it will make the lines of the adjoining residence look weak, and the garage, rather than the residence, becomes the conspicuous structure on the property. Therefore, it is wise to give the garage easy lines and to break these up by attractive plantings of trees, shrubs, vines and flowers. Some of the accompanying illustrations show how this has been fairly well done.

Similarly, light trellises break down harsh structural lines and lend an air of artistry and distinction. Windows must be placed so that they will provide light where it is wanted within; even if such an arrangement is not architecturally good, the windows may be made to appear artistic by the

judicious use of trellises and window boxes. Unusual but handy features of design often add to the garage—such as combining it with a summer house, screened porch, dove cote or room for garden tools.

Windows Placed to Provide the Best Possible Light May Be Made to Appear Artistic by Judicious Use of Trellises or Window Boxes.

If there is any choice as to location of the garage on the property it should be exercised carefully. The garage should be placed with cautious regard for appearances, but not without keeping in mind protection against burglars and fire; convenience and accessibility; possible limitations of the driveway, such as curves and grades and provisions for heating from the house, if any is desired. The garage should be in view of the house.

The location selected must allow plenty of room for a paved area sufficiently large for use as a washing floor, and in the case of a double or multiple car garage, to permit moving cars easily from one stall to another. If it is not desired to build a full width driveway, tracks should be constructed as shown in the accompanying sketch. A low curb, frequently 4 inches to 6 inches high, may be placed along the outer edge of the tracks should there be a dangerous incline near, or the possibility of colliding with near-by structures or objects.

If possible, place the garage so that there may be flower beds or other plantings on two or three sides. Since the appearance of any garage can be improved by surrounding it with foliage and flowers, builders should encourage owners to use these very effective but inexpensive measures.

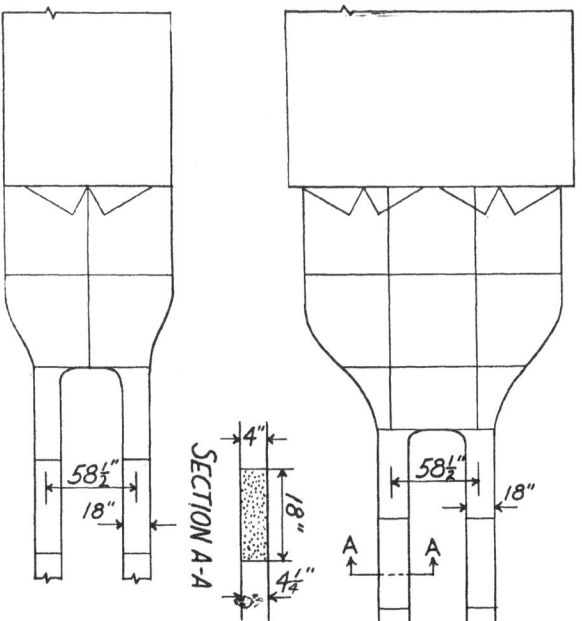

The Concrete Driveways and Paved Areas Must Be Properly Laid Out for Convenience and Maximum efficiency. Each slab should be laid independently, the arrangement being about as shown.

The Architecture of the Garage Should Conform to that of the House—Here Is a Pleasing Structure Showing the Spanish Influence.

Modern Plumbing in Kitchens and Laundries

DOMESTIC SCIENCE experts all agree on one subject: kitchens should be built around the kitchen sink. Plumbing fixture manufacturers have recognized this fact and the remarkable improvements they have produced in this most necessary article is indicative of their thorough study of the trend of modern living conditions.

It is good salesmanship to sell your customer what he wants. In fact, it is the one sure way of building a permanent business.

America has been struggling with the servant problem these past ten years and those contractors who keep this thought continuously in mind when planning homes are sure to achieve the kind of living quarters people want.

The help problem starts in the kitchen, and a practical, efficient kitchen sink will go a long way towards lightening the burden of the continuous tasks that are performed in this laboratory of the home.

The modern kitchen sink is, first of all, a beautiful and attractive piece of furniture; it is either solid vitreous china or snow white enameled iron; and it is

big and roomy; it invites working at it; it embodies the spirit of efficiency.

The chief characteristic of the most recent models is they are built in one piece, with either single or double drain board; with deep, wide basins. Some sinks are equipped with adjustable legs, a feature that has much to commend it; the sink may be set at the height that makes the work most comfortable and convenient.

In apartments the kitchen sink serves the double purpose of both kitchen sink and laundry tubs. These are made in the same material as found in the regular sinks. The white enamel covers of the laundry tubs become either the drain board for the kitchen sink or a work table for the kitchen. These are very attractive in appearance and in their combined utility are a great labor and space-saving arrangement for apartment homes.

Plumbing supplies have kept stride with the fixtures; the new kitchen sink faucet has become a single spout on a swivel joint; it is long enough to swing over the outside of the dishpan, to rinse the dishes and when not in use may be folded against the back splash board. The mechanics of these spouts have been improved; the best ones now supply water in a smooth running stream, without splashing.

It is a little thing but very important to those who work in the kitchen. There is also another variation of the swivel faucet. This one has an extra outlet with a rubber hose connection with a small spray similar to a shower head. This is found a great convenience in cleaning vegetables and rinsing dishes.

Then there's the special sink for washing vegetables always found in the big kitchen; these are usually made to order for each job; the sink has a divided compartment and is lined with german silver or white metal. They are very practical and much in demand in homes that boast of a chef.

In these same homes the butler's pantry contains a sink that is used for washing silver and the table glassware. Special tops of composition material are provided for sinks of this kind that insure glassware against breakage. While classed as luxuries in smaller homes, these sinks are necessities in the big houses and there is a definite demand for both of them.

Modern plumbing has another important function in the kitchen; a drain built into the floor for the ice box. This equipment has so much in its favor that we believe every contractor will realize its value and

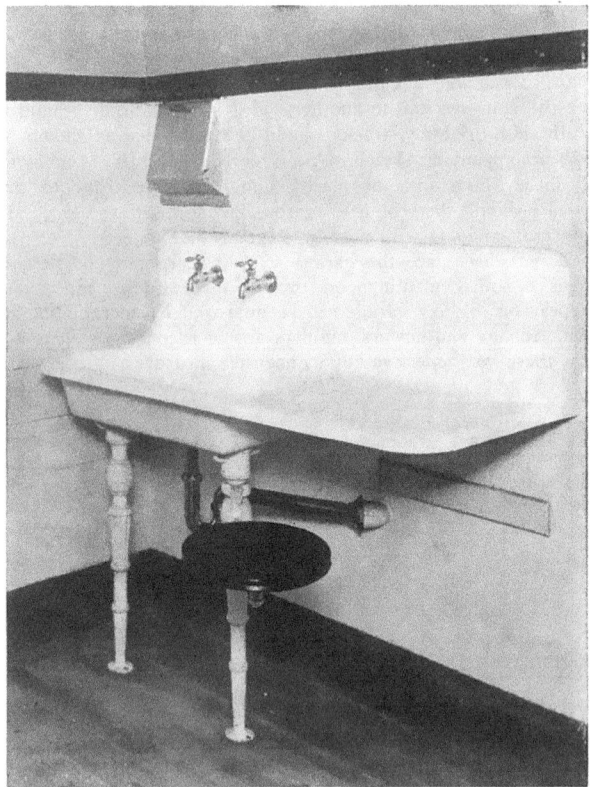

Just Below the Moulding in This Illustration Is Shown the Incinerator Opening. Kitchen refuse deposited here is disposed of finally.

appreciate its selling force as standard equipment in almost every type of home.

Garbage incinerators are rapidly becoming a staple part of kitchen equipment and come under the head of plumbing supplies. While this item has been considered an innovation and is now only installed in the finest buildings, their practicability and usefulness is so apparent that they are finding their way into modest bungalows and apartments.

Only second in importance to the sink in the kitchen is the supply of hot water and here, too, we find manufacturers have anticipated the need. There are dozens of water heaters that deliver water as hot as may be wanted, and what is more important, instantaneously, when it is wanted.

This is a subject that contractors should study very carefully. The average woman knows the relative merits of the several advertised water heaters and the builder who is wise will install only those which have a reputation.

Of course, the water heater is of more concern to the individual home owner than to the apartment dweller. In apartment houses, the water heater usually is an integral part of the heating plant, and supplies the entire house; but for residences and bungalows a water heater is an object of real concern; the contractor who is foresighted enough to install a practical and reliable outfit will make friends at once with prospective owners or renters.

And as the hot water heater is usually located in the basement, let us follow it downstairs and look at the plumbing requirements of the cellar and basement.

Good Plumbing in the Laundry

While it is true that a great majority of all kinds of homes are equipped with slate laundry tubs, still there is a very definite trend to the all-white tub, and reason enough. There's an air of cleanliness about white china or white enamel tubs; they add a note of cheerfulness to the laundry that make them attractive to women and to attract is the first step in salesmanship.

However, white tubs are also as practical as they are ornamental; they are easier to keep clean and clothing is not likely to become spotted with rust. It is easy to understand that a woman would trust her daintiest garments to be washed in a spotless white laundry tub.

Plumbing manufacturers are showing some beautiful and practical laundry tubs both in vitreous china and white enameled iron. Here, too, some manufacturers have wisely adopted the adjustable legs so that washing may be done at the most comfortable height.

These modern tubs are equipped with sparkling nickeled faucets and soap dishes that do not rust and these lighten the drudgery of wash days.

Laundry tubs may be had single or double or three in a row, and are equipped with strong board to hold the wringer.

In planning the laundry and cellar the builder should never fail to include a toilet in the basement, as prospective home owners will immediately see the value of this convenience; the toilet may be located in the cellar in a stall and the investment will pay for itself many times over in its comforts and the saving of steps.

In this article we haven't mentioned costs, for the reason that good plumbing may be had nowadays for almost any reasonable price you wish to pay. Of course, the better class fixtures cost more than the cheaper grades, but the character of the house should determine the quality of the plumbing and let us finish by saying that no builder ever lost out using the best grades of plumbing material and fixtures. As we have said in previous articles, the public has become educated to the hygienic value of good plumbing.

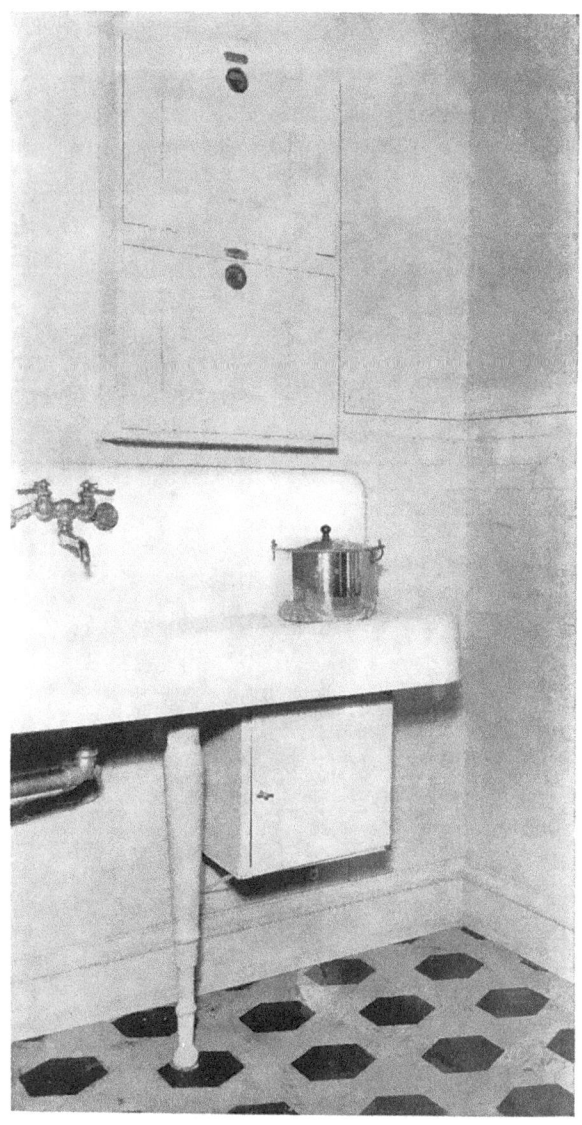

This One-Piece Sink, Adjusted to the Height of the User, Is Equipped with a swivel Mixing Faucet.

Plumbing Accessories Can "Make" the Bathroom

THE finest plumbing equipment can be marred by the wrong accessories. And on the other hand with carefully selected accessories, you can make a medium priced bath room look like a de luxe outfit.

It is only recently that this question of bath room accessories has been brought to public notice and even now a good percentage of the better grades are only installed because of direct selling efforts on the part of manufacturers.

These articles are prepared from the building contractor's point of view; it is our firm belief that if this subject receives as much consideration as it deserves, builders generally will profit much by the information.

Recently it was the writer's privilege to visit several of New York's newest and finest apartment houses. They had every one of the latest ideas in home comfort; the plumbing fixtures in particular were of the best, and big substantial tub, lavatory, built-in dressing table, shower-stall, all gleaming white and nickel, individually presented a beautiful picture. But their value and appearance as a whole was ruined by cheap, thin, poorly made towel bars, soap dishes, tooth brush holders and so on. It was a pathetic picture. The contractor did not even notice the effect himself until it was pointed out to him; he was so pleased with the beautiful tile floors and walls and the good grade of plumbing fixtures he had selected, he did not consider the accessories important at all.

On another occasion while visiting some new bungalows, where only a moderately good grade of plumbing fixtures were installed the happy selection of accessories somehow made the bathrooms look as if they might have cost two or three times the price paid.

With the present demand for the maximum in beauty and utility, manufacturers have developed accessories for every kind of bath room. Solid china accessories, nickel plated brass and enameled iron represent the best grades.

Solid china accessories that match the whiteness of the plumbing fixtures are usually built in the wall at the time the tile is laid. Recessed soap dishes and sponge holders, paper holders in this material give a fine effect of substantiality and luxury. Also of china are towel bars and hooks for wash cloths, hot water bottle and clothes. These are also built-in the wall when the tile is set.

There are also white china accessories that may be installed after the bath room is completed. These are as substantial and as attractive as the built-in ones and offer the builder a wide range from which to choose. They are of the same fine china as are the built-in fixtures; their chief advantage is the smaller cost, both in labor and installation, and they may be set after tile work is completed. Some of these exposed china fixtures have special seals to fasten them to the walls permanently.

The nickeled brass fixtures make a beautiful effect. The better grades come with glass towel bars and when the contractor decides upon these fixtures care should be taken to select only those made by high grade concerns, otherwise the nickel plate will peel off and tarnish and nothing looks quite so bad as tarnished and peeled nickel fixtures. Several good brass accessories manufacturers have achieved a new process of white enameling their fixtures which is very practical and finds favor among builders who have limited equipment budgets.

Several manufacturers produce enameled iron accessories which are beautiful in design and may be used in any type of bath room. This process of enamel-

Built-in Bathroom Accessories, Recessed Soap Dishes, Paper Holders and Medicine Cabinets Give an Effect of Substantiality and Luxury and Are Usually Built Into the Walls at the Time the Tile Is Laid.

The Neat Effect of Built-in Soap Dishes and Medicine Cabinet Is Evident Here and the Well-Placed Lights Will Appeal Especially to Men.

Medicine Cabinets and Mirrors

All steel medicine cabinets built into the wall not only are decorative but are practical as well. Every household requires lots of space in the medicine cabinet; clean bath rooms require ample storage space so that every article is out of sight; therefore the larger the cabinet the more pleasing it will be to your prospective customer. Wood cabinets, enameled white, are obtainable and many of them are substantial and practical for use when it is not possible to use the built-in models.

The bath room should have at least two mirrors. There is, of course, one in the medicine cabinet, but there should be another. A happy arrangement is a pier glass built the whole length of the door, but if this is not practical then some mirror should be placed in the bath room, preferably opposite the cabinet mirror.

Your plumbing supply dealer and the plumbing contractor are fully alive to the necessity for better accessories and will co-operate with you in making the correct selection.

You'll find it pays big dividends to put in the best accessories. And the more you put in, the better appointed will be your finished job; and just as women appreciate extra closet space just so will an extra towel bar or clothes hook often get your job a consideration that may help close a sale.

ing is exactly the same as that used in making enameled iron bath tubs, sinks and so forth. These may be had in either the built-in or exposed type. They are, of course, very durable and not too expensive.

Toilet Seats

We have been speaking of accessories and describing towel bars, soap dishes and so forth, but there is one item that, although not mentioned until now, should have a chapter all its own.

Toilet seats should receive a considerable amount of attention. The market is flooded with them at any price you want to pay. But if there is one place where the price indicates quality it is in the toilet seat. A good one costs money, but it is absolutely worth it.

The constant use, and the scrubbing and cleaning that toilet seats receive is reason enough for selecting the strongest and best. Then, too, the seat should harmonize with the balance of the bath room equipment.

Several of the better manufacturers are now advertising their seats to the public and the results are very satisfying, but there is a very important lesson to the builder in these results. It demonstrates that the home owner wants good toilet seats that are dependable and will stand up under much use.

Accessories Which Are Installed After the Bathroom Is Completed Can Be Obtained and Are Quite as Substantial and Attractive as the Built-in Type While Having the Advantage of Lower Cost.

The Adams

Plans for English Type Home Provide for Stucco on Hollow Clay Tile or Metal Lath Over Frame Construction

For Perspective in Full Colors see page 111

A HOME of beauty and satisfaction, suitable for any part of the United States, is presented in colors on page 111 and with a photographic reproduction at the bottom of this page.

The exterior has dignity, with its interesting planes and well placed doors and windows. The chimneys, with their ornamental caps are decidedly decorative and the long slopes of the roof offer attractive opportunity for the use of colored roofing material.

An interesting feature is handling of the garage which is placed at the right of the house and forms an integral part of the home. With the almost universal demand for garages these buildings are receiving increasingly more careful attention in the matter of design.

The interior is so planned that a hall separates the living room from the kitchen and dining room. The living room is notable for the lighting and ventilation from three sides. The kitchen and dining room are liberal in size and conveniently appointed.

All of the three bedrooms on the second floor are of adequate size, generously ventilated and well provided with closets.

Working plans to scale are presented in the four following pages, with cross sections presenting both the hollow tile and the frame and metal lath constructions.

Notice that the garage shown in the illustration is designed to agree with the house in architectural detail.

THE ADAMS; The Inviting Doorway, the Decorative Use of the Brick at the Ground Line and Under the Windows and the Tall Columns of the Chimneys are Touches which Make this Home Attractive. Consider the possibilities of a solid color or multi-colored roofing material. For working drawings, see the four pages following.

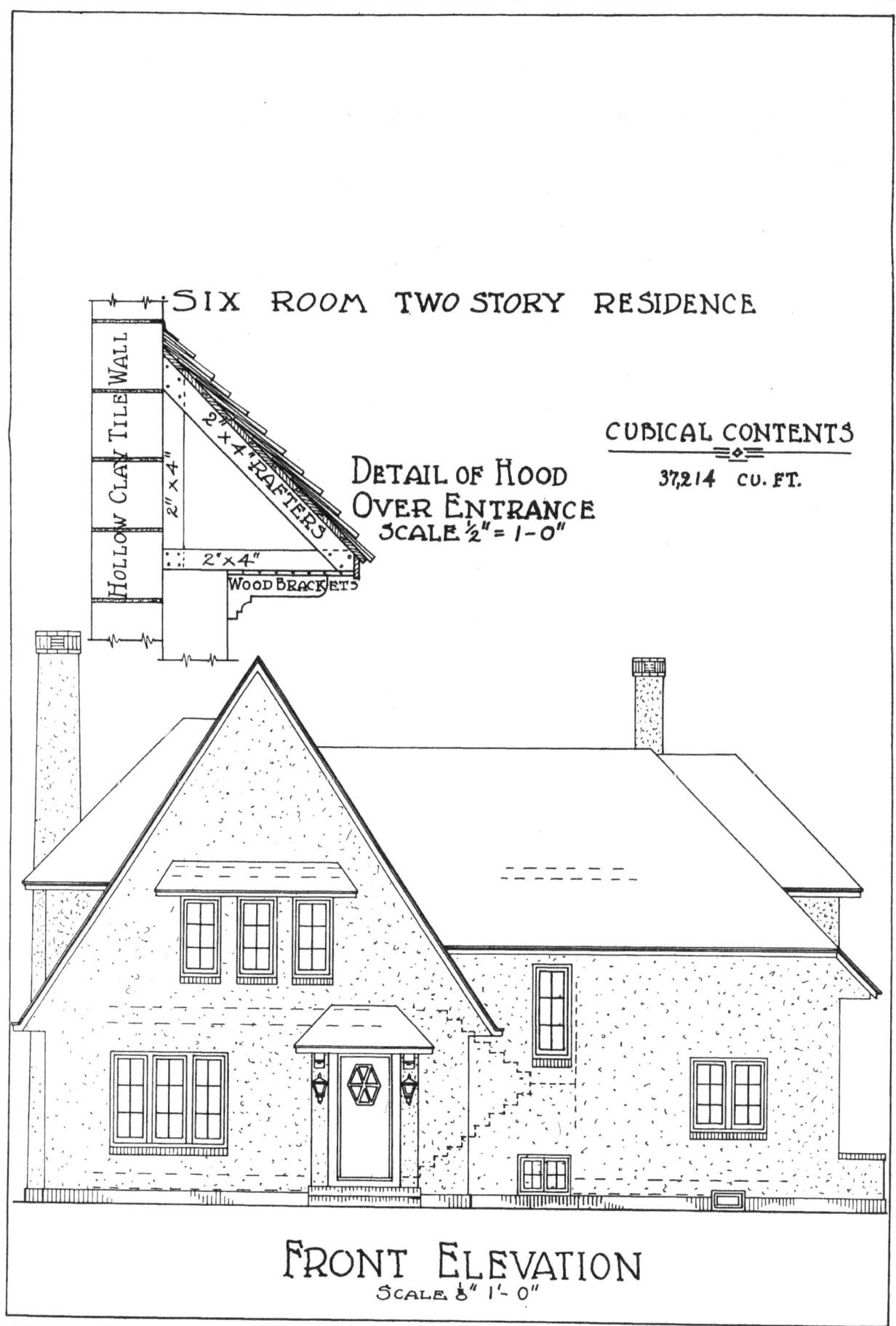

SIX ROOM TWO STORY RESIDENCE

Hollow Clay Tile Wall

2" × 4"

2" × 4" RAFTERS

2" × 4"

WOOD BRACKETS

DETAIL OF HOOD
OVER ENTRANCE
SCALE ½" = 1'-0"

CUBICAL CONTENTS
37,214 CU. FT.

FRONT ELEVATION
SCALE ⅛" 1'-0"

THE ADAMS; Front Elevation and Detail of Hood Over Entrance. Note the simple, pleasing proportions of the home and the skilled and well balanced placing of the windows.

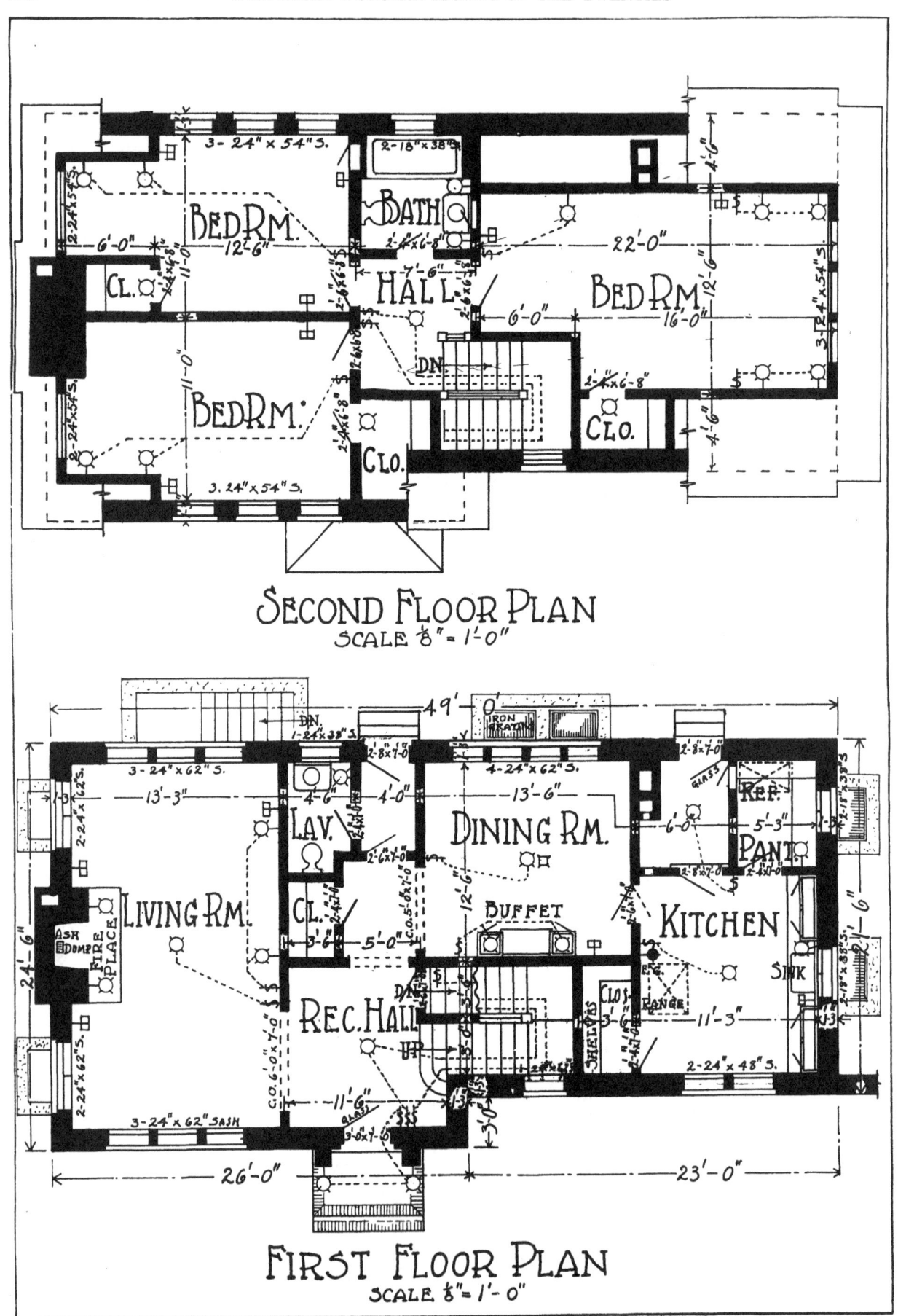

SECOND FLOOR PLAN

SCALE ⅛" = 1'-0"

FIRST FLOOR PLAN

SCALE ⅛" = 1'-0"

THE ADAMS; The Grouping of the Rooms on the First Floor Is Especially Attractive. Note the reception hall with the open stairway and the convenient closet for wraps. The kitchen and dining room arrangement is efficient.

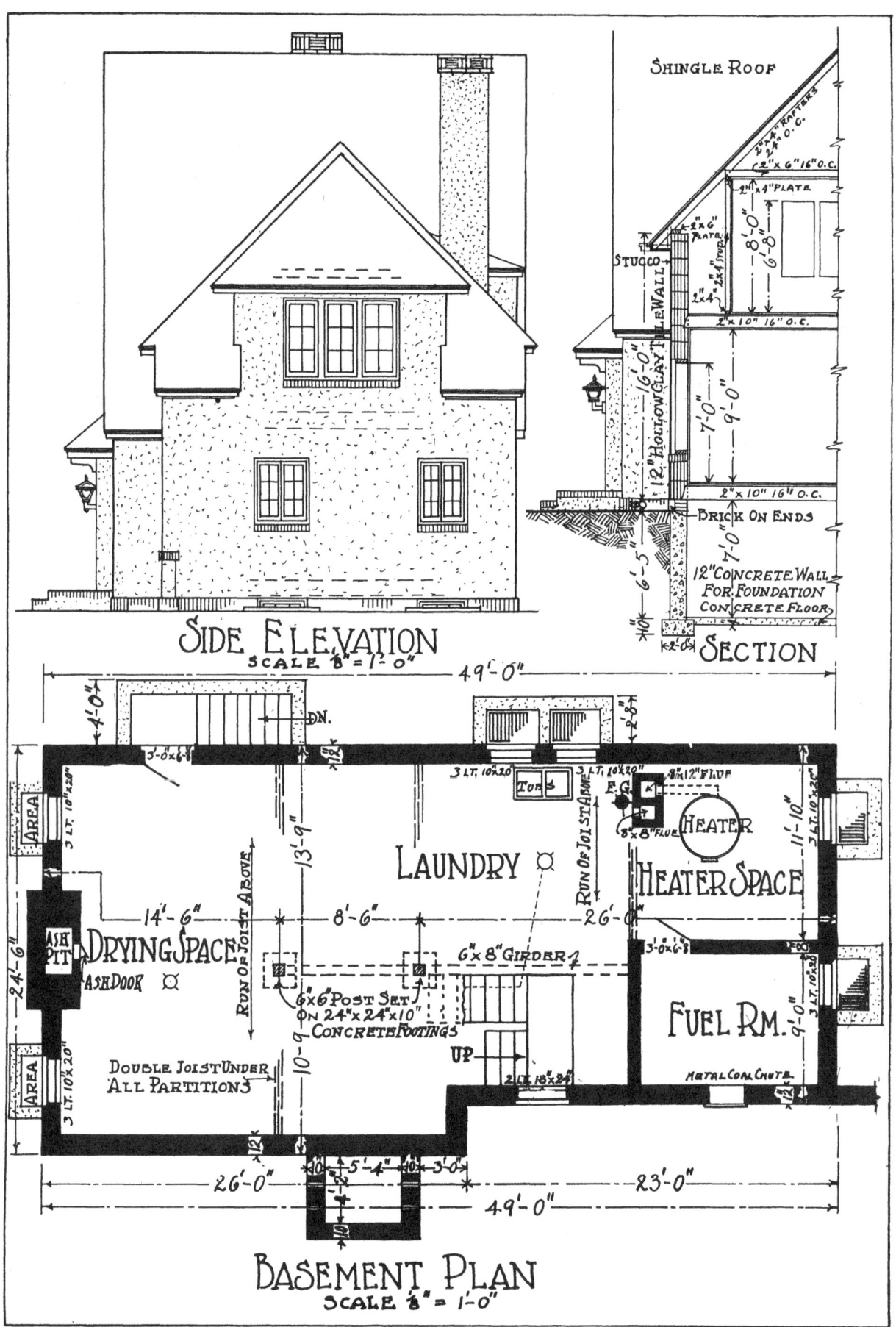

SIDE ELEVATION
SCALE ⅛" = 1'-0"

SECTION

BASEMENT PLAN
SCALE ⅛" = 1'-0"

THE ADAMS; The Basement Plan and Side Elevation with Cross Section Showing Hollow Clay Tile and Foundation
Detail. Provision is made for daylight lighting of the basement.

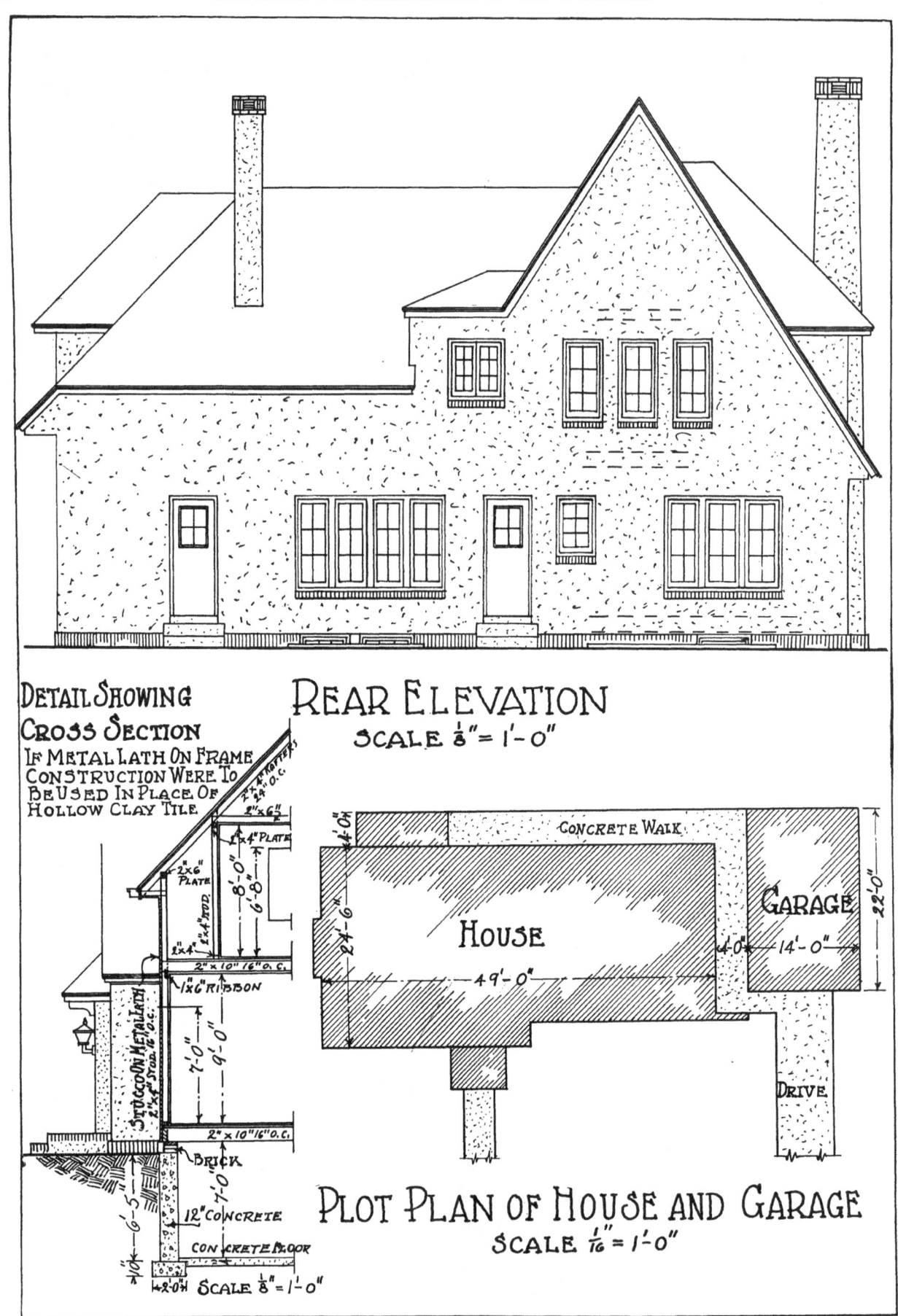

DETAIL SHOWING
CROSS SECTION
If Metal Lath On Frame
Construction Were To
Be Used In Place Of
Hollow Clay Tile

REAR ELEVATION
SCALE ⅛" = 1'-0"

PLOT PLAN OF HOUSE AND GARAGE
SCALE 1/16" = 1'-0"

THE ADAMS; Plot Plan for this Home, Showing the Arrangement of the Garage, the Walks and the Driveways,
with the Rear Elevation and Details of Metal Lath on Frame Construction.

The ADAMS

A HIGH Gable English Design of Stucco. For Complete Building Plans-Working Drawings to Scale See Pages 107, 108, 109 and 110.

The ALMA

A DELIGHTFUL Dutch Colonial Home. For Complete Building Plans Working Drawings to Scale See Pages 114, 115, 116 and 117.

The Alma

Charming Home of Dutch Colonial Design Gives Seven Well Arranged Rooms in Space 32 x 39 Feet

For Perspective in Full Colors see page 112

THE charm of the Dutch Colonial or gambrel roof style comes from its low, broad lines. In this home, illustrated so strikingly in full colors on page 112, and in the photograph below, the side walls run straight through to the upper eaves. The lower eaves coming between the first and second floor windows are simply nailed on without serving any structural purpose. They are for design only and serve effectively to produce that low, broad effect which is so much desired. The same can also be said of the roof projection at the gable ends. The front and rear walls carry right through to form the sides of the roof dormers. In other words, this is a straight gable house as far as construction is concerned, with a Dutch Colonial necklace hung around it to give it grace and beauty.

The room arrangement makes good the interesting promise of the exterior. The living room and dining room are of generous size and well placed. There is a cheerful little breakfast room and an efficient small kitchen. The maid's room and bath on the first floor are exceptional features in a house of this size. The stairway is given an inconspicuous position and leads up to a central square hall communicating with three large bedrooms, and a sewing room. Two bathrooms and three clothes closets are provided.

On the four pages following, working plans, one-eighth inch to the foot, are presented, showing in detail the construction of this home.

THE ALMA; Working Plans and Construction Details of This Attractive Dutch Colonial Home Are Presented on the Four Pages Following.

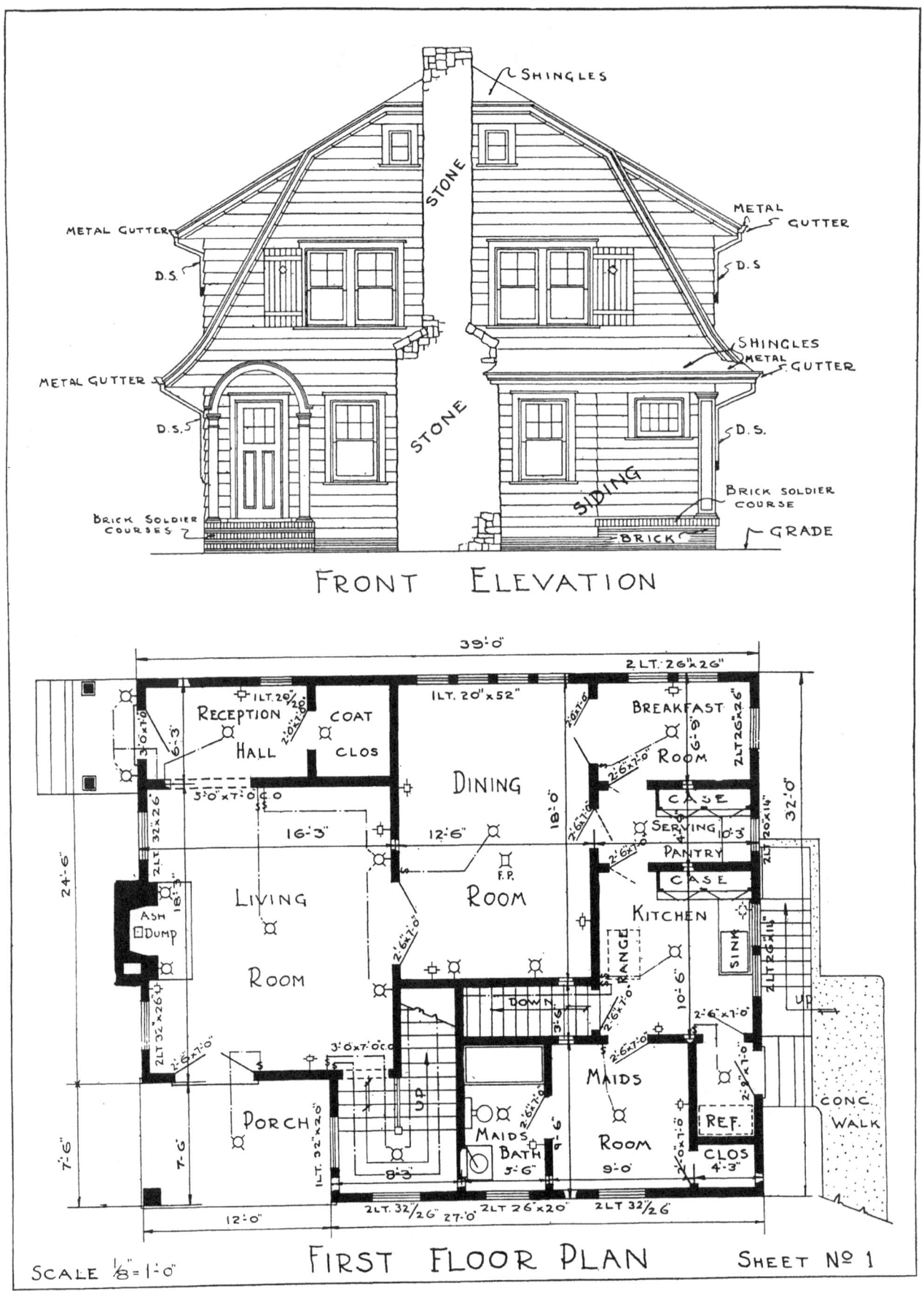

FRONT ELEVATION

FIRST FLOOR PLAN

SCALE ⅛"=1'-0"   SHEET № 1

THE ALMA; Working Drawings to One-Eighth Inch Scale of First Floor Plan and Front Elevation of the Dutch
Colonial Home Illustrated in Full Colors on Page 112.

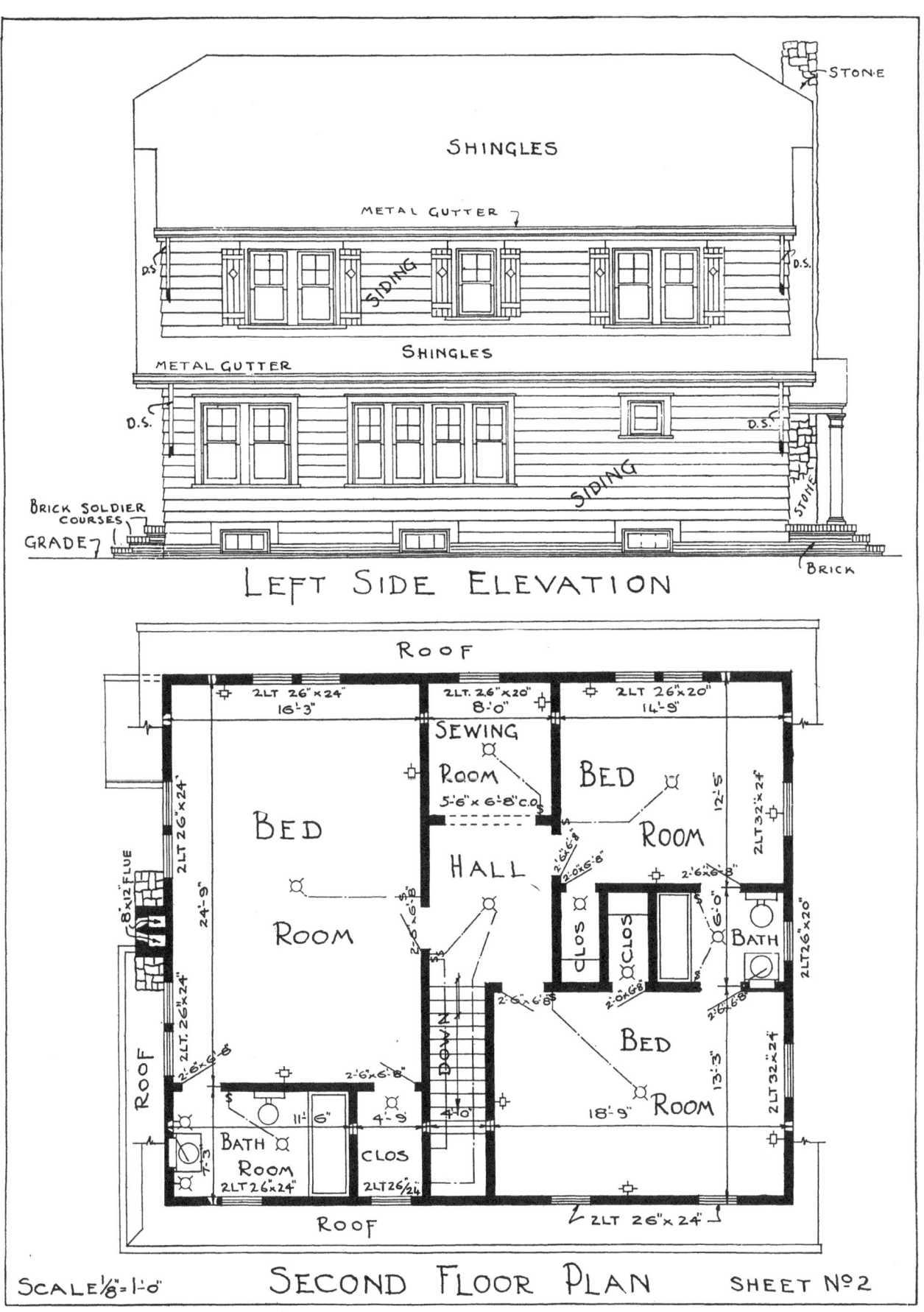

LEFT SIDE ELEVATION

SECOND FLOOR PLAN

SCALE 1/8" = 1'-0"   SHEET № 2

THE ALMA; This Dutch Colonial Home Measures 32 by 39 Feet and Contains Seven Well Arranged Rooms.

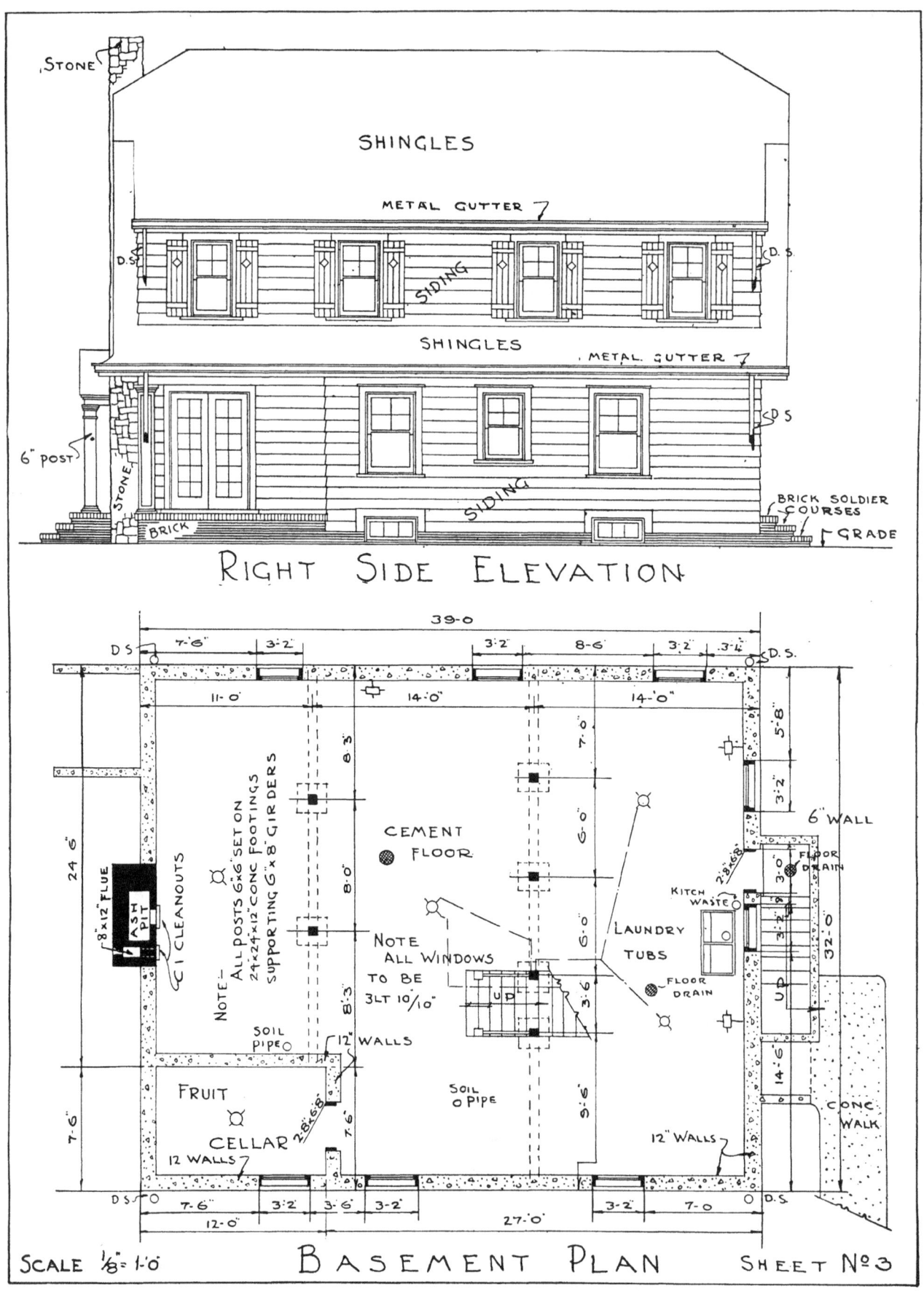

RIGHT SIDE ELEVATION

BASEMENT PLAN

SCALE ⅛=1′0   SHEET №3

THE ALMA; Basement Plan and Side Elevation Show the Good Design of This Building.

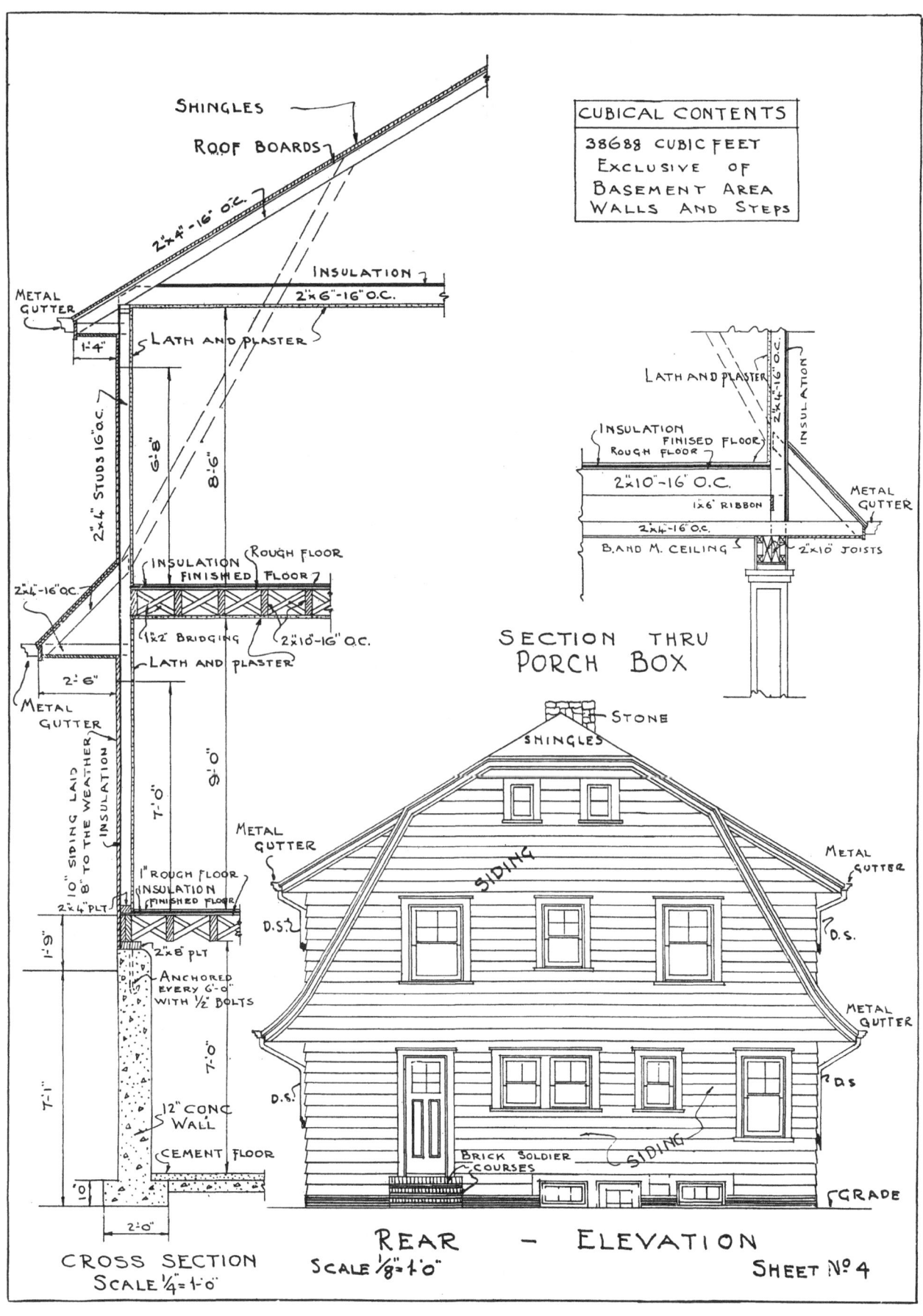

SHINGLES

ROOF BOARDS

2"x4"-16"O.C.

METAL GUTTER

1'-4"

INSULATION

2"x6"-16" O.C.

LATH AND PLASTER

CUBICAL CONTENTS
38688 CUBIC FEET
EXCLUSIVE OF
BASEMENT AREA
WALLS AND STEPS

6'-8"

8'-6"

2"x4" STUDS 16"O.C.

INSULATION
ROUGH FLOOR
FINISHED FLOOR

2"x4"-16"O.C.

1"x2" BRIDGING

2"x10"-16" O.C.

LATH AND PLASTER

2'-6"

METAL GUTTER

9'-0"

7'-0"

2"x10" SIDING LAID 8" TO THE WEATHER

INSULATION

METAL GUTTER

1" ROUGH FLOOR
INSULATION
FINISHED FLOOR

2"x4" PLT.

1'-9"

2"x8" PLT.

ANCHORED EVERY 6'-0" WITH 1/2" BOLTS

7'-0"

7'-1"

12" CONC. WALL

CEMENT FLOOR

'0"

2'-0"

CROSS SECTION
SCALE 1/4"=1'0"

LATH AND PLASTER

INSULATION

FINISED FLOOR
ROUGH FLOOR

2"x10"-16' O.C.

1"x6" RIBBON

2"x4"-16' O.C.

B. AND M. CEILING

2"x10" JOISTS

METAL GUTTER

SECTION THRU
PORCH BOX

STONE

SHINGLES

SIDING

METAL GUTTER

METAL GUTTER

D.S.

D.S.

METAL GUTTER

D.S.

D.S.

BRICK SOLDIER COURSES

SIDING

GRADE

REAR - ELEVATION
SCALE 1/8"=1'0"

SHEET No. 4

THE ALMA; The Good Construction of this Home Is Illustrated in This Cross-Section Detail. The Scale is One-quarter Inch to the Foot.

Built-in Bookshelves

Easily Accessible Height Imperative If Bookcase Is To Be Really Useful, and Architectural Results Must Be Cared For In Advance

OF all the various forms of built-in furniture that the home-builder knows today, none is better liked than the bookcases that are part of the house.

The first point to be decided is whether the bookshelves shall reach from floor to ceiling or only part way up. This must be determined by the number of books to be accommodated, and must be answered if possible by the prospective occupants of the house. It would be unwise to have shelves the full height of the room unless it were expected to fill them, and it would be equally unwise to build them only part way up if inadequate facilitites were the result.

When you have a choice between having one wall completely filled from top to bottom, or two walls each partly occupied by shelves, the latter arrangement would ordinarily be more acceptable. All the books would thereby be kept in reach, and space would be left for window openings above the shelves, to admit more air and light. The library that is lined with books from floor to ceiling sounds picturesque and inviting, but it is really an annoyance in practice, as many of the books are always inaccessible.

You will next have to determine whether the shelves are to be built out into the room or flush with the wall, and this is based largely on preference. To me there seems a far greater intimacy and companionableness in the projecting shelves. You would not know a person very well if you could see only his full face and never his profile, and similarly, you do not appreciate a shelf of books to the limit of its possibilities unless you can see its three dimensions.

The projecting arrangement has the further advantage of providing a top shelf standing out from the wall and upon which one may conveniently place a book for a moment out of one's hands.

There is another consideration, and that is the fact that the shelves built into the wall so that the books are flush with it, are usually more expensive to construct, and less flexible in case a change should be desired. You could hardly take them down and use

We Like This Room, Not Because It Is So Palatial, but Because These Books "Belong." How can one tell? Ah, there's the rub! Notice that these books were bought, one at a time, over a period of years, and not all at once like a load of potatoes.

the wall as a solid background for another purpose should it become necessary.

Architectural results must be cared for before final plans are decided. Shelving built up to the ceiling gives a sense of height to the low room. Shelves built into the wall add somewhat to the apparent floor space what they detract from intimacy or coziness. But flush shelving is entirely good form and good taste, and when properly considered as suggested herein, is architecturally commendable.

All books should be within convenient access, both the low ones and the high ones. They should not be stacked from the floor level, and the shelves may well start above a low dado usable if desired as a chest or closet for the storage of infrequently wanted things. It is also a mistake to place the shelves too high. Aside from the inconvenience of having to stretch on tiptoe or mount a chair in order to reach the volumes, the books will be subjected to a higher temperature the nearer they are to the ceiling. Continuous heat, enough to give comfort to the people in the room, is certain to be hot enough above to injure the bindings. A leather binding loses all its natural oils by

A Good Arrangement of Built-In Bookcases, Flanking Either Side of a Living Room Window.

long exposure to much heat. Dampness is also harmful to books, moisture causing the glue that fastens the cover to soften, and both paper and bindings become mildewed. It therefore seems advisable when possible to select an inside wall for the flush shelves as they are better protected against rain.

It is well to build adjustable shelves which rest on pins that may be screwed into holes at different heights provided for the purpose. If shelves are constructed of soft wood of about $\frac{5}{8}$ inch in thickness, they should not be much more than two feet in length. If they are longer, they will gradually bend in the middle under the weight of the books.

To Set Building Standards

The standard of American homes built in the future can be raised by penalizing poor construction in charging a higher rate of insurance than that placed on good construction, "pedigree" of merit, issued to good houses will encourage the building of better homes, and home ownership in the United States can be encouraged by doing away with excessive fees for obtaining and renewing mortgage loans according to resolutions presented to the National Conference on Home Building, held in Chicago during the Fifth Annual "Own Your Home" Exposition.

The electrical industry, the plumbing trade, the heating and piping contractors and many of the other trades now issue individual certificates that give the home buyer or builder only the assurance that his house is good in one particular and the conference proposes to combine their efforts and achieve 100 per cent houses.

The conference called by the National Association of Real Estate Boards to debate on how to raise the standard and lower the cost of American homes built in the future was composed of delegates from more than twenty national allied professional and trade organizations and associations and pledged itself to combat loan sharks, unscrupulous contractors, manufacturers of shoddy materials and others who prey on the unsuspecting home buyer and builder.

It is proposed to make this conference a permanent organization to meet each year in one of the cities where the national "Own Your Home" Expositions are held.

To Case or Not to Case—That Is the Question. Whether the books should be behind glass or no is purely a matter of taste—and local atmospheric conditions.

The Altavista

Italian Architecture and Stucco Beautify This Home

THE sunny skies of Italy, the blue waters of the Mediterranean, the gardens and flowers surrounding Italian villas—all these enhance the beauty of Italian house designs. But the architecture itself is graceful and appealing and many new homes in the United States are being modeled along these lines.

An instance of this is to be found in a new Wheaton, Ill., home. The architecture is after the Italian, with many arched entrances. Even the full length casement windows of the lower floor are set in arches and, in the upper part of each is a piece of decorative terra cotta, to suggest the sgraffitto decoration usually executed in special stucco for Italian villas. Outside of each of the casement windows is a wrought iron railing.

Owing to the lack of local facilities this had to be hand wrought by the "village blacksmith."

No photograph can do entire justice to this **fine** home, the charm of which is due largely to its coloring and special stucco texture.

Close-Up View Showing Texture of Stucco Work.

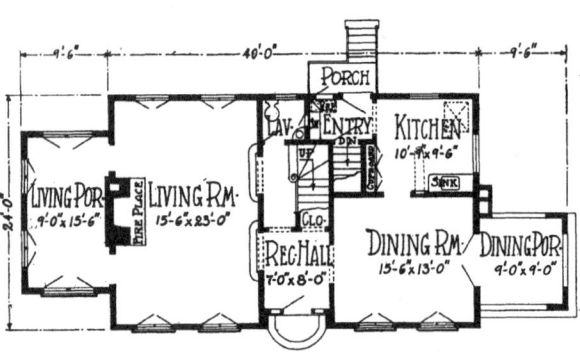

First Floor Plan.

THE ALTAVISTA; Ornamental Terra Cotta in the Window Arches, a Special Tint and Texture of Stucco, a Red Tile Roof and Italian Architecture Feature This Modern Home.

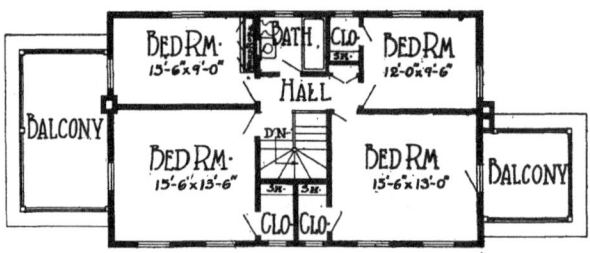

Second Floor Plan.

The roof is of Spanish red tile, which gives a rich effect against the background of summer foliage. The stucco has a special sweep and curl which provides a valuable texture effect and the tint is a warm sienna —one of the lighter orange tints. This stucco is of magnesite mixed with calcium chloride, which gave rise to the fiction that it was mixed with fuel oil. A broom and a wire brush were used to secure the desired sweep. The stucco finish was carried out on the under side of the eaves along the front and back of the house.

When our photographs were taken, the grading had just been completed and, shrubbery and bulbs have since been set out in large number, which will give the house a setting of great beauty. The land slopes sharply to the south and here the owner plans to install an outdoor swimming pool of concrete which will be 65 feet long by 35 feet in width. The ground floor dimensions of the house are 40 by 24 feet or 59 by 24 feet, including the porches, one of which is enclosed. This porch is connected with the living room and is floored with red tile. It is heated—as is the entire house—by hot water radiators and special vapor system valves, which heat the house at extremely low pressure. The building is of hollow tile construction, stuccoed, and is heat-insulated with a fiber insulation. The interior plaster has a sand float finish, painted and all interior trim is mahogany. The floors are oak, unstained, with wax finish. A special decorative fireplace adds to the appearance and cheeriness of the living room, which measures 23 feet by 15 feet 6 inches.

Fine electric light fittings adorn the house, many of Butler silver finish. The window draperies are of fawn-colored silk and the furniture is handsome and appropriate. The living room and enclosed porch are

Above: The Fireplace with Ornamental Mantel Adds to the Attractiveness of the Living Room in the Upper Picture. Below: Arched door openings give glimpses of hall and dining room beyond.

on a slightly lower level than the other rooms with a step down from the reception hall.

A fine vista through the rooms on the ground floor is visible through the arched openings, which are without doors. A partition in the basement shutting off the boiler room and laundry provides space for a billiard room.

A two-car garage at the back is finished in the same tint and texture of stucco as the house. The property, complete, represents an investment of well over $25,000.00.

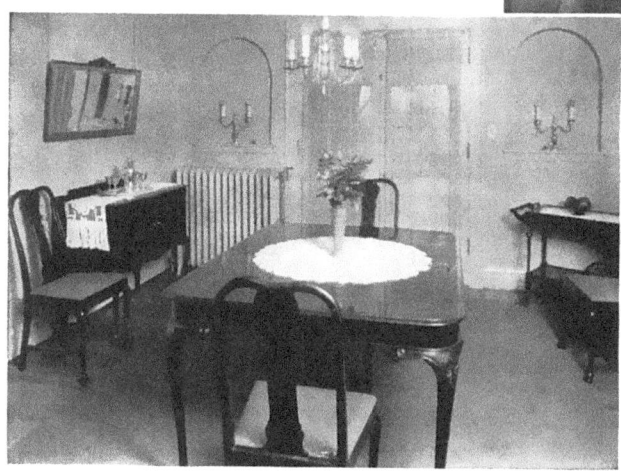

A View of the Dining Room Showing Glassed Doors to Dining Porch.

The Alcorn

An Attractive, Well-Planned Home of Spanish Design

PARTICULARLY charming is the outside appearance of the little one-story house illustrated herewith, by floor plan and photograph. It, in fact, is of quite unusual design, possessing an especially well-developed individuality. Effective indeed are such details of treatment as the turned-over edges of the roof above the gables, the arched and neatly bordered open doorway to the entrance vestibule, the use of full-length windows in the front walls, the entrance lighting fixture comprised of a tall wrought-iron standard and white globe, the little medallion ornamentation of the main front wall, and so forth. In the recessed front corner, before the three French window of the living room, is also effectively placed a little circular lily pond.

The exterior walls are of light buff-toned cement-stucco over frame construction, with the border of the entrance doorway done in light brown and dull green and the wood trimming painted greenish brown. The shingled roof is green, and the entrance vestibule is paved with red tile, while brick is introduced for edging the lily pond, front walk and otherwise as masonry trimming. Off one end of the dining room, accessible from it thru French doors, and comprising the entrance from the automobile driveway is a small side porch, floored with cement, and in the rear, with

doors opening to it from each the kitchen-entry porch, a small breakfast room and sleeping porch is still another porch, which also is floored with cement.

The interior is exceptionally well planned, as reference to the accompanying floor plan will show, and it

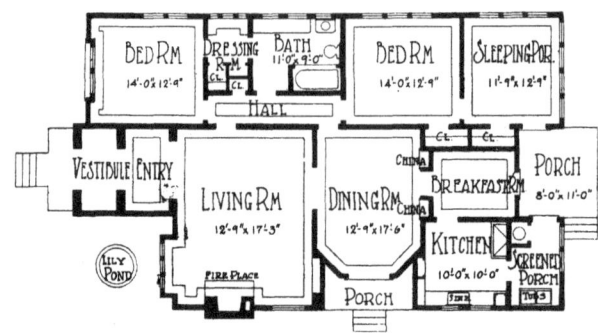

Floor Plan

is also very attractive in finish and decoration. The front door, which is of paneled oak, opens into a small entry, lighted by a tiny arched window, and an open arched doorway leads, in turn, into the living room.

The living room is designed with a chapel ceiling, and a fireplace with a wood and tile mantel.

THE ALCORN; A Los Angeles House, Designed in Light Buff-Toned Cement Stucco Over Frame. It has no basement or cellar, and is equipped with built-in gas radiators for heating.

The Allendale

A Country Estate Residence. Farms and Smaller Country Places Provide a Fitting Setting for the Type of Home Originated by Dutch Colonists

FEW moderate sized houses embody greater charm of composition with convenience of arrangement than this simple roof-dormered dwelling. Built to suit a particular site on Long Island, it was planned on simple lines as befitted an

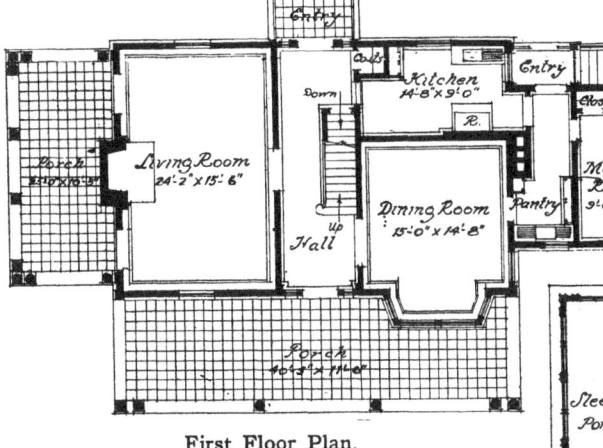

First Floor Plan.

environment that once sheltered the early Dutch settlers and also to take advantage of a fine view of Long Island obtainable from the commanding point on which it was located.

Attached to a small estate, it was desired the house should be planned to suit the living con-

ditions which included a moderate amount of entertaining.

While the design savors of the Dutch Colonial to a pleasing extent, it follows in the main the lines of the early farmhouse type, to which has been introduced the long, low roof dormer and the overhanging roof to enclose the porch. The glass-enclosed porch built on at the left balances the "L" at the right.

The floor arrangement is convenient. The living room occupies one end, with the dining room, service portion and maid's room opposite.

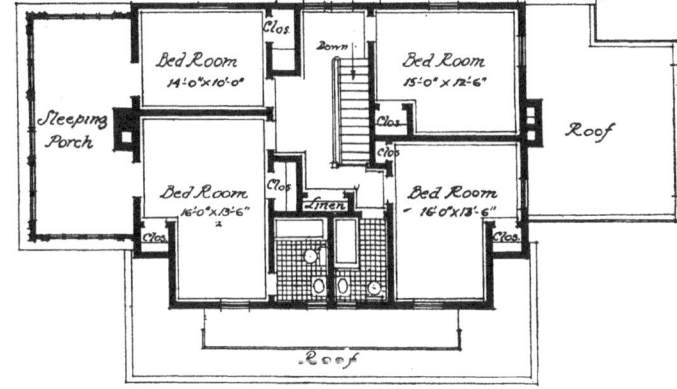

Second Floor Plan.

THE ALLENDALE; A Charming Rural Residence on Long Island, Which Finds Its Inspiration in the Dutch Colonial.

The Antioch

An Attractive New England Farm House Design Notable for the Convenience of the Room Arrangement and Generous Porches

For Perspective in Full Colors see page 129

GREEN shutters against wide, white siding; attractive porches with simple but carefully worked out ornamentation and the pleasing door, with its effective sidelights are details adding much to the good proportions of this Colonial home, which shows to particular advantage in its setting of foliage as pictured in page 129.

The front entrance admits one to an attractive reception hall, with a Colonial stairway leading to the second floor. On one side, in the usual Colonial manner, is the living room, with the sun porch adjoining and adding materially to the usable space. The window seat, with built-in book cases at each side, is a good feature worth copying.

The other side of the reception hall is the dining room, reached through French doors. This room is reached from the kitchen through an unusually con-venient serving pantry, which contains a work counter, a case and the refrigerator, which it is planned to have iced from the rear porch. A first floor lavatory is a feature which should not be overlooked. It is accessible from both front and rear of the house.

The second floor may be finished in either of two ways, as shown on page 126. The builder may install three bedrooms, one to be a master chamber, extending the full depth of the house, with its private bath and two generous closets. The other two rooms provided by this plan are of generous size and are well provided with closet space.

The alternate floor plan shown gives four bedrooms, all of adequate size and with cross-ventilation. In this plan a bath is placed directly between each two bedrooms and can be reached from either without the necessity of going out into the hall.

THE ANTIOCH; The Manner in Which the Porch Is Housed Under the Main Roof of This Home Makes It an Integral Part of the Home, Instead of Giving It the Effect of Being Added as an After Thought. Full working details of this attractive Colonial home will be found on the four following pages.

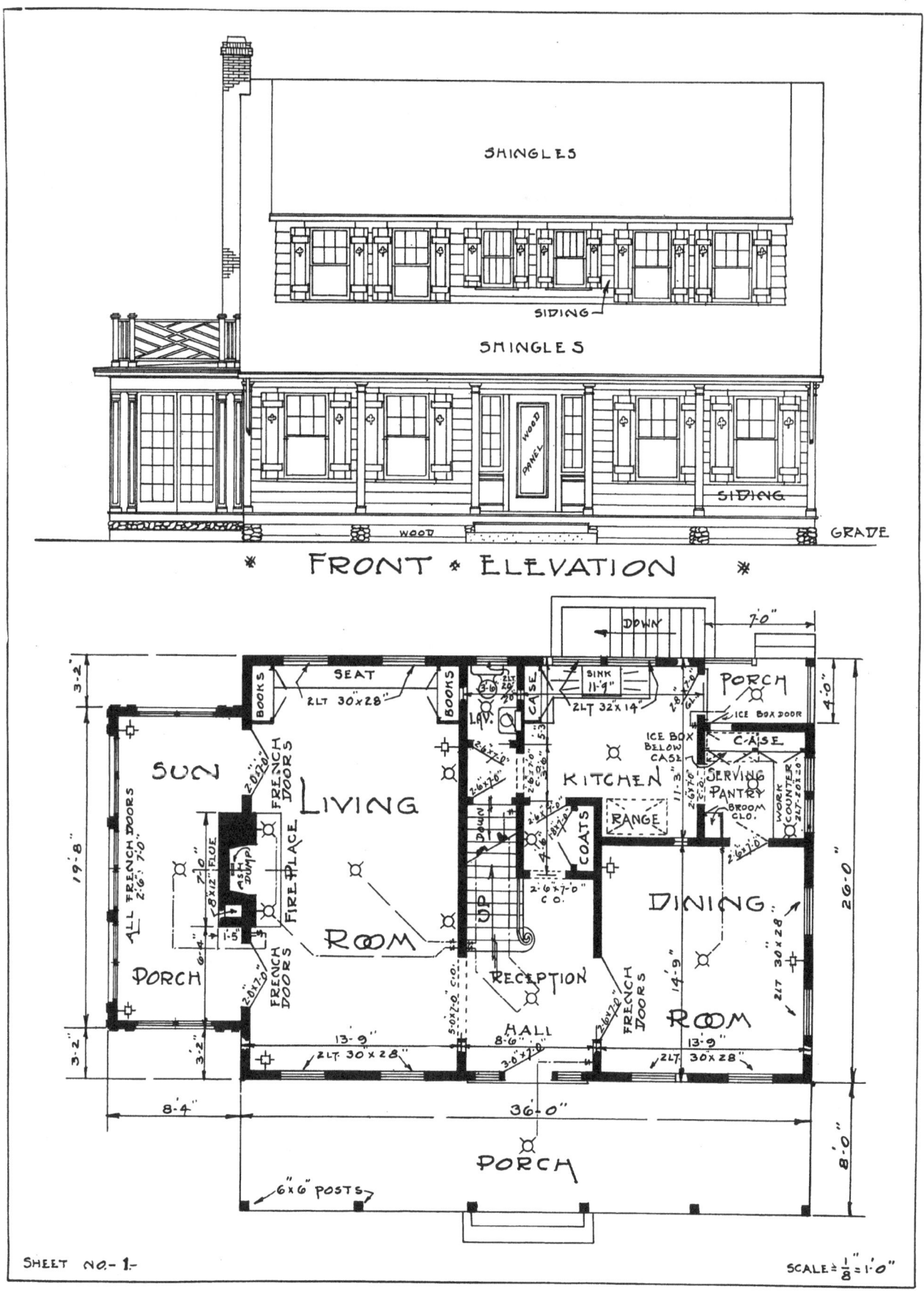

SHINGLES

SIDING

SHINGLES

WOOD PANEL

SIDING

WOOD   GRADE

❋ FRONT ❋ ELEVATION ❋

DOWN   7'-0"

3'-2"

BOOKS   SEAT   BOOKS   PORCH

2LT 30"X28"   SINK   4'-0"
                              11'-9"

LAV.   CASE   2LT 32"X14"

ICE BOX DOOR

ICE BOX BELOW CASE   C-ASE

SUN   SERVING PANTRY

LIVING   KITCHEN   BROOM CLO.   WORK COUNTER

19'-8"   ALL FRENCH DOORS   FIRE PLACE   FRENCH DOORS   RANGE   COATS   26'-0"

8"X12" FLUE

ROOM   DOWN   DINING

FRENCH DOORS   UP   14'-9"   2LT 30"X28"

RECEPTION   ROOM

PORCH

3'-2"   3'-2"   13'-9"   HALL   FRENCH DOORS   13'-9"

2LT 30"X28"   8'-6"   2LT 30"X28"

3'-0"X7'-0"

8'-4"   36'-0"   8'-0"

PORCH

6"X6" POSTS

THE ANTIOCH; The Scale Drawing Shows How the Details of the Wide Siding and the Well Proportioned Shutters Are Worked Out. The living room, with the fireplace homes one side and the window seat flanked by built-in book cases at one end, is an unusually pleasant room. Two plans for arranging the second floor are presented on the following page.

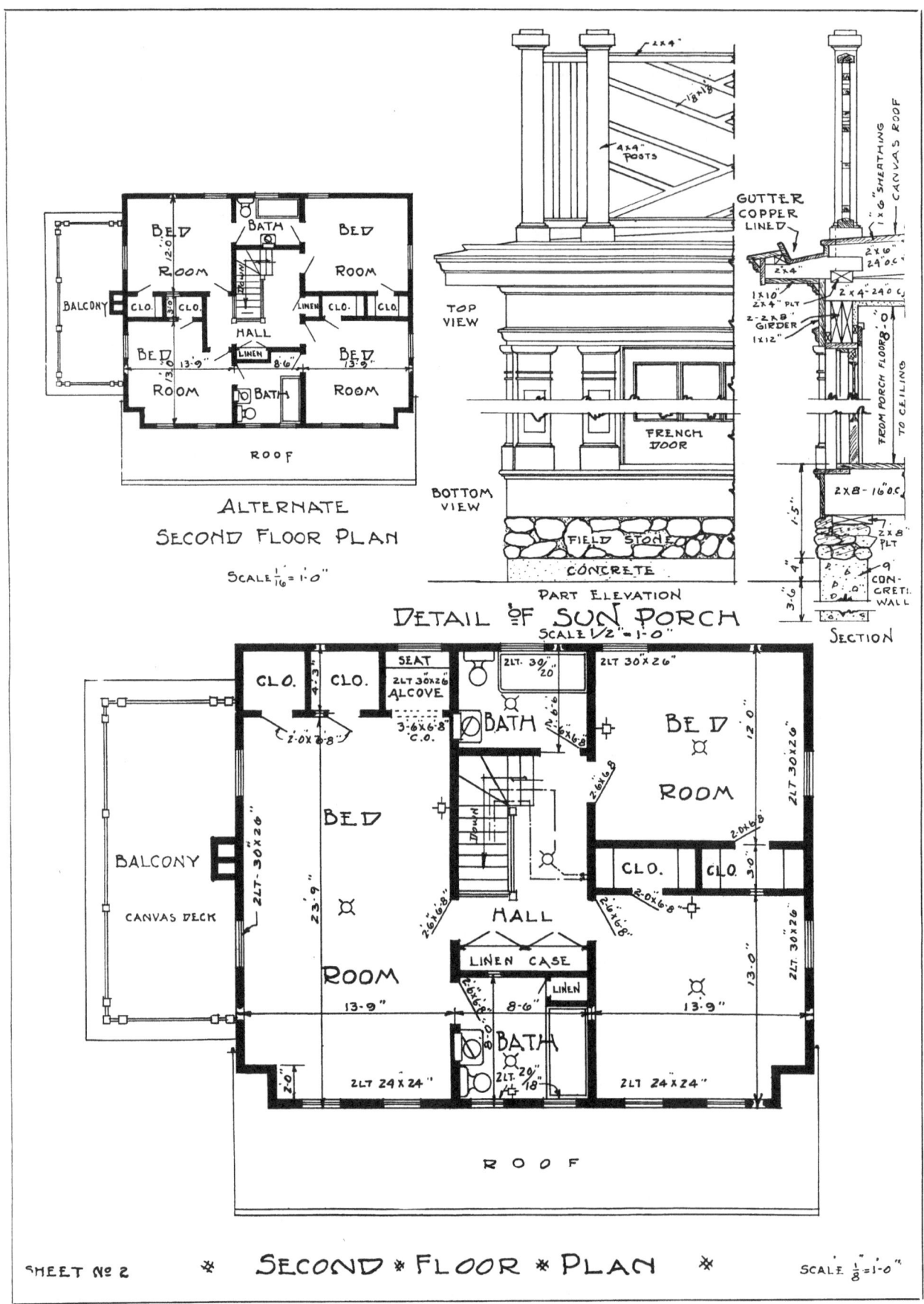

ALTERNATE SECOND FLOOR PLAN
Scale 1/16" = 1'-0"

DETAIL OF SUN PORCH
Scale 1/2" = 1'-0"

PART ELEVATION

TOP VIEW

BOTTOM VIEW

FRENCH DOOR

FIELD STONE

CONCRETE

GUTTER COPPER LINED

CANVAS ROOF

SECTION

BALCONY
CANVAS DECK

HALL

LINEN CASE

BATH

ROOF

SHEET № 2 ✻ ✻ SECOND ✻ FLOOR ✻ PLAN ✻ ✻ SCALE 1/8" = 1'-0"

THE ANTIOCH; A Large Master Bedroom, with a Private Bath is Provided in the One Plan for the Second Floor. This plan also gives two more bedrooms of good size, both with cross ventilation and lighted from two sides. The alternate floor plan gives four bedrooms, two grouped about each bath room. The basement plan and side elevation of the home are on the next page.

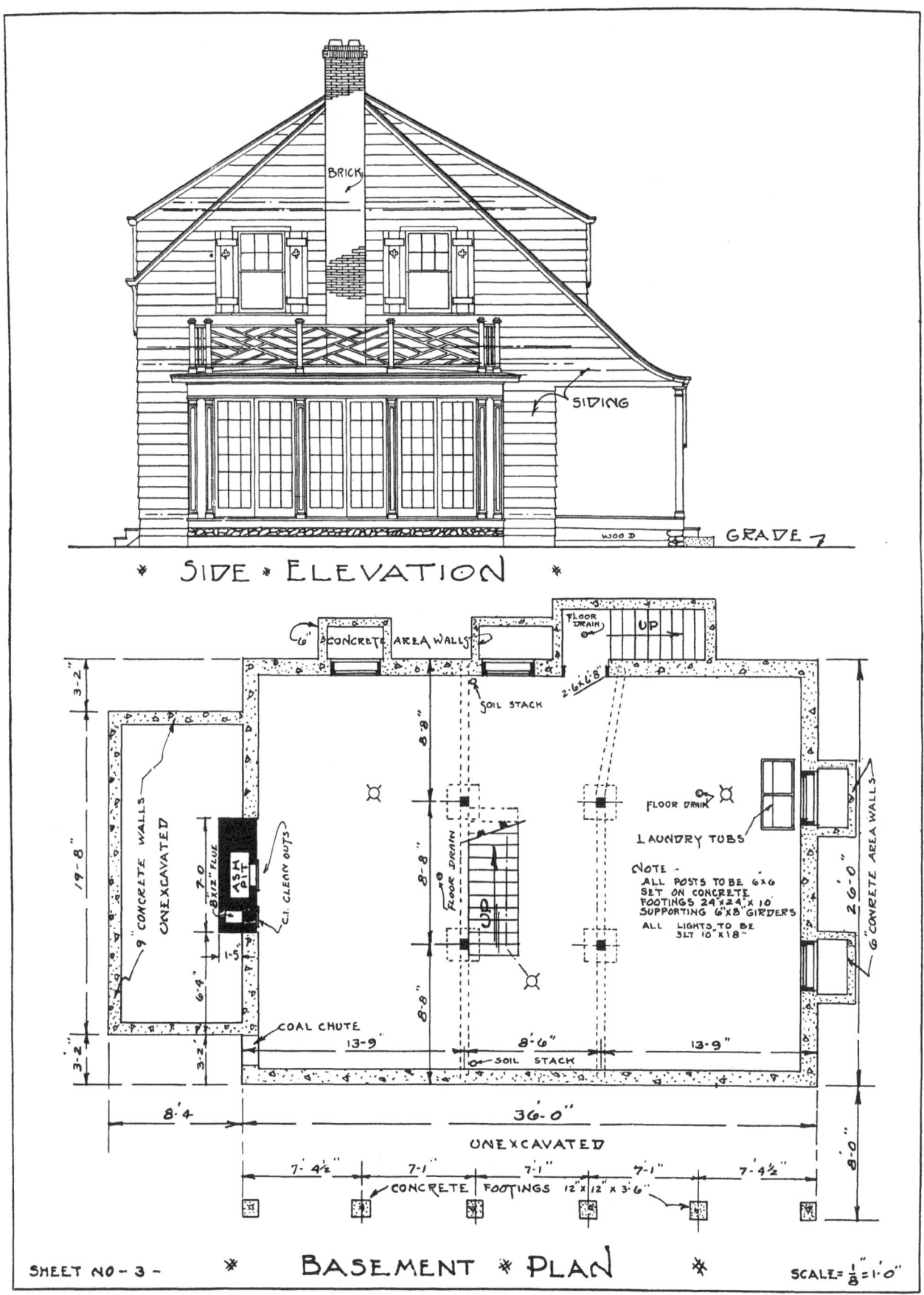

BRICK

SIDING

WOOD

GRADE

✳ SIDE ✳ ELEVATION ✳

CONCRETE AREA WALLS

FLOOR DRAIN

UP

SOIL STACK

2-6"x8"

FLOOR DRAIN

LAUNDRY TUBS

NOTE –
ALL POSTS TO BE 6x6
SET ON CONCRETE
FOOTINGS 24"x24" X 10"
SUPPORTING 6"X8" GIRDERS
ALL LIGHTS TO BE
3LT 10"X18"

9" CONCRETE WALLS

UNEXCAVATED

ASH PIT

8"X12" FLUE

C.I. CLEAN OUTS

6" CONCRETE AREA WALLS

19'-8"

26'-0"

7-0

6'-4"

1-5

3-2

3-2

FLOOR DRAIN

UP

COAL CHUTE

13-9

8'6"

13-9"

SOIL STACK

8-8"

8-8"

8-8"

8'4"

36'-0"

8-0"

UNEXCAVATED

7'-4½"

7'-1"

7'-1"

7'-1"

7'-4½"

CONCRETE FOOTINGS 12"x12" X 3'-6"

THE ANTIOCH; The Basement May Well Be Divided into the Well Lighted Laundry Indicated, with Its Built-in Tubs, a Section for the Heating Equipment and Coal Bins and a Section for Storage Purposes. A detailed cross section of this home is given on the following page.

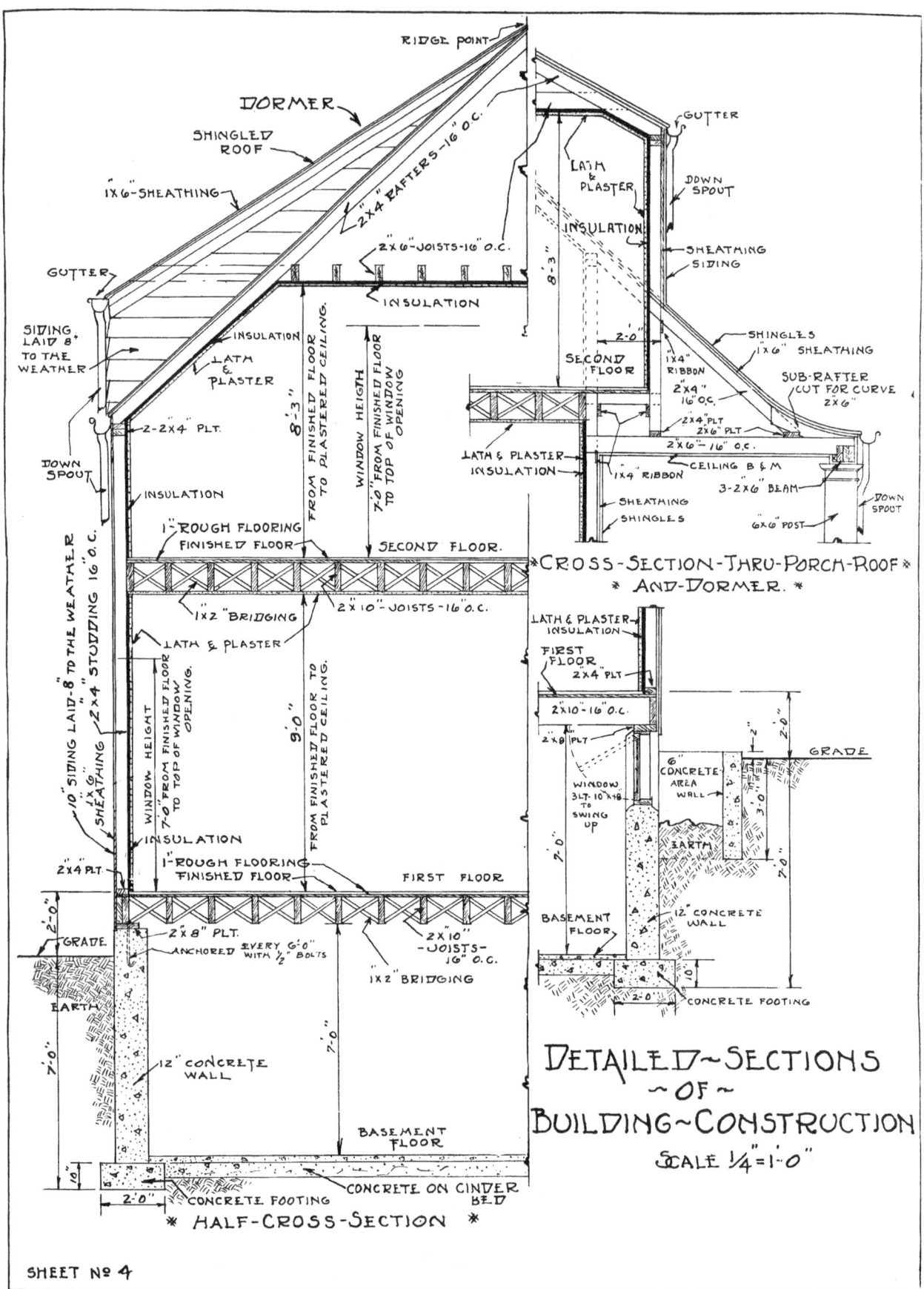

THE ANTIOCH; Details of the Construction Are Presented in This Cross Section. Note that the 2-foot concrete footings and the 12-inch basement walls provide an adequate foundation for the building. Side wall and ceiling insulation is utilized to make heating easier and less expensive.

The ANTIOCH

A NEW England Farmhouse Design. For Complete Building Plans-Working Drawings to Scale See Pages 125, 126, 127 and 128.

The ALLIANCE

A STRAIGHT Gable Colonial. For Complete Building Plans-Working Drawings to Scale See Pages 132, 133, 134 and 135.

The Alliance

Straight Gable Colonial Design Is Liked by Everyone and Delivers Most House for the Money Invested

For Perspective in Full Colors see page 130

HERE is a delightful Colonial—white with green shades and an open entrance approached by brick steps and wrought iron hand rails in the approved Colonial manner.

This house measures 25 feet by 36 feet 6 inches; 9-foot ceilings for the first floor, 8-foot 6-inch ceilings for the second floor. So this is not a large house and should not be expensive to build. At the same time, a surprising amount of good, livable space is provided, as a study of the floor plans will show.

This design follows the approved arrangement, with central reception and stair hall, the space to the left being given over to the large living room, 14 by 25 feet, and the space to the right being shared between the dining room and the kitchen. Directly back of the reception hall is the service entrance and the stairs to the basement. On the second floor the stairs come right to give a central hall which really takes up little space and yet carries an impression of size and dignity. To the left of the hall is a large bedroom with private bath, and a large well-lighted clothes closet or dressing room. To the right of the hall are two smaller bedrooms, each with clothes closet. Two closets also open off the hall and the general bathroom is at the rear. The basement nicely provides for the laundry with set tubs and electric outlet for washing machine and electric irons. The heating plant is at the other end of the basement near the fuel room, which is provided under the side porch. This would be convenient either for storage of coal or for oil tanks and pumping equipment if fuel oil is to be used.

The four pages of working drawings which follow are very practical, in that they are presented here to an exact scale as marked and are complete enough so that this beautiful Home could be actually built from these plans.

THE ALLIANCE; In Colonial Style, White with Green Shutters, Brick Steps and Wrought Iron Hand Rails to the Entrance, this Home Is Roomy but Inexpensive. Working plans for this house are shown on the next four pages.

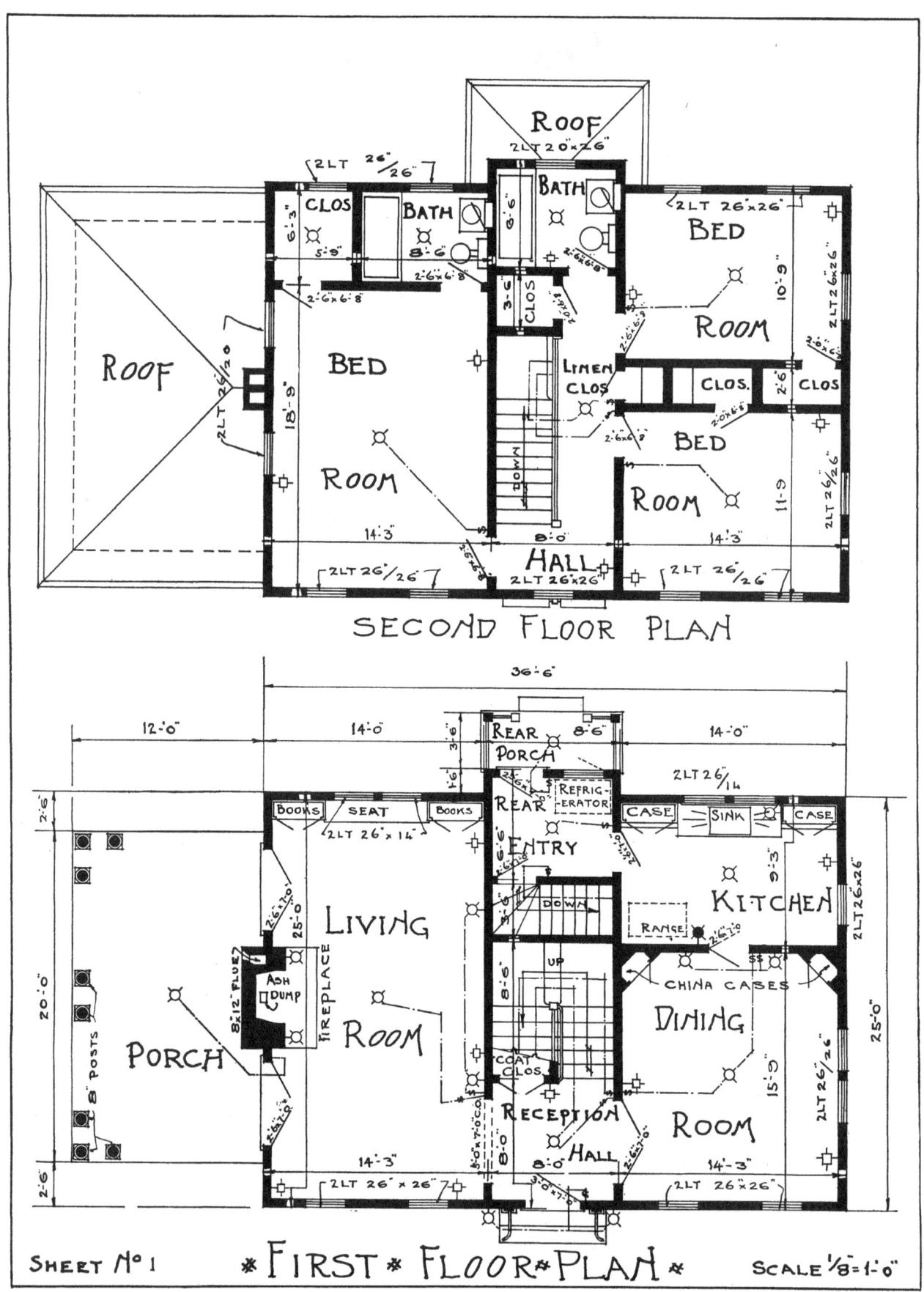

SECOND FLOOR PLAN

SHEET Nº 1   ✴ FIRST ✴ FLOOR ✴ PLAN ✴   SCALE ⅛=1'-0"

THE ALLIANCE; A Large Living Room with Fireplace, Window Seat and Built-In Book Cases Is the Most Striking Feature of the Well Arranged First Floor, While a Large Bedroom with an Extra Bath Is the Feature of the Second Floor. On the opposite page will be found the basement plan and front elevation.

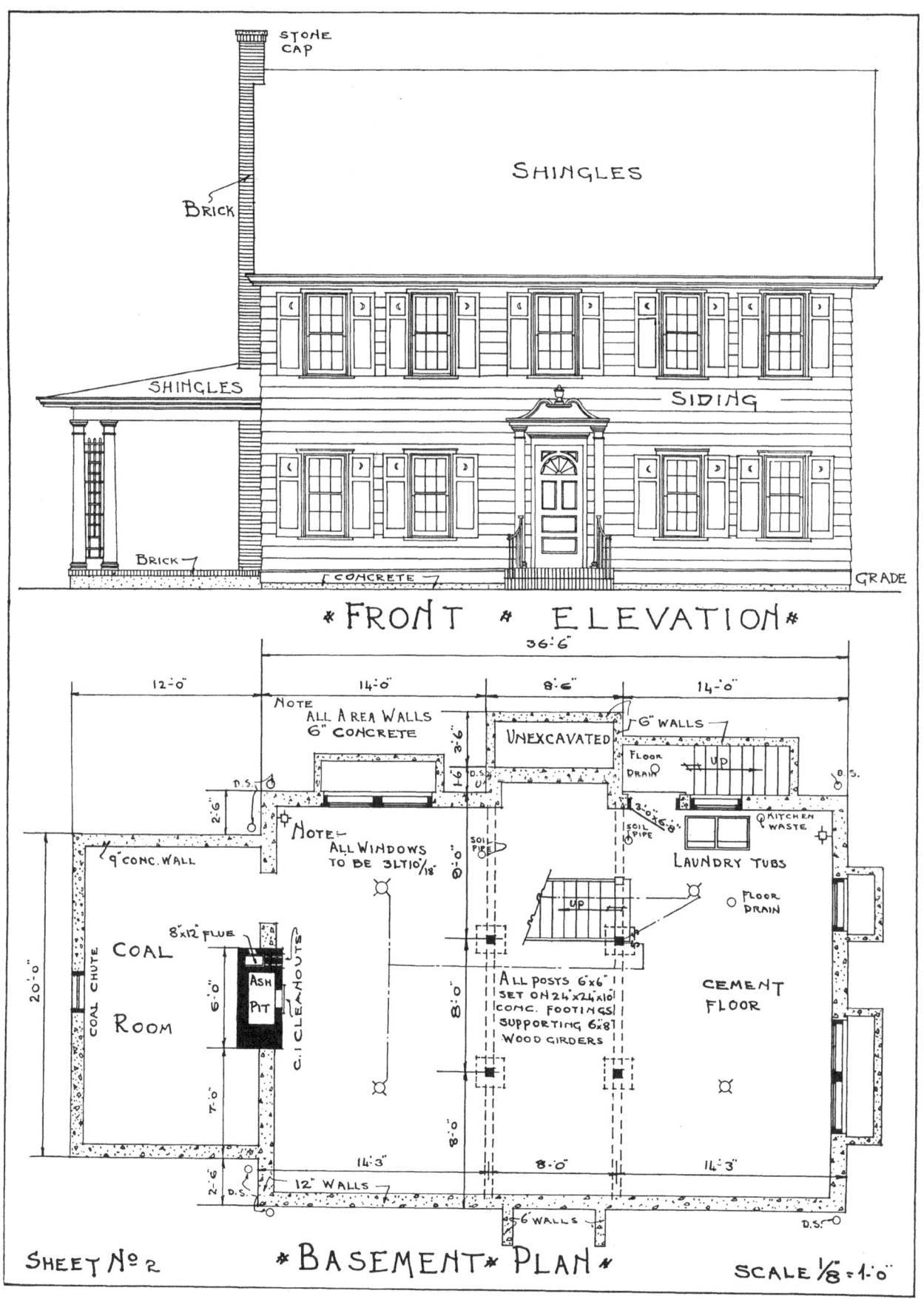

FRONT ELEVATION

BASEMENT PLAN

SHEET Nᵒ 2

SCALE 1/8ʺ=1ʹ0ʺ

THE ALLIANCE; The Basement Plan Shows the Division of This Space with the Laundry Well Separated from Furnace and Coal Room. The front elevation, above, gives the placement of windows and design of the front entrance. On the next page are the left side elevation and detailed sections of construction.

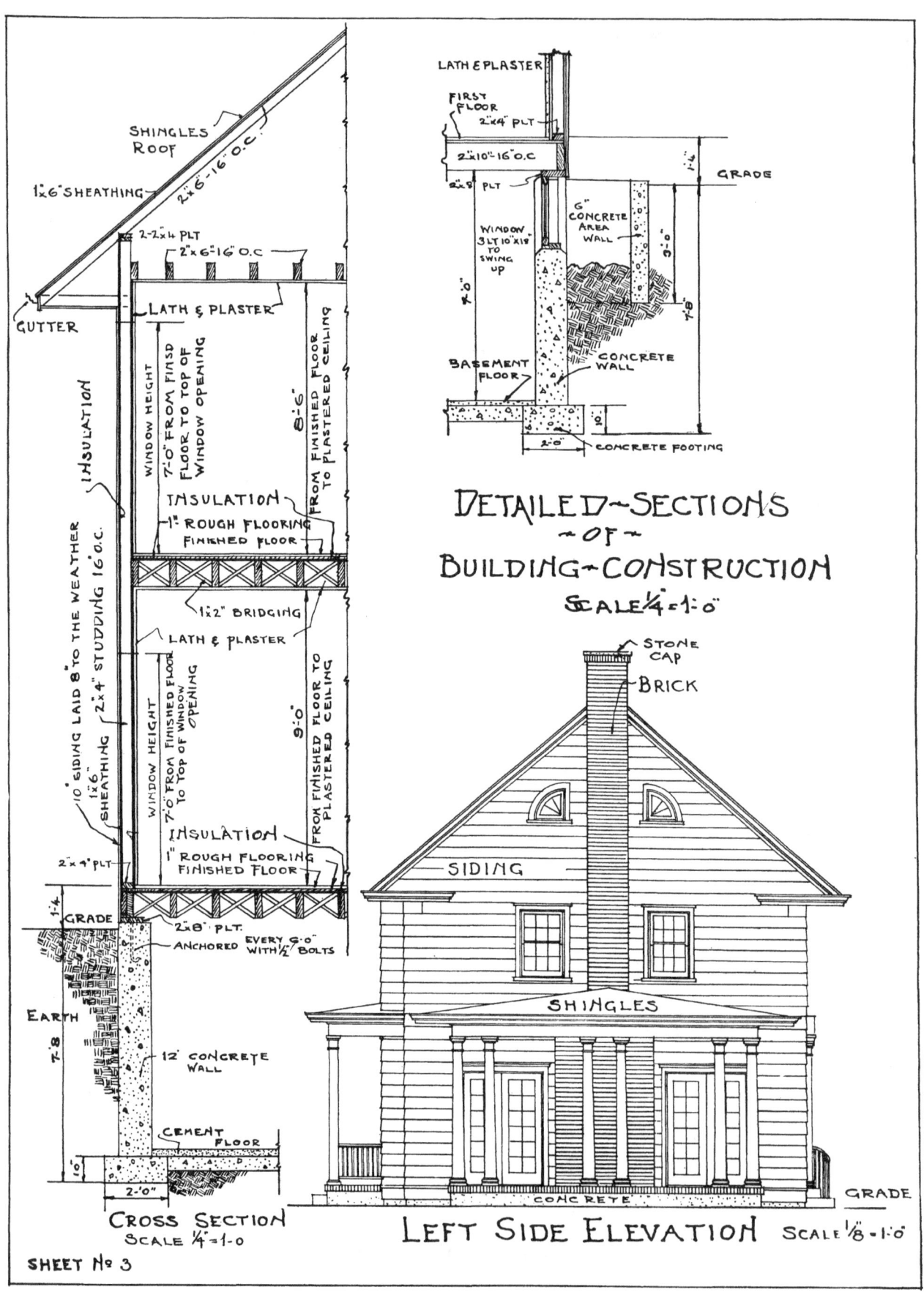

DETAILED-SECTIONS
~OF~
BUILDING-CONSTRUCTION
SCALE ¼"=1'-0"

CROSS SECTION
Scale ¼"=1-0

LEFT SIDE ELEVATION   SCALE ⅛"=1'0"

SHEET № 3

THE ALLIANCE; The Left Side Elevation Shows the Relation of Porch, Chimney and French Doors. The sectional views furnish construction details of the walls, floors and foundations. For the right side elevation and construction details of porch roof and cornice see the next page.

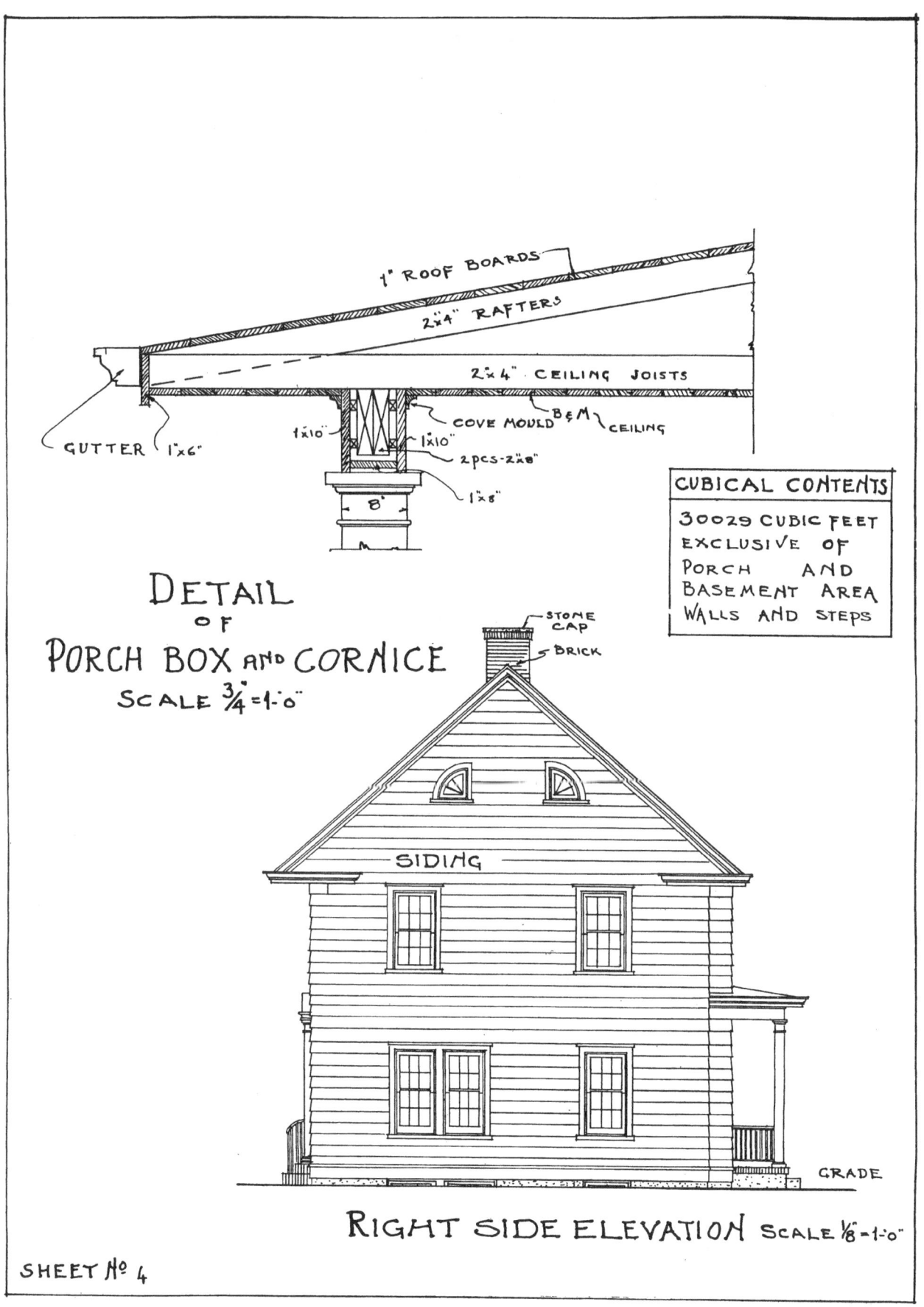

1" ROOF BOARDS

2"x4" RAFTERS

2"x4" CEILING JOISTS

COVE MOULD B&M CEILING

GUTTER 1"x6"

1"x10"

1"x10"

2 PCS-2"x8"

1"x8"

8"

DETAIL
OF
PORCH BOX AND CORNICE
SCALE 3/4"=1'-0"

CUBICAL CONTENTS

30029 CUBIC FEET
EXCLUSIVE OF
PORCH AND
BASEMENT AREA
WALLS AND STEPS

STONE CAP

BRICK

SIDING

GRADE

RIGHT SIDE ELEVATION SCALE 1/8"-1'-0"

SHEET No 4

THE ALLIANCE; In the Right Side Elevation the Wall Is More Simple. The basement windows are placed below grade in concreted area ways. Above are the construction details of the porch roof and cornice.

The Acme

A Dutch Colonial Demonstration House Which Is Said To Be "The Prettiest House in Galesburg"

"THE Prettiest House in Galesburg" was erected by an enterprising Lumber Company, to show people how to build and get the most for their money. The style is pure Dutch Colonial. The nearly square shape takes advantage of every foot of space. The house is quite roomy and yet can be built on a 40-foot lot. It includes six rooms, breakfast nook and bath, ten good closets, a full basement and an attic. The complete built-in equipment of the kitchen won unlimited praise from all the women who inspected it. It would be hard to improve on the plan for the purpose for which it was intended. There is not an inch of waste space anywhere. The house is commodious, compact and yet inexpensive to build.

It was built of frame construction, insulated throughout, with wide siding, shingle roof, brick base, chimney and steps. It was painted white, with green blinds to contrast with the white side walls.

Furnishings, even to phonograph and radio set, were supplied for the demonstration by local merchants who welcomed the opportunity to co-operate in such an exhibition. Cards were placed throughout the house showing the names of the merchants who had furnished the various pieces of equipment and this proved to be a valuable advertisement for these merchants. A beautiful phonograph, with a large assortment of records, was included among the furnishings.

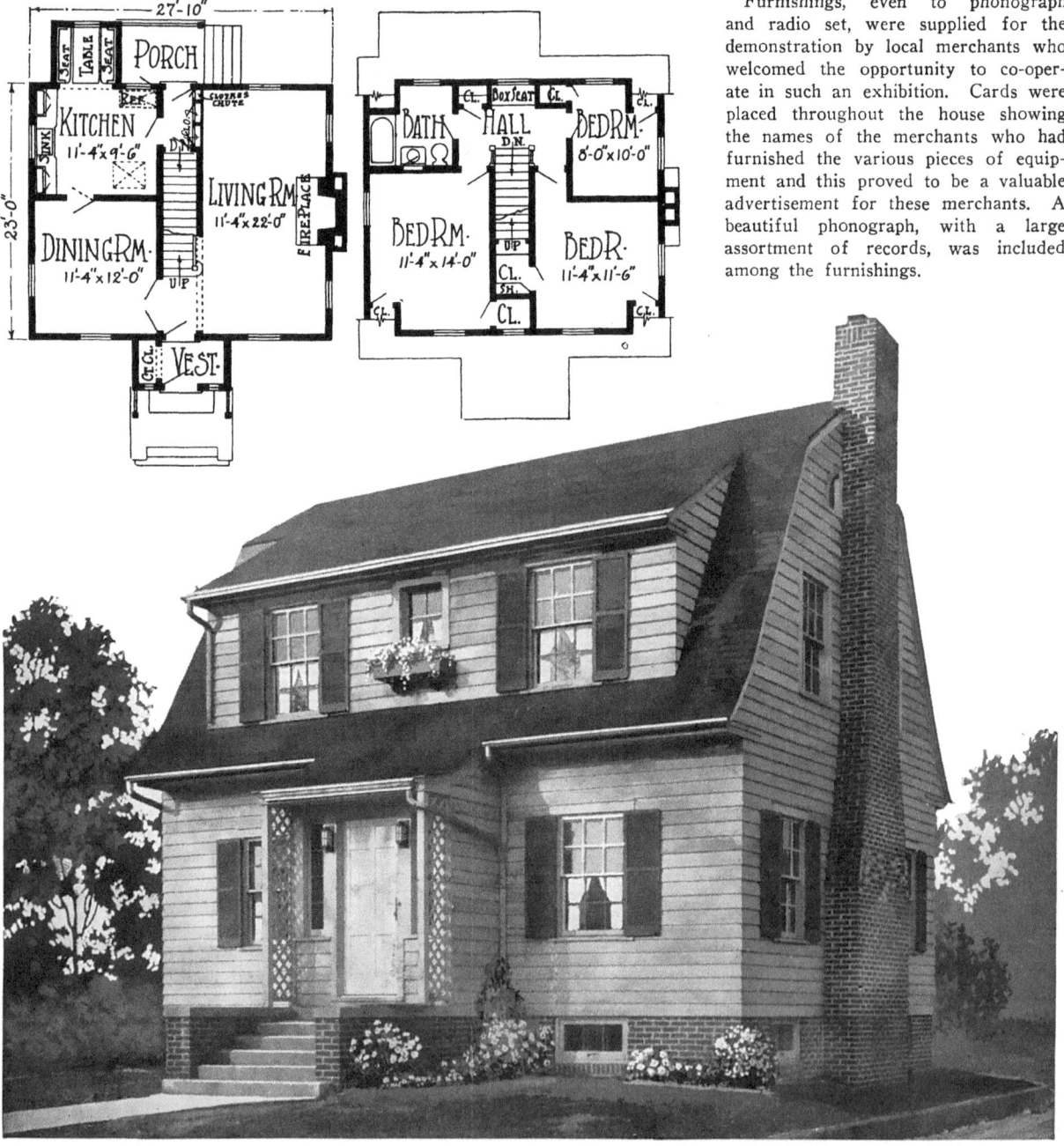

THE ACME; A Combination of White Paint, Green Blinds and Red Brick in this Dutch Colonial House Won the Approval of the People of Galesburg, Ill., Where It Was Built as a Demonstration House. The floor plans show the economical use of floor space in this style of building.

The Algona
A Pennsylvania Farmhouse Type of Home

AFTER all, what type of house is more pleasing, more homelike and fitting for a rural setting, than the good old fashioned Pennsylvania farmhouse?

It seems at once to appeal through its quiet dignity, as a place to live—a home that is truly American. This type of house of course requires generous grounds, that is, it should not be crowded in closely between neighbors, it demands free space on all sides. It is distinctly a rural house and not one for the thickly settled suburbs or the city.

The house herewith illustrated, carries out the simplicity and good taste of the farmhouse type. There is no detail on the house that does not serve a useful purpose, nothing applied for show. The setting is also approximately simple, the large oak trees were the deciding factor in locating the house and the yard was developed as an unbroken lawn, no formal gardening having been attempted. It is this simplicity, held to throughout, that gives much of the effect of fitness, a quality always to be sought in a home.

The simplicity of the exterior and the landscape work is also to be found in the interior, even the plan arrangement is symmetrical and direct. A very fine porch is a noteworthy feature here, of generous dimensions, part of it open, part closed.

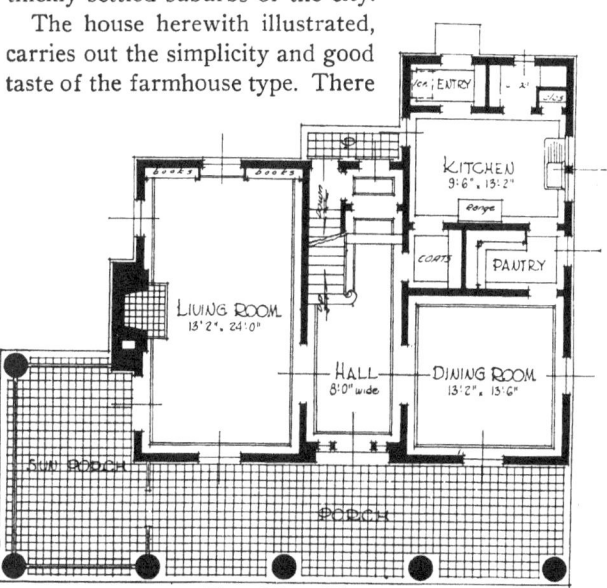

First Floor Plan.

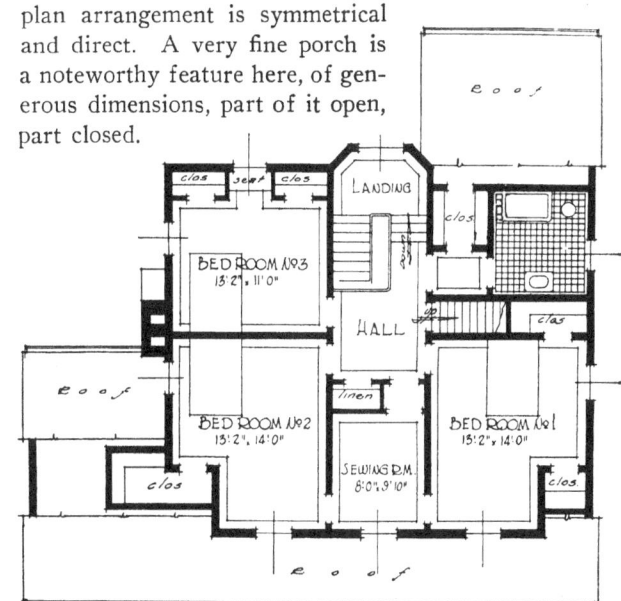

Second Floor Plan.

The Advance

A Hillside Home in Hollywood

THERE are plenty of houses built *on* a hill; but this is about one which is built *in* a hill; the home of an architect, in the foothills of Hollywood, California. It is built on three levels, with the living-room on one, the dining-room on another, and on the third the sleeping rooms and bath room. The third level is fully sixteen feet higher than that of the living-rooms, the main entrance being on the middle level. Living or sleeping rooms are reached by flights of steps leading from an entrance hall triangular in shape. On the dining room side, the wall of the living room wall is carried only to the level of the dining room floor. Here it is surmounted by a railing which gives the effect of a balcony and, through the timbers of the living room, can be seen a vista of the succeeding flights of steps leading to the upper levels.

The lot is pie-shaped—or should one say like a *wedge* of pie?—being about seventy feet wide at the rear and narrowing toward the front, with a grade rising about five inches in twelve.

The interior walls are finished in texture plaster, being putty finished and troweled down—the texture having the appearance of being applied over stone or adobe. Floors are dark, filled with a blue paste filler, coated with shellac and with a couple of final coats of wax. The fireplace is a roomy affair, four feet in width, five in height and two in depth; red

The Entrance to the Hillside Home Is Made Unusually Pleasant by the Steps and Walk Beside the Rough, Vine-Grown Retaining Wall.

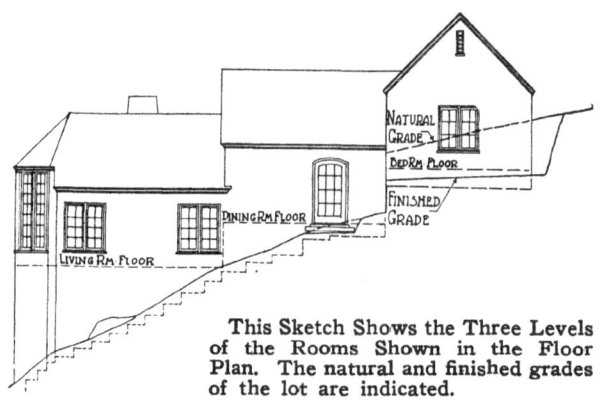

This Sketch Shows the Three Levels of the Rooms Shown in the Floor Plan. The natural and finished grades of the lot are indicated.

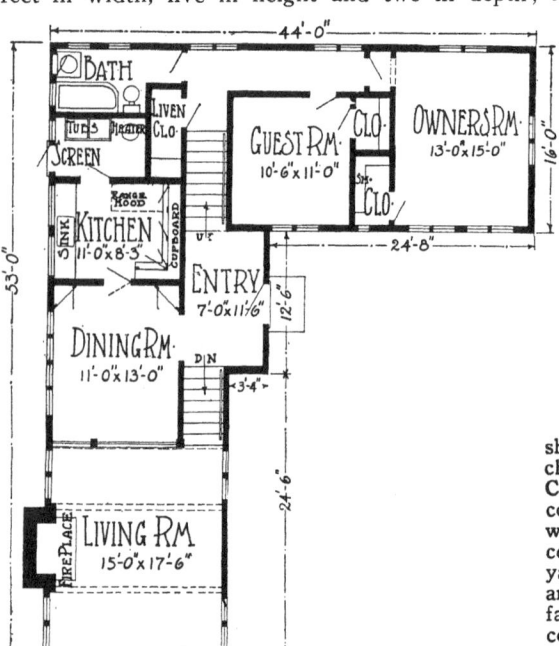

THE ADVANCE; This Unusual Floor Plan Fits Well the Peculiar Shape of the Lot on Which the Home was Built.

The exterior is finished in shingles and the windows are shaded by gayly striped awnings adding that touch of cheerful color which is so characteristic of the present-day California home. The entrance is reached by a series of concrete steps which rise along a vine-covered retaining wall of picturesque, rough stone construction. These steps continue on up to a side yard on the third level. In this yard, and all about the house, flowers, shrubbery, vines and trees have been planted and, encouraged by the famous California climate, have thrived and already become an inseparable part of the picture formed by house and garden.

This Side Yard, Reached by Concrete Steps, Is on the "Third Level" of the Home.

brick set in a herringbone pattern form the fire back, and then there is a stone lintel and a bronze plaque of Breek-Assyrian design, flanked by torchieres of wrought iron.

The kitchen is painted a canary yellow, with black outlines on the cupboards; blue crepe being employed for the window curtains, and on the floor is a blue covering.

A trussed ceiling in the living-room with timbers stained by over-glaze treatment has resulted in a hard wood effect. This over-glaze means first: a dark oil stain, then a coat of shellac, and finally a coating of gray paint—immediately rubbed off with a rag—thus aging the timber. That's a wrinkle which may be utilized by many home planners.

The walls of the master-bedroom are of orchid, with furniture of lavender-gray; while the guest-room has cream walls, rag rugs and rose accessories.

The house has windows of the casement variety—swinging inward—and taken altogether it is a very appealing home both inside and out, and presents a most striking example of the adaptation of the house design to the site which it is intended to occupy. This latter is the first point of consideration in the planning of any new home even though the site does not present such an unusual problem as in this case.

THE ADVANCE; The Living Room of the Hillside Home Is Reached by a Flight of Stairs Down from the Entrance Which Is on the Dining Room Level. This room can be seen to the rear of the picture, as can the stairs to the sleeping quarters, which are on a level still higher than the dining room and kitchen.

The Abbott

A House That Will Need No Repairs

WHEN building costs are high, one should build well and permanently, that is, sound, substantial construction around an economical plan, so as to avoid the expense of repairs and also to make every foot of floor space count as usable room.

The house herewith illustrated embodies these requirements.

The construction is of hollow tile stuccoed outside and plastered inside, the roof is slate. The only work which will require painting is the small amount of wood trim.

As to the plan arrangement, the architects have worked it out along lines of real economy. The entrance is into a small vestibule with coat closet adjoining, thus the usual hall space is given over to the living room.

The stairs go up from the rear of the living room while also serving the kitchen, giving the advantage of a service stairway without extra cost.

On the second floor are three bedrooms, a bath and plenty of closets, all conveniently arranged about the small center hall.

A small balcony over the front entrance connects to the two main bedrooms of the second floor, it is a convenience for these rooms as well as making an attractive feature on the exterior.

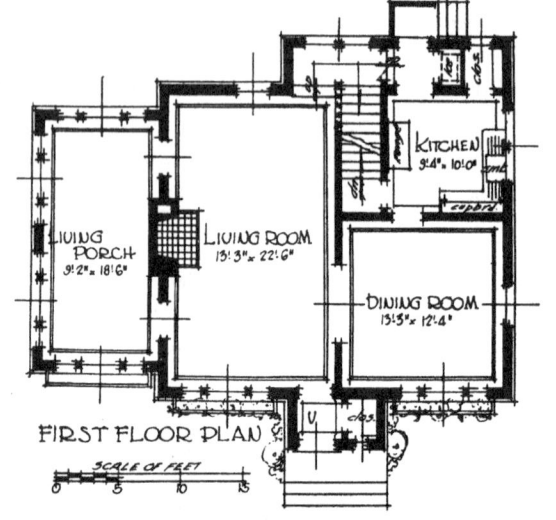

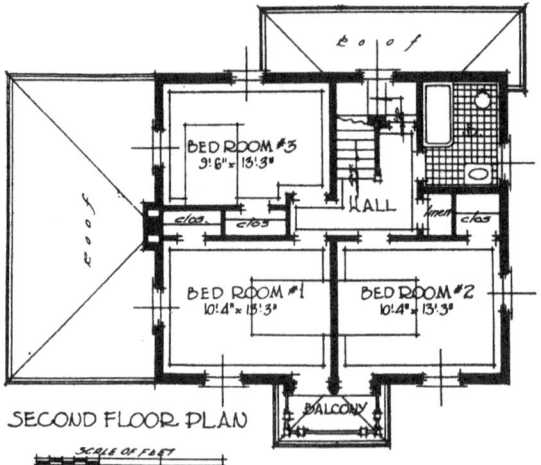

THE ABBOTT; Photo and Floor Plans of Good House Designed Without "Gingerbread" Elements Which Usually Are Causes of Early Repairs.

The Azalea, an Italian Villa

Residence in Which Spaciousness and Beauty of Detail are Perfectly Blended

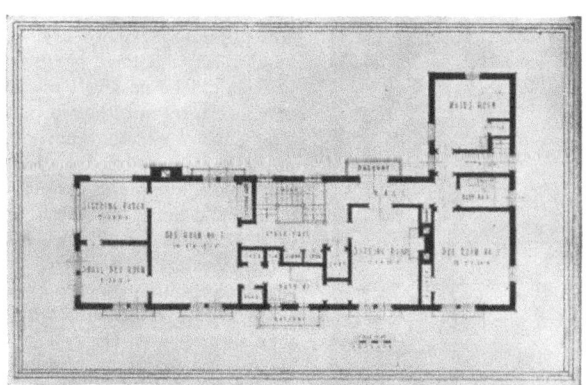

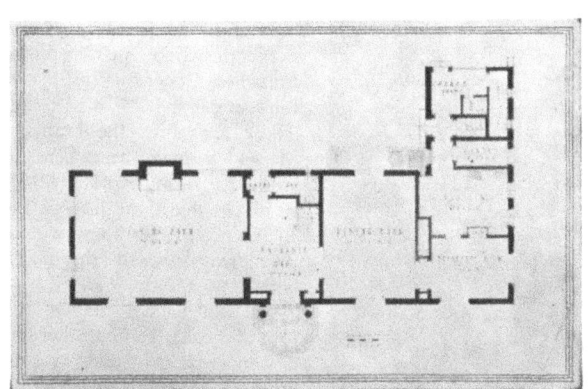

THE AZALEA; Above Is Shown the Front of the Italian Villa. Below is a closer view, showing in more detail the window balconies and French doors, with ornamental trellises. The floor plans give an idea of the simplicity and spaciousness of the arrangement of rooms. The living room is 19 by 27½ feet with a large fireplace at one side.

LANDSCAPE ARCHITECTURE

AND

THE HOME

Selecting the Home-Building Site

IN the thrill of planning our first home, we too often forget that this home, which may be the only one which we will build, is to have a permanent setting, a place in the sun, which is different from that of any of its neighbors. Too many of us plan the house first, long before we have decided on the lot upon which it is to be placed. We do not always realize that the direction in which the lot faces, the grade of the lot, the trees and the rock outcrops, the hills and valleys, are all factors which are intimately connected with the kind of a home which we are to build.

Let us imagine that we are about to select such a lot, before we have designed our home. We will choose a general location which would be convenient to our place of business. The location should also be in a section of the community where the prevailing winds do not send the smoke, odors, or gases from nearby manufacturing plants into our living-room or bedroom windows. In some of the smaller communities this smoke factor may be serious; and we would like to avoid being too near the railroad with its noise and soot. Manufacturing plants always reduce the value of a piece of property for residence purposes.

In the vicinity of large cities the matter of transportation to and from our work is of concern to the home owner. When we are so situated that we can have both an automobile and a home, then the country or suburban sections have many advantages. Here we can usually find good educational advantages for our family, well designed churches, a library and other community features which will give to our children surroundings which they can happily remember, and perchance come back to when their schooling is over.

We expect, and that rightly, a good clear water supply, a well-managed and carefully designed sewerage disposal and refuse disposal system.

This Terraced Entrance to the Flower Garden and Greenhouse Is Most Invitingly Framed with Rose Bushes Which Adds to the Attractiveness of the Home.

We need well-lighted and adequately policed streets, with paving smooth and safe for driving. We may have parks, playgrounds or perhaps a fine bathing beach if near a lake or river.

We have now disposed of the question of where we would like to live, and our next thought is of the lot upon which we will build this dream-home. Where the country is flat, little can be done except in the style and design of the house, to relieve it of monotony. We can by grading, if it be properly directed by real imagination, re-create a new scene about the house.

We can look for trees upon such a lot, trees whose welcome shade and spreading limbs give shelter and a feeling of permanency to the finally completed home. We may be fortunate enough to have several different varieties of trees on our lot, and their preservation should be no small matter of concern to you, their owner. Too many trees, however much we may admire them, only make our home dark and damp, and must be sacrificed in the beginning, before we grow too attached to them.

Some communities take great pride in the trees with which they have been blessed, and take great pains to preserve them. Many of these old forest monarchs have an interesting history. There is an old elm in Cambridge underneath whose spreading branches General Washington took command of his troops. There are elms, the branches of which have been bent in youth at right angle to their trunk, to mark the line of the Indian trails, as they wound their way toward the north lakes.

Our lot should not be too low in grade, so that there is a tendency of the surface drainage, the rains and melting snow of spring, to flow into our cellar, or to make of our entire lot a wet, unhealthful place in which to live. The low lot may also be difficult to build upon, due to the average shallow depth of the sanitary sewers in the street. It seems to the writer to be wise in the purchase of the lot, to be sure that the first floor grade of your home can be set at such a height that the house need not be put upon stilts, or on high foundations or terraces, to keep the basement level above the sewer grade.

Most of us know that low wet land is apt to be foggy and unhealthful. Pockets of this kind also encourage damage caused by early and late frosts, which may take all of our fruits or late maturing vegetables, or our choice and cherished late asters. In the spring late frosts also ruin many an otherwise promising fruit crop by killing the blossoms. A friend of mine, who lives in the state of Washington, now noted for its fine apples, was asked why he seldom had frost difficulties in the spring when all of his neighbors were losing large sums in frozen blossoms. "That," said he, "is because as an early comer I chose my home-site, and my orchard site with care, on a high level plateau, where the sun beats warmly down even in early spring."

A Natural Feature of Great Beauty May Be a Spring Fed Brook or Pond. Here mirrored rhododendrons and willows frame the charming view of this country home.

A Home Built Upon a Terrace, at Some Height Above the Street, Gains Prominence and at the Same Time Improved Views from Its Windows.

If your lot is high, with a knoll seeming the best place for the house, let the building seem to build up out of the ridge. Do not let it seem to be in danger of sudden displacement during the first wind-storm, perching on the top like a brown derby on a tiny head. Rather, if the hill be high and the house be large let the style be kept low and rambling, with rooms on different levels on the first floor, if necessary, and with terraces of sufficient width to hold the house where it belongs.

A lot with steep slopes to the house and to the garage from the street, is one which may necessitate much grading down to make the ascent an easy and a safe one for either the motor car or for the visitor on foot. This requires no little ingenuity and cleverness in design, but may be the means of giving you an individual final result with the garage placed at a lower level than the first floor grade of the house. The entrance walk may lead upward in long ramps, rather than short flights of steps, until the house terrace or porch is reached.

Another natural feature of great beauty which is an attraction sought by the nature-lover, is a spring-fed brook or a wide lagoon, or a low piece of land with a valley so placed on the lot that it might serve when dammed at the lower end, as a site of a lake where summer swimming can be enjoyed, and where skating in winter gives zest to the day's joys. A more inviting scene, one more restful, can scarce be imagined.

As long as there is some motion to the water, even though the stream be artificially fed during a part of the day, little danger need be expected from mosquitoes, those pests of the summer evenings. Fish life would keep down the larvae, and provide much happiness to the small boys of the neighborhood. The reflection in the depths of the lake of the flowering shrubs along the banks, of the sunset glow, and of the warm light in the windows of the home you love, is a sight which pulls the heart-strings.

In digging the excavation for the basement of his home, a friend of mine found two large boulders of granite of brilliant hues, which his contractor advised be buried to get them out of the way. Both these rocks were saved. One was made the center,—and a popular center it was,—for a bird-garden and wild retreat, where it its hollowed top the old rock held cool water for the feathered visitors through the hot summer days.

The other boulder, even larger than its fellow was dragged within the shade of an old hemlock. Its rather irregular top was cut into a rustic seat, from the enveloping arms of which on many a summer evening weird tales were told around a crackling camp-fire at its base. Thus unexpected beauties and joys may be found on even a dismal and ordinary appearing site, if we have imagination and the courage to apply it to our lot.

Think in the beginning of the views of your new home which to you seem the most inviting, and frame them with attractive planting. Screen the views which are unattractive, especially those sections which are devoted to the service portion, the drying yard and other unsightly portions of the lot. These screens may be walls, lattice, or planting as has been suggested. Remember that in our northern climate many months are spent within the cozy walls of our home, and thus the best of the views from the windows can be framed, emphasized, and made restful and inviting. Evergreens and architectural features aid in making less bleak the winter's scenery.

Adapt your new home to the site which you have chosen. Adapt the arrangement of the rooms, their size and contents, to both the lot exposures and to the needs of your family. Adapt the materials of construction to those in common use in the community, preferably as permanent as possible. Do not select a freakish style of architecture just to be different from your neighbor. Above all adapt your home and its contents to your pocketbook, so that its final purchase, interest on your investment, taxes, and other fixed and seemingly inescapable charges will not take all of the pleasure out of the ownership of your dream-house.

Fitting the Home to the Lot

TO the home owner, and especially to one who owns a lot, however tiny the plot of ground may be, and who is about to build a home, comes a new undreamed sensation which stirs him as nothing else in his life has moved him. You who have gone through this experience know that in your haste to complete this home of yours you often hurry too fast in the preparation of plans, or perhaps you make no definite plans at all, at least until you have actually started the building. Without a studied plan no real progress can be made, and it is here that the architect can best realize your needs, and with patience and with due knowledge of your wishes mold the results into a home of which you will always be proud.

Relation of Rooms

Without in too much detail thinking of the plans and specifications, the elevations and style of our home (for within the covers of this magazine and within the brains of many architects are many splendid examples of home design) let us think for a moment of the rooms, their outlook, their relation and arrangement as they affect each other. The elevations and materials of construction really determine the architectural style or character of the final result. The plan may be ever so convenient, ever so well carry out your ideals, and yet due entirely to the elevations, the home into which you finally move may be far from your expectation of the home you had hoped for. Thus it is wise to study the probable future appearances of the house with the plan in mind, with the elevations shown from different points of view. A perspective study helps very much in arriving at the probable future appearance of the house, but the writer has found that a model in clay or in other plastic medium, worked out carefully at a usable scale, will often make changes in the elevations seem wise and essential before the home is actually erected.

Divisions of the Lot

In a general way this lot of ours upon which we are to build our home, whether the lot faces north or south, east or west, falls into three divisions. There is that portion to the front of the house which is open to the public, an area which gives little if any privacy, and which, like our faces, is usually kept smiling, clean and bright to give our guests the happiest memories of their visit. Then there is that part of the lot which is so placed at either side of the building that by planting or by use of a lattice fence or by other methods, the area can be made partially private. The third section of the lot, which should be entirely screened from the street, is the one place which the owner, a mere man, can call his very own. Hence so far as is possible with the more or less crowded conditions of our suburban sections, he can proudly say that he is master of all which he surveys, to the fence enclosure. This area may be, and usually is, at the back of the house, which should make the study of that elevation of the building one of much thoughtful planning. Indeed it seems to the writer that instead of calling this the rear elevation of our home, we should think of it, should plan it, as the GARDEN elevation or GARDEN side of the house. Mayhap this would bring a new charm, a new lightness, a beauty and liveable gardenesque character to this, the living side of the home.

Location of Service Station

Too often to the rear of the house are relegated the most unsightly of the necessary service sections of our home, sections which could as well or better be placed at the side. I refer to the service entrance, from which ashes and other wastes of the establishment must be carried, where the foodstuffs are delivered, and through which the family washing is brought out into the sunlight of the drying yard. Where the garage is detached it would logically be placed at the rear of the lot, with a drive of adequate width, and a turn-around of sufficient size to permit of backing around upon your own lot.

Homes Crowded

Our great difficulty in America is that of placing a large home of sufficient area to care for the needs of the average family upon a narrow and oftentimes shallow lot into which our country and suburban sections are being divided. Thus houses are placed close together, as close as fire risks will permit, in some cases so close that they lose their individuality as they march in close formation down the street.

A Secluded Corner of the "Outdoor Living Room" with a Sheltered Bench on Which the Home Owner May Rest and Enjoy the Contact with Nature When Tired from Working Over the Favorite Plantings of His Garden.

Individuality

It is to avoid this monotony, this similarity, that heroic measures are at times adopted by our architects and builders to eliminate this tendency or at least to differentiate between the homes. It is only by designing our homes to fit the lot as well as the needs of the family that we can avoid the sometimes freakish results of the vain effort to have our home entirely different from that of our neighbors.

The Living Room

Turning now to the arrangement of the rooms for a moment, bearing in mind that we are to have a garden side to our home from which the garden should be directly reached, let us strive to build our house around the living room, yes, about the fireplace of the living room as the *heart* of the entire home. The fireplace usually works out best if located at one end of the room, especially if the room is rather narrow, for this arrangement permits of the grouping of chairs, a sofa or other inviting group about that end. Wherever the fireplace is located take care not to have two doors leading into the dining room or into the hall or to any part of the house at either side of this retreat. The

at least have stepping stone paths set in the turf, so that one may walk dry shod after a heavy dew or rainfall. The paving may be of brick, slate with its variegated colors or of other material which is in keeping with the architectural character of the house.

Dining Room

More and more, except in the larger homes, the dining room, once one of the important and carefully studied rooms of the entire home, is becoming less and less an essential. In the smaller homes, the bungalows and the cottages, the dining room has been entirely displaced by the dining alcove. The space before devoted to dining room may become a library, or a library and sewing room combined. The windows of the dining room should face east to give us a cheery start as the day begins.

The kitchen, that necessity in every home of whatever size, should be so placed that the smoke and odors from the cooking foods are carried away from the rest of the house. Thus it would in many cases be at the northern end of the place, where the prevailing winds in our climate at least would blow the aromas away from the other rooms. The kitchen may very happily be designed toward the front of the house, especially if the house faces north, and there

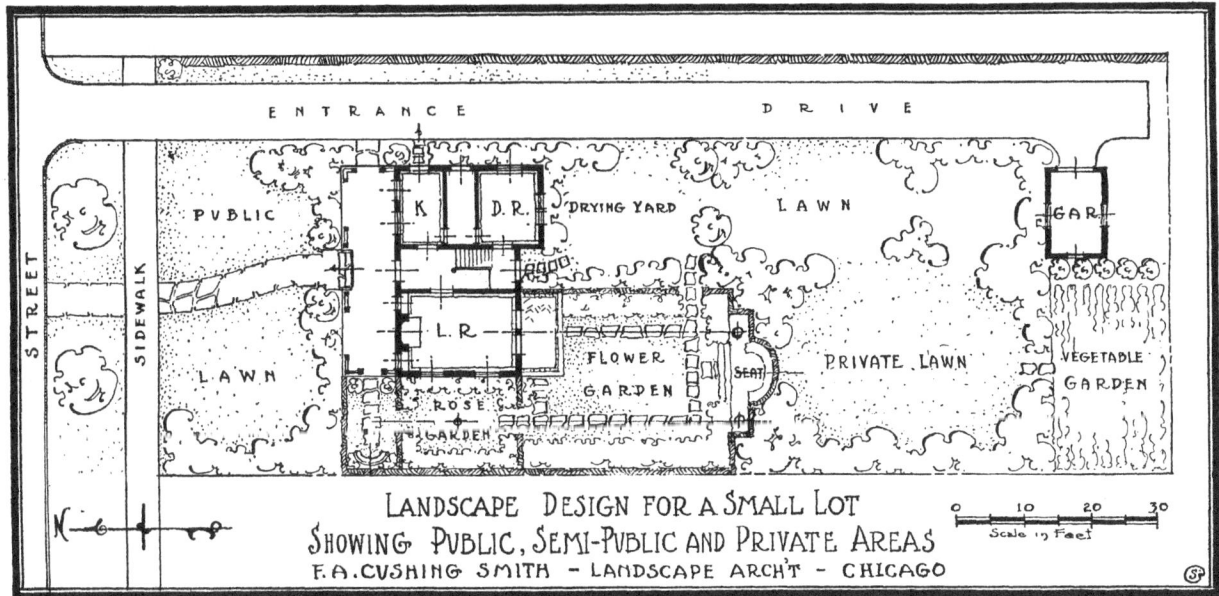

The Public Parts of the Grounds Are Usually Kept at Their Best for Guests and Passers-by, but the Private and Semi-Private Parts May Be Equally Attractive and Justify the Term "Garden Elevation" to Replace "Rear Elevation," Thereby Adding a New Charm to the Home as a Whole.

arrangement cuts in two or three parts the group that might have enjoyed the blaze and crackling of the logs on the hearth.

Sun Room and Terrace

The fireplace located on the north end of the living room which runs north and south will give the rays of the setting sun an opportunity to brighten the late afternoon hours and will permit of the south opening, through wide French doors, out upon a terrace, or even upon a sun room where in the winter the room is filled with blossoms. Here, too, is the transition from the more formal interior of the indoor living room to the less formal and more open outdoor living room—the garden.

Use of Terrace

Outside of the sun room or the garden end of the living room a terrace will give, upon its broad expanse, a spot for a tea-table and chairs, from which our garden may be studied and enjoyed. The terrace should be paved, or

can be no possible objection to such a design. The service entrance may be at the side of the building, the drying room, and the service yard being enclosed within a lattice wall, a stone wall or a high hedge.

The Outside Living Room

Considering the outdoor living room on the garden side of the house, we want this room to afford us the same privacy which our interior living room gives. It would be preferably enclosed, whether of the formal or informal type, by lattice, hedge, wall or a combination of these materials. There might be a summer house, a pool with a fountain which quietly plays upon its bright surface. There would be seats, for the worker in the garden tires often in the labors of love in weeding the flower beds. The kinds of flowers, their color of bloom, their height and time of bloom, the varieties which look well together, the edging of the planting beds, all these factors enter into the successful outdoor living room. We will, in a later article, take up various details of the garden.

The Allenhurst
A Well Designed Small House

THE design of this house is simple, direct and pleasing. It has good character.

The walls are white shingles, giving a good foil for the rough vari-colored stone chimney and a crisp contrast with the rural character of the setting.

The plan arrangement shows clearly the disposition of the different rooms, a layout that is convenient and economical. A cellar is provided under the full area.

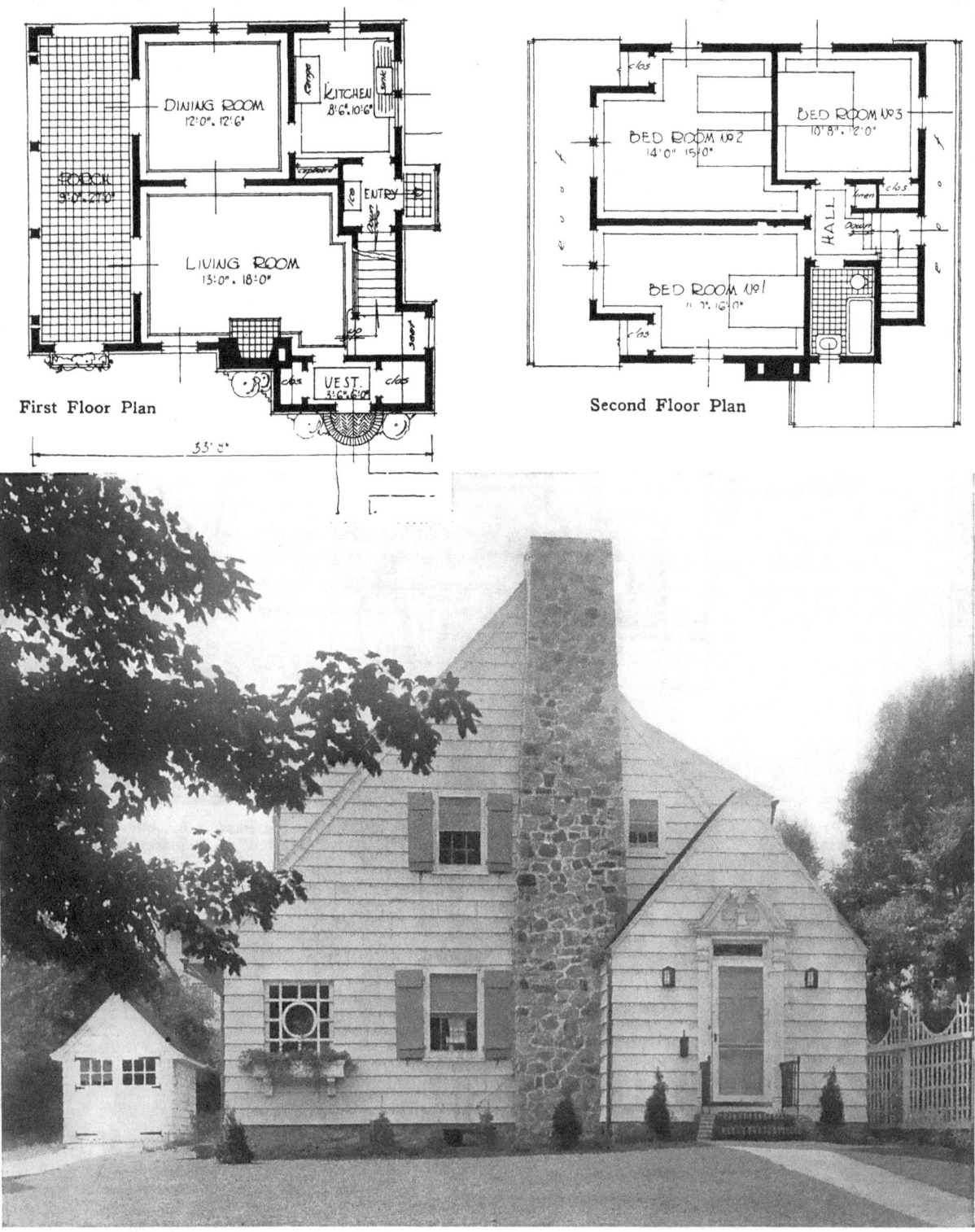

First Floor Plan

Second Floor Plan

THE ALLENHURST; The Entrance Doorway of This House Is a Study in Refinement. It shows how full size details, properly worked out by the architect, and executed with precision give the right character expected. The graceful entrance contrasts well with the rugged chimney, lending variety to the front, without conflict of parts.

The ALLEGAN

KITCHEN
SERVING PANTRY
CASE
BUFFET
DINING ROOM
HALL
BATH
MAID'S ROOM
LIVING ROOM
PORCH
FIRE PLACE
FIRST FLOOR PLAN

BED ROOM
BATH
LINEN
BED ROOM
SEAT
CLO.
HALL
BATH
CASE
BED ROOM.
BED ROOM
SECOND FLOOR PLAN

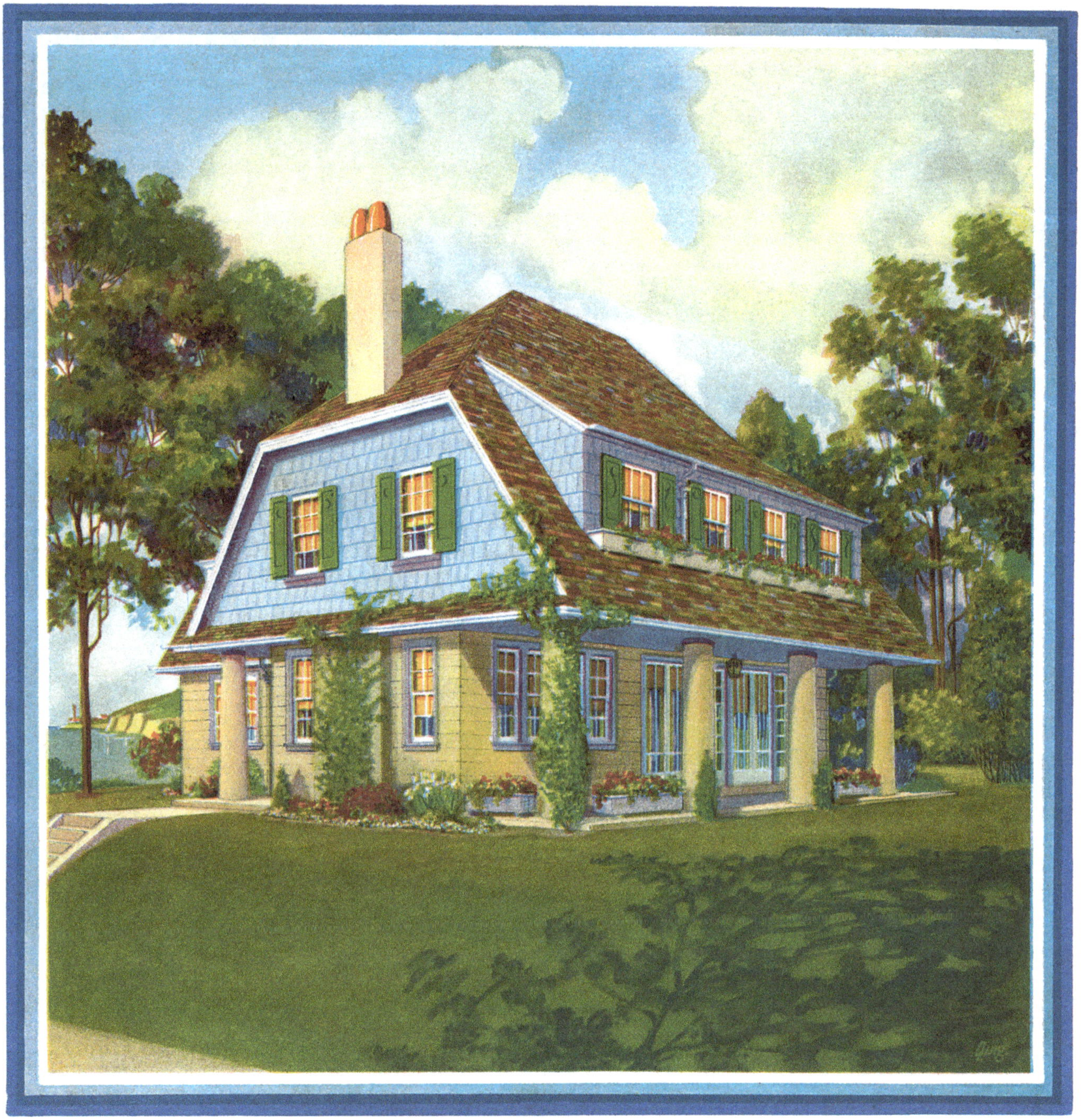

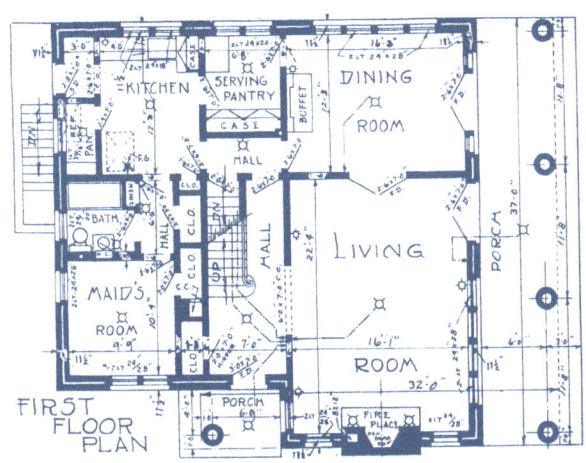

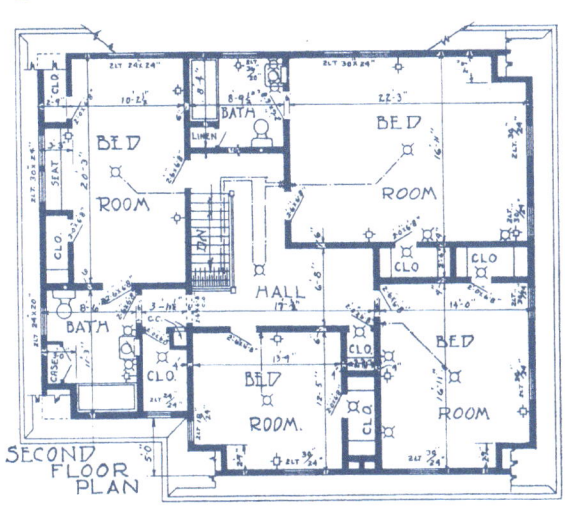

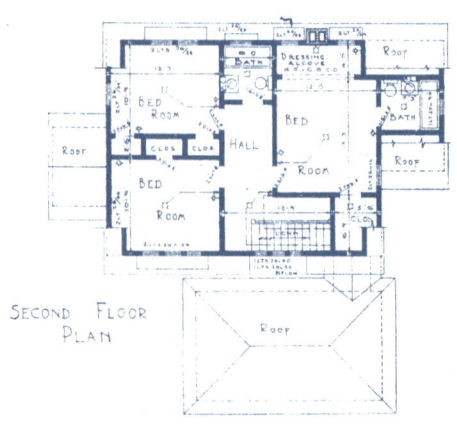

The *ADDISON*

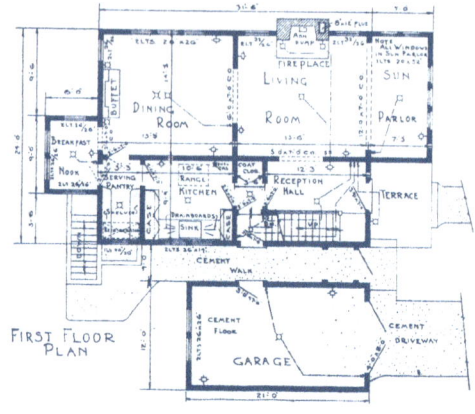

FIRST FLOOR PLAN

SECOND FLOOR PLAN